Is it Rape?

On Acquaintance Rape and Taking Women's
Consent Seriously

JOAN McGREGOR

ASHGATE

Published by
Ashgate Publishing Limited
Gower House
Croft Road
Aldershot
Hampshire GU11 3HR
England

Ashgate Publishing Company
Suite 420
101 Cherry Street
Burlington, VT 05401-4405
USA

Ashgate website: http://www.ashgate.com

British Library Cataloguing in Publication Data
McGregor, Joan
  Is it rape? : on acquaintance rape and taking women's rape seriously.
  – (Live questions in ethics and moral philosophy)
  1. Aquaintance rape 2. Sexual consent 3. Rape – Philosophy
  I. Title
  345′.025232

Library of Congress Cataloging-in-Publication Data
McGregor, Joan.
  Is it rape? : on acquaintance rape and taking women's consent seriously/Joan McGregor.
    p. cm. – (Live questions in ethics and moral philosophy)
  Includes index.
  ISBN 0-7546-5065-0 (alk. paper) – ISBN 0-7546-5066-9 (pbk. : alk. paper)
  1. Acquaintance rape. I. Title. II. Series.

  HV6558.M34 2004
  362.883—dc22
                                                2004005412

ISBN 0 7546 5065 0 (Hbk)
ISBN 0 7546 5066 9 (Pbk)

Printed on acid-free paper

Reprinted 2005

Typeset by Tradespools, Frome, Somerset.
Printed and bound in Great Britain by
Antony Rowe Ltd., Chippenham, Wilts.

To Don, Clea, Sage, and in memory of
George A. McGregor

Contents

Acknowledgments

This book has been in the pipeline for a number of years since I first started thinking about rape in the early 1990s. In many ways my interests grew out of my doctoral dissertation work on coercion. In that research I was concerned about the subtleties of coercion and particularly the role of power differentials in coercive relationships. Power differential or bargaining power differences arise in most acquaintance rape cases as well. My supervisors were Joel Feinberg and Jules Coleman and I benefited immeasurably from working with them both.

I would like especially to take this opportunity to thank Joel Feinberg not only for his advice but also for his example as a philosopher. After being in the profession now for many years, I have come to realize what a rare philosopher he was. Not only was he a brilliant man but he was a generous and gracious one as well. I will always be grateful that I had the opportunity to work with him. I am certainly also indebted to many others. Their ideas and comments over the years have helped me think about the difficult issues in rape.

My colleague, Jeff Murphy, has always been a formidable critic, and even when we are not discussing philosophy I imagine his challenges. Delegates at the University of San Diego law school conference organized by Larry Alexander in the mid-1990s, including Stephen Schulhofer, Alan Werthelmer, Heidi Hurd, and Heidi Malm, spurred me to see the richness of the topic and the diversity of views on rape. There were many other venues and people, including an APA Symposium on rape with Larry May, Marcia Baron, and myself, that helped shape my thinking about rape. All of these discussions and arguments have only reinforced my view that rape, particularly acquaintance rape, is an extremely contentious and intractable issue. I have stuck with the topic of rape because I believe that it is an incredibly important one for all women and I believe that women will only be treated as equals in society when all rape is taken seriously.

I also want to thank Sandra Woein, my Research Assistant, who was very helpful in the preparation of this manuscript. I am also thankful to my husband, Don Senneville, for listening to me discuss the complexities of rape for so many years.

Chapter 1

What is Wrong with the Criminal Law of Rape?

'I didn't hurt nobody. Nobody has a black eye or broken ribs.'

Mike Tyson at his sentencing for rape.
(Cynthia Tucker, 'Rape does Hurt Somebody,' *San Francisco Chronicle*, 6 April, 1992)

The boxer Mike Tyson's words unfortunately echo a sentiment that is well entrenched in legal practice and in society at large. In the absence of obvious violence or an explicit credible threat of extreme physical force, people question whether it is rape. Add to the mix that the man and woman know each other and the assumption is that, whatever happened, it couldn't amount to criminal rape. Rape is conceived of in legal practice and in the minds of many in society as a *violent* assault by a *stranger*. Nonviolent nonconsenual sex with someone you know – your boss, co-worker, or date – is not rape. Even when it is not so 'nonviolent,' if the sex is with an acquaintance it is not conceived of as rape. Not so long ago in the American legal system, husbands could beat and 'rape' (engage in forcible nonconsenual sex) their wives without the law recognizing any wrong to the women. These assaults against women went unrecognized and unprotected by the criminal codes. Historically, rape was not acknowledged unless there was extreme force by the aggressor, and 'utmost resistance' by the victim (and *de facto* the two were not acquaintances). The contemporary landscape is not much better. Consider these cases:

> A 19-year-old sophomore at a Pennsylvania college one afternoon went to the dorm where her boyfriend lived. While waiting for him to return she entered the room of an acquaintance, Robert Berkowitz. She sat on the floor and talked with him for a while. He sat next to her and began kissing and fondling her. She protested his advances and said that she had to go. Berkowitz disregarded her protests, got up and locked the door, came back and pushed her on to the bed, lay on top of her, removed her clothes, and penetrated her. Throughout she was saying 'no.' Berkowitz said that he took the 'no's to be passionate moaning. He was found not guilty of rape because there was no *forcible compulsion*.
>
> (*Commonwealth v. Berkowitz*, 1994)

> The pregnant ex-wife of the defendant verbally resisted his sexual advances but did not physically resist because in the past he had been extremely violent toward her and she feared for her own and her fetus's safety. The court found no rape since there was no force.
>
> (*Commonwealth v. Richter*, 1998)

Cases with no obvious physical force and/or with timid, scared victims who put up no resistance mean no rape. Even more bizarre are cases involving unconscious victims or those with disabilities, where no force is required. In some jurisdictions they cannot be raped (*Davis v. State of Florida*, 1989). In other examples where the victim was so intoxicated that she could not resist, no rape is found (see p. 79). In other words, if there was no 'legally' recognized force, there was no rape.

In this book I want to consider how the law treats cases of nonconsenual sex, particularly between acquaintances. I will argue that the law has wrongly excluded nonconsenual sex without legally recognized force from criminal protection. Criminal rape laws are too narrow in capturing only cases where there is clearly recognized physical violence *and* resistance from the victim (and when the two agents know each other it is even more difficult to get a prosecution, even with these factors present). The statutes and legal standards are a major problem. However, societal attitudes and myths about women and sex exacerbate the problem. People's attitudes about what rape is, who rapists are, and what women's responsibilities are with regard to men and sex greatly affect whether any given incident will be acknowledged, prosecuted, and found guilty. These social attitudes influence whether women themselves view what happens to them as rape, and how they view their own responsibility. What I want to explore is whether, all things considered, the law should protect women from nonconsenual sex with acquaintances, whether or not there is any attendant violence.

Historical Factors

Historically, even when rape was acknowledged it was thought to be an offense against the woman's father or husband as opposed to an injury to her. Women didn't have an interest in their own bodily integrity, but fathers had an interest in their daughters' chastity for their marketability as brides; and husbands had interests in ensuring that any progeny of their wives were biological theirs. Current criminal laws have rectified some of these abuses and omissions. For instance, most jurisdictions do not statutorily exclude wives from the set of possible victims (although it is still entrenched in societal attitudes that a man cannot rape his wife), and they do not require 'utmost resistence' – physical resistance to the point of death – by the victim. Many criminal rape laws, however, retain the conjunction of 'against the will or without consent' *and* 'force or threat of force' – that is, rape defined as 'sexual intercourse with a woman, against her will or without consent and with force or threat of force.' Legal practice and social attitudes have trouble recognizing as legally impermissible a wider range of sexual interactions, for example, nonconsensual sex without force (force in criminal law is conceived quite narrowly usually referring only to extreme physical force), which often includes acquaintance 'rapes'. In these cases, even when there is force, given that the two are acquaintances the law does not recognize them as 'with force' – quid pro quo sexual threats in the workplace, fraudulently optioned sex, and sexual relationships between individuals with wide differences in power (priest/parishioner, lawyer/client, teacher/student, therapist/patient).

The Facts about Rape

The facts in America are that most rapists are not prosecuted because somewhere between 60 and 90 percent of rape victims don't report the crime. So-called 'date rape' or acquaintance rape is one of the most unreported crimes. Unreported rape is complicated by the problem of victims not labeling their experience 'rape' or 'attempted rape,' even though the events fit the statutory definition of rape. Mary Koss's extensive research on the hidden crime of acquaintance rape has changed the understanding about the frequency of rape and about its perpetrators. Koss's research on 3187 female college students showed that one in four had experience rape or attempted rape, that 84 percent of those raped knew their attackers, and that 57 percent of the rapes had occurred on dates. The reception to these findings was fascinating in that they were met with incredulity and attacks on the researchers and their work. For example, Neil Gilbert argued that Koss had manufactured a 'phantom epidemic of sexual assault.' Katie Roiphe then published *The Morning After: Sex, Fear, and Feminism on Campus*, arguing that the statistics must be distorted and a product of post-coital regret and not real rape, and further that feminism was hurting the cause of women: for example, that rape-awareness education on college campuses was not empowering women but promoting the image to women that they are weak, dependent and without sexual desires.

The Problems with our Views about Rape

At this point I don't want to defend the numbers, it is sufficient to acknowledge that there is much more sexual assault occurring in America than has been recognized. The reasons that women don't report their rapes include the fear that the criminal justice system will not believe them, fear that they will be blamed for the events – the belief that they were responsible for what happened to them and could have controlled it. Finally, many victims of acquaintance rape don't label their experience as rape at all. They often believe that the law does not protect them against the acts of acquaintances. These fears and beliefs are in fact warranted. Under prosecution of rapes often results because police frequently fail to list victims' reports as rapes since the police themselves think that the charges are false or that the victim precipitated the rape.[1] If a rape case gets to trial, the conviction rates are lower than for other crimes and the victim is often 'raped again' by trial procedures.[2] Police, prosecutors, judges, and juries are either unlikely to believe victims, or they are likely to hold women responsible for what happened.

The upshot of this system is that the law and society at large are not backing up women's rights to control access to their bodies. Consequently, I will argue that the law is not protecting women's sexual autonomy. Part of the problem is that society in general, including women, does not see nonconsensual sexual intercourse with an acquaintance as rape – a criminal offense. Two problems persist. First, aggressive sexual activity by an acquaintance is not *viewed* as rape. The law permits quite a lot of coercion in sexual relationships between acquaintances. The law is not going to see forcible sex – a man holding a woman down with his superior strength – as rape when the parties are acquainted. Society's image of rape is of a stranger using physical violence or threats of violence. Consequently, cases that diverge from this paradigm are not treated as crimes and as 'real rapes,' as Susan Estrich pointed out (1987). The second problem lies with cases where there is no overt force by the man, but the woman does not consent. She may say 'no' and yet he goes ahead and has sex with her and she doesn't stop him, possibly because she is too frightened. She may just cry. Regardless, there is no consent. These cases do not meet either the statutory language of rape or societal notions of rape, despite what the statutes say.

What I want to explore in this book are the issues surrounding nonconsenual sex with an acquaintance. The data show that the prevalence of these offenses is high, and yet the criminal justice system is not prosecuting these assaults. One reason they are not prosecuted is that these incidents tend not to involve 'force,' or at least what is legally recognized as force. Nonconsenual sex alone is not a criminal act under many statutes; force is also a necessary factor in the crime of rape. Another reason is the question of what the law and society understand as force or threats. Leaving aside the use of a weapon or a severe beating (or explicit threats of these), other power relationships are not conceptualized as force by the law. Finally, even if there is force, if the sex is between people who know each other, the law and society are unlikely to see it as criminal in nature. Exacerbating the difficulty of acknowledging acquaintance rapes as rapes are the differences in the perceptions of men and women about what occurred. Consider these cases:

> Denise was raped in the mid-1970s by a 'friend of a friend' in her own apartment. He ignored her protests, pinned her to the bed with his body, and choked her. When he fell asleep after ejaculating, she escaped and drove to a female friend's house. The two women returned to Denise's the following morning. The man was gone. 'He left me a note with one of those smiley faces drawn on it. The note read: 'Denise, I woke up and you were gone. Catch ya later! Have a nice day! Bob' ... Minutes later, the phone rang. The voice belonged to a cheerful Bob. I think I called him a bastard or a fucker and I told him not to ever call me again, and then hung up. He called back, sounding surprised, asking, 'Hey, what's the matter?'

> April, too, was raped by a man who showed no evidence of understanding what happened. He was a recent acquaintance ... he pushed her onto the floor, slammed her headfirst into a corner, and they struggled until he raped her. 'The penetration was very violent,' she says. 'When it was all over, he asked me if I usually fight so much during sex. I don't think it ever occurred to him that he had raped me.'
>
> (Warshaw, 1994: 91)

Men and women perceive certain behaviors and communication as meaning very different things in the sexual situation, even excluding when they are not being honest about events. Putting aside the disingenuous cases, consider the differences in perceptions about sexual communication – starting with men not taking 'no' to mean no. Part of the cultural message about sex is that men are aggressors or initiators of sex and women are not supposed to be eager about sex, so they need to be persuaded or 'forced' into it. Adding to the problem are a significant number of women who say 'no' but still desire sex and may later consent to sex. Men are taught to be the aggressors and to be persistent, and women are taught to be passive and appear reluctant. These stereotypes about sexual behaviors are also reinforced in the media. For example, we are all familiar with the famous scene from *Gone with the Wind* (1939) where, ignoring Scarlett's objections, Rhett carries her to the bedroom and forces sexual intercourse upon her. Magically, in the morning Scarlett is a radiant and happy woman. From this model we get 18-year-old Sam saying, 'I used a little bit of force once where I overpowered a woman. She didn't mind it after it was over. If she'd started crying or something, I would've stopped' (Beneke, 1988: 36).

In modern times, rock and rap lyrics, as well as popular men's magazines, exalt the sexual dominance of men over women – the view that women are there for the sexual service of men. Discussing these difference perceptions, Robin Weiner claims:

> Men and women frequently misinterpret the intent of various dating behaviors and erotic play ... a woman may believe she has communicated her unwillingness to have sex—and other women would agree, thus making it a 'reasonable' female expression. Her male partner might still believe she is willing—and other men would agree with his interpretation, thus making it a 'reasonable' male interpretation. The woman, who believes that she has conveyed her lack of consent, may interpret the man's persistence as an indication that he does not care if she objects and plans to have sex despite her lack of consent. She may then feel frightened by the man and submit against her will.
>
> (Weiner, 1993:147–9)

The research backs up this divide between men and women's acceptable sexual behavior, including when women are consenting and when sex is forced. In the case above the woman would believe that she had been raped or had engaged in nonconsenual sex (if she didn't label it rape) and the man would believe that he had engaged in normal sexual interaction. The perceptions of the activities are truly split.

Even if we agree that she didn't consent – which people and the law, given its interpretation of consent, dispute – criminal law looks to what the *man believes* about the situation. Did the man believe that the woman wasn't consenting to sex? If he didn't believe that, then he believes she is consenting. Consequently, if such a case made it to trial the man would likely be acquitted for lacking the *mens rea* or mental state for the crime of rape. The law requires for criminal conviction that the defendant be *at fault* for the offense; and he is only at fault if his mental state includes an awareness of wrongdoing. What about the Casanova who believes that every woman wants to have sex with him and consequently believes that all women are consenting to sex with him? What about the men who raped Denise and April? Was their behavior at fault? Should the law reward with acquittal men who remain oblivious to what women are communicating? We could require the man's belief about the woman's consent to be not only *honestly* held, but also *reasonable*. Thus you would think that this might stop that Casanova who honestly believes that any and all women are consenting to sex with him, no matter how unreasonable that belief might be. For example, the woman said 'no' and pushed him away. This would seem a good resolution to our problem of inconsiderate and self-absorbed men. However, reasonable beliefs are often tested against societal attitudes about norms of sexual communications – going back to norms about male dominance and persistence and female submission and reluctance. So in the society where it is understood that 'no' means 'yes' and women feign reluctance, men may 'reasonable believe' that the woman is consenting even in the face of resistance.

The other piece to this puzzle is the research data about whether there is any justification for the commonly held belief that women say 'no' when they mean 'yes.' Muehlenhard and Hollabaugh (1988) studied college women to find out whether they ever said 'no' when they intended to have sex with someone. They found that 39 percent of the students reported that they had said 'no' once or only a few times when they intended to have sex with the person. The reasons for this behavior, according to the study, were: fear of appearing promiscuous, moral reasons, and what they called manipulative reasons, the desire to be in control. Other interesting facts about the women who had said no while intending to have sex were that they were more likely than other women to view romantic relationships as adversarial – to see that men were entitled to use force to get what they want, to think that women like forceful men, and to see token resistance as common. These are women who have internalized the Scarlett/Rhett conquest model of sexuality.

Some of the obstructions to rape reform are that many statutes don't include nonaggravated nonconsensual sex; that interpretations of the statutes don't include women's perceptions of what is frightening or intimidating, and women's normal reactions to those circumstances (for example, submission or crying); and that there is a gender split about sexual communication leading to differences in beliefs about sexual events. The questions I want to explore is whether there are good reasons for excluding a range of nonconsensual sexual activity from criminal law? Why not treat as criminal all nonconsensual sexual activity and worry about what circumstances and conditions undermine consent? What role, if any, should force play in the crime of rape? And what difference should it make that the victim knew the assailant? These are the questions that I will take up in this book to ultimately argue that nonconsenual sex should be a crime, whether or not there is recognizable force. Forcible sex should be distinguished from nonforcible but nonconsenual sex. But both should be treated as crimes. Distinguishing the different types of cases will allow us to clarify the elements of the crimes, one focusing on the issue of sex without consent and the other focusing on the forceful or violent nature of the sex. Separating the offenses allows us to be clear about the harm involved and the severity of each offense. Nevertheless, whether we are talking about aggravated or nonaggravated rape, the fact that the victim knows her assailant should not change the law's reaction to the crime. We no longer accept that a husband can legally beat his wife; no more should we accept that a boss, date or husband can rape his subordinate, date, or wife.

The Plan for the Book

I will begin by considering the history of rape law, which I will argue protected male interests in sexual access and avoiding prosecution at the expense of female interests in protecting their autonomy. The law required 'utmost resistance,' in other words, for women to fight to the point of death or face the assumption of consensual sexual intercourse. Added to this is the requirement of corroboration by an independent witness, and the existence of extreme force. These factors made it unlikely that there would ever be a conviction for rape. Although some of the more egregious requirements imposed historically have been eliminated, the reforms have only gone so far; in particular they have not resolved the problems of prosecuting acquaintance rapes. There continues to be resistance to changes to the rape statutes that would capture this wider range of cases involving acquaintances and no force.

What I ultimately argue for is expanding our conception of rape to include all nonconsenual sex, including that which is perpetrated by an acquaintance. The focus of my argument will be on a robust notion of consent. I will analyze consent as an act using the performative account of language. But before I can get to those positive arguments, I need to address the powerful issues that challenge the rape reform that would include nonaggravated (nonviolent) nonconsensual acquaintance sexual activity. The objections are as follows:

1. *No serious harm objection*   Philosophers such as Michael Davis have argued that 'rape is *not* a *very* serious crime' (1984: 62). For Davis the forced penetration of nonconsenual sex is not very serious. He is not referring to what the law often calls 'aggravated rape' that would include additional assault, for example, a beating along with the rape. Jeffrie Murphy (1994) analogized forced sexual intercourse with forcing someone to eat sushi, taking something that is normally pleasurable and forcing it upon someone. Again the implication is that rape is not as serious as other crimes since a constituent part of it is pleasurable. This reinforces the opinion of Joe, who said 'There has to be some point in every rape where the woman relaxes and enjoys it. I'm not saying that ladies *want* to be raped *because* they enjoy it, but there has to be some point where they enjoy it, because it's enjoyable. Sex is enjoyable' (Beneke, 1988: 54). Particularly when we focus on acquaintance rape it is commonly believed that there is no serious harm involved, and consequently it should not be treated as a crime.

2. *Lack of clear distinction objection*   This focuses on the lack of clear criteria to distinguish nonaggravated yet nonconsensual sex – what I'll call for simplicity 'acquaintance rape' – or not fully consensual intercourse (that should count as rape) from nonaggravated yet non- or not fully consensual intercourse – what the courts have called 'unscrupulous seduction,' 'reluctant submission,' or just regretted intercourse (Panichas, 231).

3. Mens rea *objection* A third objection is argued by Doug Husak and George C. Thomas III, who raised worries that expanding the definition of rape beyond explicit threats or physical violence would be unfair to defendants who base their actions on social conventions about how women consent to sex. Husak and Thomas (1992) argue that it is reasonable for a man to believe that a woman is consenting to sex even when confronted with 'no's' or other kinds of rejection behavior, including physical rejection.

4. *'Paradox' of acquaintance rape* A fourth argument against expanding the definition of rape is that women in unaggravated situations with acquaintances are often uncertain themselves as to whether they were 'raped.' Peter Westen calls this the 'paradox' of acquaintance rape and asks what causes survivors of acquaintance rape to be normatively ambivalent about whether they were raped. If the victims themselves are uncertain about the interpretation of events, then the law should be reticent to forge ahead and expand the territory of felonious sex.

5. *Patronizing to women objection* This final objection was raised by a group of critics of rape reform, including writers such as Katie Rophie and Camille Paglia. They argue that the inclusion of acquaintance rape undermines women's equality by making them out to be incompetent, implying that women cannot take care of themselves and are in need of protection by the state. Consequently, I'll call this the 'patronizing to women' objection since it rests on the claim that expanding the rape law is in fact patronizing to women. These critics argue that women can (and should) take care of themselves. Women should be clear about their desires and make sure their partners know

what they want and don't want, and not rely on the law's protection of their sexual lives.

Are these good reasons for excluding the range of nonconsensual sexual activity from the criminal law? These objections embody substantive worries about the harm of nonaggravated rape, about the ability to draw clear lines and procedural concerns about the fairness of imposing rules that cannot be followed or are out of step with social conventions. If women themselves report that they sometimes say 'no' when they are interested in sexual activity, then why shouldn't the law be skeptical about protecting women against these behaviors. Further, if women don't always consider themselves as rape victims when they have experienced nonconsensual sex, then again why should the law treat nonconsenual sex as a felony. A final significant objection is the history of the law's treatment of women – viz., that many rules instituted to 'protect' women in fact functioned to treat them as 'different' and 'inferior' because of their need for protection. Many times women's behavior was curtailed in the name of protecting them; society then continued to see them as inferior to men. So if changes in the statutes would result in infantilizing women, treating them as if they couldn't take care of themselves, that would be a serious argument against the changes.

Whether and why we should expand the criminal law's protection against nonconsensual sexual activity is the focus of this book. There are, maybe needless to say, powerful arguments on both sides of the current debate. Asking for more regulation is particularly difficult for liberals, who are generally committed to less coercive regulation by the state. The criminal law's aim in a liberal democracy is the provision of the conditions for individuals' self-determination and the pursuit of their own conception of the good. Since in the liberal state the conditions for individual autonomy are the primary goals of law, this leaves the state with the role of ensuring that personal autonomy is protected. Its secondary role is to facilitate autonomous development by ensuring the social and political environment most conducive to individual self-determination and well-being. How that is done is that at minimum the criminal law ought to protect against harm to others. Even in cases where there is harm to others, however, we only want to engage the coercive power of the criminal law when the harm is *serious* as having the law meddling in all kinds of trivial harms would encumber our lives too much. Liberals have not wanted to expand the reach of the criminal law because they believe that the state will do more harm than good in interfering with individuals' chosen actions.

The reason the state should protect against harm and threats of harm is that such harm to our important interests makes us fearful and often forces us to constrain our activities and ambitions, which in turn frustrates our ability to pursue our ends – to live autonomously. Harms the criminal law sees as serious enough to encompass are those that violate or threaten personal autonomy. These would include offenses against the body and personal property, actions that undermine our capacities to choose rationally, including undermining our sense of self-respect and self-worth. Only those we recognize as *wrongful* harms are protected by the criminal law, and then only if serious. Joel Feinberg has written the classic work on the theory of harm and what he calls 'the moral limits of the criminal law' (1984: 34–35). Feinberg gives credence and substance to John Stuart Mill's theory that the legitimate limit on the criminal law is harm to others, the so-called 'harm principle.' For Feinberg, two conditions are necessary in applying the harm principle: a harm must be 1) a wrongful act that 2) sets back or invades the interest of another person. The first condition focuses on those harms which are also wrongs. Many things can be harmful, for example, actions to which we consent can literally harm us. However, not all harms to us are wrongs. The harm principle, argues Feinberg, is mediated by the *volenti non fit injuria* maxim, meaning 'To one who consents, no harm is done.' So, for example, consenting to a surgical procedure that has a 50 percent failure rate may result in actual harm – the patient may be worse off than before the surgery. If I gave my informed consent (I was told the benefits and risks and was competent to consent and did consent) then, even if I am harmed by the surgery, I would be one of the 50 percent who were harmed by the procedure. Therefore I am not wronged and have nothing to complain about since I consented to the surgery knowing the risks. Consent plays an important role in determining whether a harm is wrongful. Consent is the vehicle through which we express our autonomous wishes, so by getting consent one does not wrong that person.

The second condition states that for the action to be a harm it must set back another's interests. There are a number of ways of understanding what an interest is, including one based on well-being and another based on rights. Well-being covers a large variety of types of interests – stealing someone's property, beating them up, terrorizing them all affect their ability to live their life. Feinberg discusses two kinds of well-being interests: welfare interests and ulterior interests. Ulterior interests arise from an individual's particular goals and ambitions. My life will be better if I realize my particular ends – those are my ulterior interests. This is assuming that my ulterior interests remain fairly constant over time. Welfare interests are those we all have that are prerequisites for any ulterior interests. These are interests in life, health, liberty, absence of fear and other psychological impairment. Rights-based interests are interests in things or states of affairs, whether or not they effect our well-being. The wealthy woman is harmed by the embezzlement of her money, even though she doesn't know that her money was taken and doesn't need the money that was stolen. She has a right not to have her money taken. These are harms that a person is entitled to be protected against and morally entitled to complain about, since the person has a right that is violated by the harm (Feinberg, 1984).

The law should protect against those wrongful injuries against interests that are critical to personal autonomy. The reformulated question of our project is: Are nonconsensual nonviolent sexual interactions between acquaintances seriously wrongful harms that violate either well-being interests or rights-based interests such that those events undermine personal autonomy and thereby should be prohibited by the criminal law?

Since women are much more likely than men to be victims of sexual assaults of any kind, violent or not, the obvious question to ask is whether the criminal law is treating women's autonomy rights equally to men's by excluding from criminal protection so much nonconsensual sexual activity? Sexual assaults are not harms that have the same impact on everyone to the same extent. Outside of prison, a disproportionate number of women are the victims of rape. Adding this to the emerging awareness that the law has not always acknowledged and protected women's and men's interests equally should lead us to be skeptical of the current law's treatment of women. Since the impact of the harm of nonconsensual sex (if it is a harm) disproportionately affects women, and given the history of unequal protection of women's interests, we will want to look more carefully at the objections to expanding rape laws to ensure that this recalcitrance doesn't simply perpetuate the historical pattern of discrimination.

It is an essential element of a just legal system that it at least recognizes and protects important interests, say autonomy interests, of everyone equally. No individual should be treated as inferior to another. One important way the law has treated individuals as inferior has been to treat the group they belong to as inferior by failing to accord their interests equal consideration. Unless individuals are sure that they and their interests are equal before the law and will be treated as such – including protecting them from violence, bodily invasions, and domination by others – they will have difficulty developing the proper amount of security, self-esteem, and respect that are required for leading an autonomous life. Societies committed to liberal principles must ensure conditions in which all individuals may develop their capacities and live autonomous lives. Treating their interests equally is one important way of doing this. I believe it is important to be clear about the role the criminal law plays in protecting autonomy and securing equality of citizens. If the criminal law does not protect women's interests in, for example, their sexual autonomy, it is not protecting them from serious harms and is thus perpetuating their unequal status in society.

In discounting or disregarding harm to members of particular sections of society, whether racial minorities or women, the law fails to treat them as equals. Legal systems that protect the interests of some but not others thereby imply the superiority of one group over another. That is, the law is treating one group as if they matter and another as if they do not. Such systems then preclude individual relationships based on equality. In this book I will consider the ways in which the criminal law has failed and continues to fail to protect women's interests, particularly in sexual autonomy, by failing to protect women from sexual violence and a range of nonconsensual sexual acts. Historically the reason for this failure arose from social and political institutions that considered women legally unequal to men. Though we have obviously progressed from those bad old days, current rape laws and their application, I will argue, continue to undermine women's sexual autonomy. The law fails to ensure that women's interests are accorded the same consideration as men's interests. What I will consider is how this treatment is a reflection of embedded ideas that support sexual inequality generally in modern (western) society. Robert Dahl (1996: 639) wrote that 'the subordination of women [is] institutional and enforced by an over-whelming array of the most powerful forces available [including] individual and collective terror and violence, official and unofficial; law, custom and convention; and social and economic structures [and is] backed up by the state itself.' I will argue that the law's treatment of rape, and society's view of rape, illustrate this institutiona-lized and enforced subordination of women. To subordinate a group is to treat them as inferior or unequal to others. Rape exemplifies the concatenation of forces that continue to support the unequal treatment of women in society. Ironically the act of rape itself, I will argue, expresses the inferiority of women, which is one of its harms.

Ultimately, what I want to consider is the proper *liberal* theory of harmful or wrongful sex, one that protects all individuals' interests equally and will provide the elements for criminal prohibitions. Liberal societies purport to have two fundamental values – liberty and equality. Liberals start with the assumption that individuals are moral equals, which merits equal liberty and opportunity. In the words of Ronald Dworkin, they are deserving of 'equal concern and respect.' All competent adults are moral agents: they have the capacity to develop and exercise moral responsibility, to develop and pursue a conception of the good. But note that the call for equality is not necessarily a call for substantive equality, say in income, for everyone. However, that conception of equality is not of interest here. The importance of equality for many groups who have historically suffered discrimination –

such as women and racial and ethnic minorities – is, as
Elizabeth Anderson (1999: 313) has pointed out, to
'abolish oppression – that is, forms of social relationships by which some people dominate, exploit, margin-
alize, demean, and inflict violence upon others ... [is]
to seek a social order in which persons stand in relations
of equality.' The aim is to end arbitrary social
hierarchies. It was because some people considered
themselves superior to others – men superior to women,
whites superior to blacks – that they thought they
deserved more social goods and freedom. That superiority was also grounds for not recognizing (or
discounting) harm to the inferior group. Historically
harms against women were not recognized partly
because women were not recognized as gender equals.
The result was that rape laws had absurdly high
standards to prove that a woman was raped. For
example, statutes required as elements of the crime that
the woman prove that the act was 'forcible' and 'against
her will,' and courts (and some statutes) required victim
resistance, expressed first as 'utmost resistance.' These
requirements weren't protecting women against harm.
They were, however, protecting men from charges of
sexual assault. Later the requirement of the victim was
then reduced to 'earnest resistance' and then 'reasonable
resistance.' The victim was in effect put on trial: either
her lack of resistance to physical violence or threats of
violence showed that she was not really a victim or, if
her resistance wasn't aggressive enough, it showed that
she didn't value her 'virtue' and thereby wasn't a victim.
This is merely one illustration of the criminal law's
failure to protect or recognize significant harms to
women, and thus its failure to protect women's sexual
autonomy and to treat them as equals.

There is a fair amount of a consensus now in liberal
societies about the historical picture, that is, that rape
laws treated women unfairly and did not protect them
from harms. Society did not 'see' certain actions as

wrongful or damaging to women. Nevertheless, there is much less consensus about current criminal laws and the need for, or the direction of, reform. Even now the idea that a husband could 'rape' his wife or that a man could 'rape' his date is met with disbelief. That sexual interaction without violence (violence understood in traditional legal terms) could be injurious is met with incredulity. It is easy to see the historical legacy as products of sexism – women's interests were not seen as equal to men's because women were viewed as less valuable – but current statutes are not thought of as resulting from sex discrimination.

What then is the argument that current criminal laws continue to fail to protect women against certain harms and thereby fail to accord their interests equal consideration? That question and its answer will form the core of this book. First I shall consider briefly the history of rape laws and how they were unfair to women's interests. I shall explore the criticism of the criminal rape laws raised by feminists in the 1970s. They exposed the fact that the laws were not protecting women from harms but instead were protecting men's interests, mainly in matters of sexual access and avoiding prosecution. Feminists pushed for reforms, arguing that the force and resistance requirements and the introduction of past sexual history, among other practices, were not protecting women from harms. Furthermore, they exposed the inherent suspicion of women that was entrenched in the system and how it worked again to protect men's interests at the expense of women's. After considering the historical records and reasons why reforms are still not protecting women's sexual autonomy, I shall outline my own strategy for reform.

Before detailing my own positive agenda, in Chapter 3 I shall expand upon the objections raised to including nonaggravated rape in criminal law. While feminists were pushing for rape reform, another group of anti-rape reform critics such as Camille Paglia (1992), Christine Hoff Sommers (1990), and Katie Roiphe (1993) argued against change. They argued against feminists' conceptualization of rape and questioned their strategy for advancing women's equality. Critics in this camp argue that the radicals' views about the pervasiveness of sexual violence and the unintelligibility of consent under the current patriarchal system actually undermine women's progress toward equality, making women out to be incompetent victims who cannot take care of themselves on dates, at home, or in the office. They argue that feminists are actually undermining women's goals of equality by enfeebling women, by portraying them once again as victims of men, and thereby in need of protection from the state. Ironically radical feminists, I shall argue, end up agreeing with some of the anti-rape reform critics on issues about the direction of reform. Liberals, though not necessarily explicitly agreeing with the substantive claims of Paglia, Sommers, and Roiphe, seem to agree with many of their conclusions. Liberals have tended to advance libertarian or libertine views about sexuality, arguing that the government ought to stay out of consensual sexual behavior and assuming that the notion of consent is unproblematic at least in the context of sexuality (Husak and Thomas, 1992 and 2001).

Who is right about the criminal law's treatment of sexual interactions? Should we expand our notion of impermissible or criminal sexual activity? Has the criminal law failed to notice harms against women, or should we keep the criminal prohibitions narrowly drawn to include only violent sexuality without consent? What role should consent play in sexual crimes? Is the notion of consent fairly unproblematic, as liberals have assumed, or totally bankrupt, as radical feminists have argued? I will argue that both the radical feminists' and the anti-rape reform critics' rejection of consent is misguided. I believe that this is a mistake and that consent is a powerful moral tool for protecting individuals. Furthermore I believe that it is important to focus our attention on so-called 'acquaintance rape.' This is where the hard questions are and it is significant that the empirical data show that the vast majority of nonconsensual sex takes place with a person that the victim knew and without any legally recognized force. Thereby the stereotype of the stranger with a weapon, which formed the basis for the elements of rape, does not help us grasp this problem. The notions of physical force and 'against the will' fit nicely into the picture of the stranger jumping out from a bush and attacking an unknown woman. A woman's date physically over-powering her is a very different picture.

After exploring the history and the contemporary landscape of debates about rape, Chapter 4 will analyze the nature and value of consent following my argument in Chapter 3 that we should separate aggravated (forcible) rape from unaggravated, what I shall call acquaintance rape since it most often involves someone the victim knows. The former should not have the element of nonconsent; rather violence, force, or the threat of force should be sufficient for criminality. Whereas with acquaintance rape the focus should properly be on consent. Consent, I shall argue, does play an important role as the delimiter of noncriminal from criminal sex because consent plays a crucial role in protecting *autonomy*. If we are going to claim that consent plays a significant role in protecting autonomy, then what counts as consent will have to be much more stringent than what is currently accepted in criminal rape proceedings. After considering various conceptions of consent, I shall argue for a performative conception of consent. Consent has normative importance since it *gives permission* for crossing personal boundaries. Consent should not be mistaken, as it has been by many, for voluntary action; nor should it be confused with submission or mere assent (as the law has done too often in rape cases).

Chapter 5 will consider factors that undermine consent, focusing on the internal characteristics of a woman which make it impossible for her to consent. Incapacitation also undercuts consent, and the question I ask is what makes a person incapacitated. The common reasons are alcohol, mental illness, and mental retardation and age. These are cases where, even if there is a 'yes,' the law should not treat that as consent. The next chapter considers the external constraints on a person's action that frustrate consent, particularly coercion and fraud. In this chapter I will analyze these concepts, arguing that background circumstances can be coercive, resulting in implicit threats, and thereby no explicit communication of the consequences of non-compliance is required for coercion. Coercion and deceit are defeaters of consent, but there is no justification to infer consent from their absence. Beyond 'no meaning no,' I shall argue that we should require a positive 'yes' in the absence of coercion or fraud and without any of the internal factors that incapacitate a person. Throughout this analysis, I shall illustrate these arguments with examples and also argue that what constitutes consent, and thereby would undermine it, varies from context to context depending on the seriousness of the activities involved, the consequences of mistake, and the opportunities of revocation, among other factors.

So far we have been discussing the elements of the crime of rape, or the *actus reus*. Let us turn now to questions about the mental state, or *mens rea*, required for the crime in Chapter 7. Is the mental state required for rape the belief that one is having sex without consent? Is recklessness sufficient? What about negligence about consent? If we suppose that mistaken belief about consent is a defense for rape, then does the mistake have to be reasonable, or is the fact that it is honestly held enough, as the High Court justices in England supposed in *Regina v. Morgan* (1976). The *mens rea* standard has a profound effect on how the law treats rape.

Chapter 8 will examine in more detail the harm of rape, arguing that rape, beyond affecting individual welfare interests, involves an expressive harm to the victim that inturn affects all women. The message that rape expresses is the inferior status of this woman and all women, that their interests don't matter, and that they exist for the sexual gratification of men. Since I have focused so much attention on the role of consent, I consider whether consent transforms *any* sexual inter-action into a morally acceptable one. In other words, is consent all that matters for morally acceptable sex? The role of consent in sadomasochistic relationships raises interesting questions for liberals and feminists. I will explore some of them. Finally I shall outline where we should go from here in terms of rape, society, and the law.

Notes

1 See 'Victims of Rape: Hearings Before the House Select Committee on Children, Youth, and Families,' 101st Cong., 2nd Sess. 5 (1990). In one study the statistics sent to the FBI showed that only 53.8 percent of rape reports filed by women were listed as rapes by the police.
2 A rape victim recalling her court experience writes: 'My experience in the courtroom was like being raped all over again, only this time it was worse because I was in front of a room full of people.' In Weihe and Richards 1995, p. 32.

Chapter 2

The Historical Treatment of Rape

A 16-year-old victim was tripped to the ground by her neighbor and he then forced himself on her. The victim screamed as hard as she could and the defendant then held his hand over her mouth. The Supreme Court of Wisconsin found that *the victim had not adequately demonstrated* her nonconsent. 'Not only must there be entire absence of mental consent or assent, but there must be the most vehement exercise of every physical means or faculty within the woman's power to resist the penetration of her person, and this must be shown to persist until the offense is consummated.'

Brown v. State, 1906

Looking back, the history of rape law is shocking and indefensible. In response to criticisms by feminists such as Susan Brownmiller (1976), many changes came about in the 1970s and 1980s. Nevertheless, even with these revisions the penal codes and legal practice continue to be infected with the history of patriarchy. The system still protects the interests of men at the expense of the interests of women (Archard, 1999; Dripps, 1992; Estrich, 1987; Henderson, 1992; MacKinnon, 1989; Schulhofer, 1992 and 1998; West, 1991). Historically, rape laws have had blatant sexist assumptions and standards that raise serious questions about the law's objectivity or fairness. There are two problems: first, the laws protected men's interests in sexual access and against prosecution. Second, the statutes and the courts employed assumptions and standards about rape,

consent, force, reasonable belief, and resistance that
failed to account for the perspective of women.
Unfortunately, those same assumptions and standards
are employed against women, to their detriment.
Feminist legal theorists have criticized standard doc-
trines in rape law, pointing out that 'utmost resistance,'
the requirements of physical resistance and corroboration, marital exception, and the routine introduction at
trial of past sexual histories in rape cases are not rational
for the legitimate ends of criminal law and are blatantly
unfair to women. The aim of this chapter is to give a
brief history of rape laws, particularly focusing on the
20th century, and then to introduce the reforms that
were meant to solve certain problems and examine how
and why they failed to do so. This will not be an
exhaustive history of rape, as for that there are some
excellent studies, for example, Hirshman and Larson,
1998.

Historical Lessons

The 18th-century definition of rape in the acclaimed
Commentaries on the Law of England was 'carnal
knowledge [by a man not her husband] of a woman
forcibly and against her will' (Blackstone, 1966). The
law statutorily exempted husbands and it required a
finding of force *and* absence of consent. The fact that
wives could not be raped by their husbands, even if they
were estranged and there was extreme force, wouldn't
be changed until the late 1970s and early 1980s.
Blackstone's definition was retained into the 1950s,
with changes from the American Law Institute's
attempt at reforming the entire criminal code, called
the Model Penal Code. Rape laws, argue theorists such
as Debra Rhode, were not designed to protect only
women's interests.[1] In *Justice and Gender* she claims:

Historically, rape has been perceived as a threat to male as well as female interests; it has devalued wives and daughters and jeopardized patrilineal systems of inheritance. But too stringent constraints on male sexuality have been equally threatening to male policymakers. The threat of criminal charges based on female fabrications has dominated the history of rape law.

(1989: 245)

To illustrate how these laws protected men's interests and not women's we must first look at how they were designed to protect men's interest in their women, in their daughters or wives. For instance, the 'utmost resistance requirement' reflected the belief that a woman should protect her chastity with her life, since female chastity was worth a lot to fathers interested in marrying off their daughters and to husbands wishing to ensure that children were biologically theirs. Rape laws protected the value of female chastity for their men rather than women's sexual autonomy or even their physical well-being. First, it could be extremely dangerous for women to 'resist to utmost' in many circumstances, and it was was also humiliating to victims whose resistance was found wanting, as they were then judged to have consented. Second, 'utmost resistance' protected men's interest in sexual access, thus making it difficult to obtain a criminal charge and conviction for rape. The result was that to prove 'forcibly' and 'against her will,' courts (and some statutes) required resistance, expressed first as 'utmost resistance.' This meant that, unless the victim used 'utmost' physical resistance in a fight to near death, the sexual interaction was not against her will. Female chastity was of the ultimate value, and women who didn't protect it with their lives must have consented to the sexual activity. Utmost resistance was considered to be the natural response of a virtuous woman, and therefore not an imposition on any woman. In the following case where the appeals court reversed the conviction of a man found guilty of raping a servant in his house, the court said,

> Can the mind conceive of a woman, in the possession of her faculties and powers, revoltingly unwilling that this deed should be done upon her, who would not resist so hard and so long as she was able? And if a woman, aware that it will be done unless she does resist, does not resist to the extent of her abilities on the occasion, must it not be that she is not entirely reluctant?
>
> (*People v. Dohring*, 1874)

The woman's behavior is judged and put on trial, even with evidence of extreme force or weapons. If she was not beaten to the edge of death, she was not raped. A Texas court said in *Perez v. State* (1906) that 'although some force be used, yet if she does not put forth all power of resistance which she was capable of exerting under the circumstances, it will not be rape.' This requirement reflected the view that it was better for a woman to die than be 'dishonored.' And the assumption was that if a women did not put up such a fight she probably was consenting and just could not admit to it.

In the case of *Whittaker v. State* (1880) where, even though the assailant had the woman's hands and feet tight so that she couldn't move and threatened her with his revolver when she screamed for help, the Supreme Court of Wisconsin reversed his conviction, saying 'this is not a case where the prosecutrix was overcome by threats of personal violence.' The court continued that Whittaker's threat to use his gun was merely 'conditional upon her attempting again to cry out ... The testimony does not show that the threat of personal violence overpowered her will, or ... that she was incapable of voluntary action.' For the court, consent which is equivalent to 'submission ... no matter how reluctantly yielded, removes from the act an essential element of the crime of rape.' The 'utmost resistance' requirement, as Schulhofer stated, 'became impossibly difficult to satisfy and dangerous to any victim who tried' (1998: 19). These were malicious standards that got worse when medical writers insisted that women had the physical means to stop rape if they so desired, by using hands, limbs, and pelvic muscles. They claimed that any woman who wasn't willing could stop any man, regardless of size, from penetrating her. The implication was that successful penetration meant that the woman was willing (*Brown v. State*, 1906). In addition to utmost resistance there was a fixation on women making up complaints of rape, with courts showing an entrenched suspicion and distrust toward female victims. Unless the victim could *prove* that she physically resisted, what reason would they have to suppose that she was not lying? 'Distrust of women victims was incorporated into the definition of the crime and the rules of proof' (Estrich, 1987: 29).

Two other requirements which suggested the unreliability of female victims were corroboration of their testimony and the prompt filing of a complaint. If the complaint was not made quickly, it was assumed that the victim was having second thoughts about her consensual sexual activity. Distrust of female victims was integrated into the instructions to the jury, who would be told that it was unsafe to convict on the uncorroborated evidence of the alleged victim. The legacy of this history is epitomized by the warning given three centuries ago by the English Lord Chief Justice Matthew Hale (1609–76), who said that rape is a charge 'easily to be made and hard to be proved, and harder to be defended by the party accused, tho' never so innocent.' This was, until very recently, recited to juries before their deliberations. Glanville Williams, a leading 20th-century jurist, said 'There is a sound reason for it [the instruction to the jury], because these cases are particularly subject to the danger of deliberately false charges, resulting from sexual neurosis, phantasy, jealousy, spite or simply a girl's refusal to admit that she consented to an act of which she is now ashamed' (1963: 159). Furthermore, it was the opinion of the jurist John Wigmore (1863–1943), author of the USA's most influential treatise on evidence (1970), that 'No judge should ever let a sex-offense charge go to the jury unless the female complainant's social history and mental make-up have been examined and testified to by a qualified physician.' Williams worries that psychological approaches such as physicians questioning the plaintiff to determine whether she is fantasizing, neurotic, and so on, may not be able to pick out all falsehoods and suggests that all female complainants should take polygraph tests.

The issue of consent being identified with submission, no matter how long or what it takes to get that submission, is patently absurd but has endured until the present. What role is consent supposed to be playing when it can be inferred from someone beaten or threatened to comply? In *no* other area would we accept such a notion of consent. The consent standard in rape was and, as we will see, continues to be unique. The law requires victims of rape, unlike victims of any other crime, to demonstrate their 'wishes' – that is, to demonstrate their nonconsent through physical resistance. Moreover, in some cases even resistance has not been sufficient to establish nonconsent. Even in contemporary cases we see the lingering effects of the attitudes explicitly expressed in academic works of the 1950s and 1960s; for example, Glanville Williams's classic textbook on criminal law warns that women often welcome a 'masterly advance' and 'present a token of resistance' (1963: 238). An article published in the *Stanford Law Review* (Dworkin, 1966) argues that, although a woman may desire sexual intercourse, it is customary for her to say 'no, no, no' while meaning 'yes, yes, yes.' Similarly, a *Yale Law Journal* article suggested that women do not know what they want or mean what they say and often require force to have a 'pleasurable' experience.[2] Rather than requiring an explicit sign of consent and worrying about the circumstances in which the alleged consent was given (for example, were the circumstances threatening or implicit threats made, was the victim intimidated), the courts have interpreted silence and nonresistance as signs of consent. In the eyes of the law consent was presumed to be present, and this presumption of consent could only be defeated by the most extreme circumstances.

Even where there is clearly overwhelming force, courts have pursued the issue of consent. In the case of *People v. Burnham* (1986) a woman was severely beaten and then forced to engage in intercourse with her husband and a dog. The court held out the possibility of consent, or at least that the defendant might reasonably believe that she was consenting.[3] So-called 'submission,' no matter how 'reluctantly given,' negated the element 'without consent.' The meaning of consent is mysterious since beating and threatening a woman into 'submission' was taken as consent.

Many of these severe rules lasted well into the 1950s and 1960s, and some persist to the present. The exception was in the case of a white woman charging a black man. In those cases, the law did not require 'utmost resistance' since it was assumed that a white woman would never consent to sexual intercourse with a black man. For instance, in Virginia in 1921 a black man was sentenced to the death penalty for the rape of a white, 'simple, good, unsophisticated country girl.' The court never looked for her 'utmost resistance' (*Hart v. Commonwealth*). This and similar cases illustrate another way in which the law has treated different groups and sections of society unequally.

The Model Penal Code

In the 1950s the American Law Institute proposed reforms to state criminal codes, including rape laws, prompted by worries about the extremely low conviction rate for rape. The Model Penal Code, however, kept the requirements of corroboration of the woman's testimony, the special cautionary instructions to the jury, the marital exception, and extended exemption to cases where the man and woman were living together. The Code suggested eliminating victim consent altogether and focusing on the man's illegitimate behavior. Changing the focus from the woman's to the man's conduct sounded like a step in the right direction as, up until then, the woman's conduct was judged and often found failing. Nevertheless, the reasons for not including the element of consent in the offense of rape in the Model Penal Code lay with sexist notions about women and consent. They were filled with the same assumptions about women: that women say 'no' and don't mean it, that women are ambivalent about consent to sex, and that women have conflicting emotions and are unable to directly express their sexual desires. What the contributors to the Code stated as their motivation was to draw a 'line between forcible rape on the one hand and reluctant submission on the other' (Section 279), and only the former was a serious crime. The focus then was on 'forcible compulsion' as a trustworthy guide to when women had not consented. Submission, usually in cases without overwhelming violence, was legitimate. However, submission through intimidation, threats, or deception is not legitimate sexual conduct, and force continues to this day to play a major part in the understanding of rape.

States reformed their statutes in the 1960s but didn't adopt the Model Penal Code's suggestions wholesale; rather they adopted parts of it, particularly focusing on 'forcible compulsion.' Most states kept the resistance requirement, the marital exception, the special rules about prompt complaint, corroboration, and the cautionary jury instruction. They reduced the utmost resistance requirement to 'earnest resistance' and later to 'reasonable resistance,' keeping to this day the question of the woman's physical resistance (Williams, 1963: 162). Current rules and practices still rely upon a woman's resistance as necessary evidence of rape. The laws continue to see rape as only a violent attack, and then only if the woman resists. Nonconsensual sex outside these parameters was not protected. Again the extreme force and resistance requirements were not applied when a black man was the defendant and the victim a white woman.

In the 1970s feminists such as Susan Brownmiller and Susan Griffin exposed many of the problems with the laws and the criminal justice system's treatment of rape victims (Griffin, 1971). The baseline assumption of consent, the corroboration rule, the routine introduction of a victim's sexual history, force and resistance, and marital exception illustrate the protection of men's interests in sexual access and not the protection of women's sexual choice. For practical purposes, the baseline apparently is one of consent rather than nonconsent.[4] Feminists argued that the rules themselves, particularly the force and resistance requirements, embodied typical male perceptions, attitudes, and reactions rather than female ones.[5] Moreover, some feminists argued that, far from protecting women, the rape laws, through their expectations of proper female behavior and their high expectations of impermissible force, actually served to enhance male opportunities for sexual access. What a woman wore or did – 'she wore a tight sweater,' 'she went to the man's apartment,' 'she drank alcohol' – led police and prosecutors to assume that she consented or had only got what she deserved because of her appearance and behavior. Feminists argued that the rape laws actually increased a woman's dependence on a male protector and thus reinforced social relations of male dominance.

If a case actually got to trial, the woman was subjected to brutal cross-examination of her life, particularly her prior sex life. No matter how violent or outrageous the alleged rape was, the object was to make her out to be a 'bad girl' who either consented to the events or got what she deserved given her 'loose' lifestyle. In the case discussed by Susan Griffin in *Ramparts* magazine, she described a rape trial where four men force a woman at gunpoint to go to one of their apartments, where all four sexually assault her. In court other women testified that the man owning the apartment had sexually assaulted them as well. The defense attorney characterized the events as consensual, suggesting that the victim was a 'loose woman.' The attorney asked her if she had been fired from a job because she'd had sex on the office couch, if she'd had an affair with a married man, and if her 'two children have a sex game in which one got on top of the other and they _____' (Griffin, 1971). All of these allegations she vehemently denied; however, the attorney had successfully created in the jurors' minds a distrust of the victim and a picture of her as a loose woman. Consequently, the defendant was acquitted. The standard trial tactic was for defense attorneys to 'put the woman' on trial, asking questions about her previous sexual experiences, whether she used birth control, whether she went to bars, what she wore, either suggesting that she consented to the sexual events or that she 'got what she deserved.' In the 1990s rape trial of William Kennedy Smith we heard, among other things, about the victim's Victoria's Secret underwear, suggesting that anyone who wears such underwear is looking for sex and thus playing to jurors' ideas about proper female behavior. Even victims who admitted consenting to sex with their boyfriends were consequently portrayed as likely to consent to the stranger who was on trial for raping them. The disappointing aspect of this is that juries accepted these arguments.

In the 1970s and 1980s, in response to feminist objections, reforms were made such as dropping the corroboration requirement and the special instruction to juries and, eventually, introducing 'rape-shield' rules to bar defense attorneys from using past sexual experiences as a way of undermining the credibility of the victim. Concern for equality led some feminists to stipulate gender-neutral statutes to replace traditional statutes which punished the rape of a woman specifically by a man. By 1980 over half of the American jurisdictions had gender-neutral statutes (Estrich, 1987: 81ff.) Support for gender-neutral statutes also arose from the following concern: 'Men who are sexually assaulted should have the same protection as female victims, and women who sexually assault men or other women should be as liable for conviction as conventional rapists' (Legrand, 1973: 941). Gender neutrality is seen as a way 'to eliminate the traditional attitude that the victim is supposed to resist earnestly to protect virginity, her female 'virtue' or her marital fidelity' (Bienen, 1980: 174–75).

Problems, however, arise from making rape statutes gender neutral as such statutes may address one set of issues but create others. Because women do not necessarily react in the same way as men, if gender-neutral statutes mean retaining male norms and reactions to rape scenarios, then women will continue to be disadvantaged. So, for example, physical resistance might be a typical male reaction to attack, but not necessarily a typical female reaction. Men are socialized to fight, to respond physically; women are not and may respond by, for example, crying or 'freezing.' Subjecting women to the resistance requirement therefore disadvantages them. Further, rape is typically something that is done *to* women *by* men. Rape is not generally a gender-neutral crime; men rape, not women. Women are overwhelmingly the victims of rape, and making rape gender neutral obscures this fact. Gender-neutral statutes are, however, the norm today.

Another move has been to re-label rape as a form of assault in order to rid the offense of 'its common law baggage of unique rules ... of resistance and proof,' to refocus attention away from the victim and place it where it properly belongs – with the defendant. The re-labeling of rape as 'sexual assault' may assume a position in the debate as to whether rape should be considered a crime of sexual desire or violence. Some feminists argue that rape is motivated by the desire to dominate, to have power, and not, as was long assumed, by uncontrollable sexual desire. Focusing on the violent aspects of rape makes it clear that the law is not trying to prohibit all sex and that violent men must be incapacitated as dangerous criminals, not treated as merely sexually aberrant. Moreover, to see rape as violence is to recognize that sex should be inconsistent with violent assault in law. The advantages of this, according to Rosemarie Tong, are: (1) it eliminates residual corroboration rules; (2) it lowers the overly high age of consent for sexual intercourse; (3) it eliminates as admissible evidence the victim's past sexual history; (4) it eliminates the marital-exception rule; and (5) it reduces the penalties for rape (1984: 113).

Reconceptualizing rape as assault has prompted some to question the seriousness of rape, particularly nonaggravated rape (Davis, 1984). How serious an assault is rape? Assaults are normally graduated in terms of the level of bodily injuries. Supporters of the change recognized that equating rape with assaultive conduct may obscure the unique meaning and under-standing of the indignity and harm of rape. Rape is different from other assaults. The reasons for the difference are complex. But then sex is different from other kinds of touching (McGregor, 1993).

It is understandable that feminist law reformers should seek to eliminate the legal rules that have made rape prosecutions more difficult to secure than prosecutions for other crimes. Their intentions, however, have sometimes been misinterpreted. Feminists are concerned that more rapes are prosecuted and hence argue that penalties for rape are reduced, recognizing that juries are unlikely to convict when the defendant faces a long sentence for a nonaggravated rape. Moreover, not all rapes are the same. Rapes which involve aggravated assault are worse than so-called simple rapes. That's not to suggest that the latter are not serious offenses and worthy of some punishment.

Conceptualizing rape as a form of assault or an act of violence presents the following problem; a man can force sex against a woman's will without physical violence. Having power over the victim will do. The definition of force – still a major component in statutes – needs to be clearly articulated and not confused with exclusively physical force. I will use force$_L$ to refer to the specialized notion of force that is used in criminal law. Threats short of physical violence should be sufficient for rape. Not all threats, however, undermine a person's freedom, for example, 'If you don't sleep with me I won't give you a fur coat.' So which threats are sufficient? This is a tough and tricky question that I will take up later. Another problem with conceptualizing rape as assault is that assaults are normally not consented to in law. Assault cannot be consented to; in other words, consensual assault remains assault. The exception is in certain sports which can, in some instances, involve what looks like assault with consent.

Feminists who argue for rape as *sexual* assault want to reinforce its violent character *and* sexual nature. Some argue that the so-called power rapists' and anger rapists' 'choice of the vagina or anus as the object of aggression is not accidental, but essential ... the rapist seeks to spoil, corrupt, or even destroy those aspects of a woman's person that should be a source of pride, joy, and power for her rather than a source of shame, depression, and humiliation' (Tong, 1984: 117).

On the other hand, rape as sexual assault focuses on women's sexuality for being particularly susceptible to attack, and hence in need of special protection. This view may reinforce the myth of rape 'according to which the invasion of sexual integrity is so traumatic that the victim's psychic wounds never heal' (Ibid., 118). The sexual assault approach may unwittingly cast women back into the position of victim, a role which many feminists would like to move beyond. With all these attempts at reforms, results were not good.

Even after the rape law reforms in the 1970s and 1980s, contemporary laws still search for victim resistance, with most US states retaining some version of it. Consider the following case. In *State v. Rusk* (1981) the victim gave the defendant a ride home from a bar where they had met through a mutual friend. The defendant invited the victim up to his apartment but she declined. After he took her car keys, she reluctantly accompanied him to his apartment. The defendant started to undress the victim, and before intercourse the victim said to the defendant, 'If I do what you want will you let me go without killing me?' The victim started to cry and then the defendant, according to the victim, started lightly choking her. The appellant court argued that she had not been raped as she had not been *forced*$_L$ because she had not resisted.

The standards used in this case exemplify what feminists label 'the male orientation to the law.' 'Prohibited force$_L$' is defined in terms of the victim's response to the situation. That response must be resistance, and resistance is interpreted to mean *physical* resistance and not merely verbal protests. If the law were simply interested in protecting the autonomy rights of women, then why not consider verbal protests as resistance? Beyond that, if the laws were interested in protecting the autonomy rights of women, it would drop altogether the resistance requirement and see verbal protests as sufficient for nonconsent. The 'physical force' and 'physical resistance' requirements in rape law embody what Susan Estrich (1987) called 'a male perception of threatening situations' and a male way of responding to a threatening situation. Physical force is seen as threatening, and one responds to the threat with physical resistance. Force translates into 'physical force' rather than into the various power relationships to which women might feel vulnerable. Being isolated, without transportation, with someone you hardly know who is physically more powerful than you are, possibly someone who is in a role of authority, all could contribute to a person feeling threatened and thereby being 'forced' into sex. The law's standard, however, of the 'reasonable person' is one who fights back, not cries. As Estrich says: 'The reasonable woman, it seems, is not a schoolboy "sissy"; she is a real man' (1987: 65). Also worth noting is that the woman's behavior, and not the defendant's, is the one that is subject to evaluation. The law is judging what the alleged victim did or didn't do to make an assessment of whether she was truly a victim or not.

When the 'physical' resistance requirement is applied to women, the results have been disastrous because many women do not respond with physical force to a threatening situation. Women, as Estrich points out, often respond by crying rather than by using force. One reason for their failure to use force may merely be the normal differentials in strength between men and women. Other reasons for women's lack of physical and sometimes even lack of verbal response are probably related to social conditioning. Women are socialized not to fight or respond physically; they are also brought up to be passive, especially around men, and particularly men they know (Warshaw, 1994: 52–

54). For a rape conviction, a victim may only fail to resist, the courts have argued, when her behavior is based on a *reasonable* fear that if she (the victim) resists, she will be seriously harmed. In *People v. Rusk*, the victim's fear was based upon being isolated, in an unknown part of town, late at night, without her car keys, with a man she didn't know. The court claimed that her fear was not reasonable: 'She may not simply say, "I was really scared," and thereby transform consent or mere unwillingness [sic] into submission by force. These words do not transform a seducer into a rapist.' Again the courts have enshrined a standard of reasonable fear that is *not* based upon the experiences of women. To whom is the fear reasonable? For some (many?) women, being isolated with a man who is larger and who has made intimidating remarks or gestures may be a frightening and unpredictable situation. Just as a man might be afraid of three big men in an alley and comply with their wishes without resistance, for many women one man may be enough.

Force$_L$ is defined in terms of the victim's resistance; if she did not resist, there was no force$_L$ – therefore, no rape. And, if the reason for not resisting is fear, then the situation must be one which is objectively threatening, that is, one which men would find threatening. Consider *State v. Alston* (1983), in which Alston and the victim had a 'consensual' relationship over a period of some months. During that relationship, Alston had behaved violently toward the victim on many occasions. A month after their relationship had ended, Alston came to the school where the victim was a student and attempted to block her path and demanded to know where she was living. When she refused to tell him, he grabbed her arm and stated that she was coming with him. At one point the defendant told the victim he was going to 'fix her face.' The defendant also told her that he had a 'right' to have intercourse with her again. The two went to the house of a friend of the defendant. The defendant asked her if she was 'ready' and the victim told him she did not want to have sexual relations. The defendant pulled her up from the chair, undressed her, pushed her legs apart, and penetrated her. She cried. The court agreed that she had not consented but, since there was no 'force,' it was not rape.

The court's conclusion that there was no force in this situation, is, according to Estrich, 'to create a gulf between power and force and to define the latter strictly in schoolboy terms. Alston did not beat his victim – at least not with his fists. He didn't have to. She had been beaten, physically and emotionally, long before' (1987: 62). Estrich goes on:

> The definition of force adopted by the *Alston* court, like the definition of nonconsent adopted by earlier courts, protects male access to women where guns and beating are not needed to secure it. The court did not hold that no means yes; but it made clear that, at least in 'social' contexts like this one with appropriate victims, a man is free to proceed regardless of verbal nonconsent. In that sense Alston was right. He did have a 'right' to intercourse, and his victim had no right to deny him merely by saying 'no.'
>
> (Ibid., 62–63)

The definition of force is extremely narrow and does not acknowledge the range of power relationships that don't neatly map onto this standard definition of force. Consider the Wyoming Supreme Court's reversal of a conviction in *Gonzales v. State* (1973). As in *People v. Rusk*, the defendant and victim met in a bar and the defendant requested a ride home. The victim refused, but the defendant got into her car anyway. The victim repeated her refusal to drive him but, after unsuccessfully trying to get him out of her car, she started to drive. He asked her to turn down a road and stop so that he could urinate. Before getting out of the car he removed her keys from the ignition. When he returned he told her he was going to rape her; she tried to talk him out of it. 'He told her he was getting mad at her and then put his fist against her face and said, "I'm going to do it. You can have it one way or the other." ' The Wyoming Supreme Court argued that the trial court's standard of reasonable fear was in error; it should not place the determination 'solely in the judgment of the victim and omit the necessary element of a reasonable apprehension and reasonable ground for such fear; and the reasonableness must rest with the fact finder.' Surprisingly the court did not find that it was a 'harmless error' since a fact finder should (if asking whether a reasonable woman would have been afraid) have found that the fear was reasonable. The court seemed to suggest that a trier of fact might not find the fear in this case reasonable. What then is the standard of reasonable? Shouldn't the courts ask whether a woman might find a situation frightening?

Again, looking for physical force$_L$ and physical resistance in *Commonwealth v. Mlinarich* (1985), where Mlinarich threatened a 14-year-old girl living in his custody with return to the detention home if she refused sex with him, the court found no forcible compulsion, hence no rape. The court said the legislature 'did not intend to equate seduction, whether benign or sinister, with rape ...' Here is an obvious power relationship where no physical force was required, but the courts still look for it. Up until the present we will find the model of rape as violent, with physical resistance, and there is still a deep suspicion of female victims.

Guilt for the crime of rape, along with most serious crimes, requires the defendant to have a specific mental state, or *mens rea*, which refers to what he actually believed or understood at the time of the crime. For rape, the defendant must have believed that his victim was *not* consenting or believed that she might not be consenting. So defendants may claim mistake about the consent of the victim, that is, claim as a defense for rape that they believed she *was* consenting. Standard *mens rea* doctrine may not apply since it is in men's interest to remain oblivious to women's desires, signs, and sensibilities (MacKinnon, 1989: 182). As long as men continue to believe the stereotypes about women, for instance, that 'no' means 'yes,' that women require some force, that women desire to live out rape fantasies, and so on, then it may be true in many cases, particularly the so-called acquaintance rape cases, that the defendants will lack the *mens rea* for the crime. *People v. Rusk* illustrates the problem with a standard of 'reasonable belief' for consent, based on what men in a sexist society would believe reasonable in the circumstances – namely that, since he did not use 'excessive' force and she did not strenuously resist, then she was consenting. The courts, with the expansive notion of 'seduction,' contribute to men's behavior toward acceptable sexuality as the standard fails to consider what women would reasonably believe in certain circumstances.[6] The episode is only considered a rape, a violation, if the defendant thought that the woman was not consenting. 'Doctrinally, this means that the man's perspective of the woman's desires determines whether she is deemed violated' (MacKinnon, 1989: 180). This is particularly a problem with acquaintance rape cases in many of which the defendant doesn't believe he is raping his victim.

Some theorists, for example, Catherine MacKinnon, argue that the defense for mistaken belief in consent should not be acceptable. Mistake-of-fact defenses in common law vitiated the *mens rea* for the crime of rape. The argument for this was: 'if D commits the *actus reus* of an offense with a factual misunderstanding he should not be blamed for the social harm he causes unless he deserves blame for making the mistake' (Dressler, 1987: 132). Whether those mistakes must be reasonable or not is, however, a controversial issue. With the mistake defense, MacKinnon argues, the law measures whether the rape occurred from the standpoint of the (male) perpetrators who are allowed to see sexual violence against women as acceptable. When a defendant is acquitted for rape 'a woman fails to prove that she did not consent, she is not considered to have been injured at all' (1989, 180). MacKinnon argues further that rape is not like other crimes of subjective intent because sexuality defines gender norms, so that the only difference:

> ... between assault and what is socially defined as a noninjury is the meaning of the encounter to the woman. Interpreted in this way, the legal problem has been to determine whose view of that meaning constitutes what really happened, as if what happened objectively exists to be objectively determined ... as a result, although the rape law oscillates between subjective tests and objective standards invoking social reasonableness, it uniformly presumes a single underlying reality, rather than a reality split by the divergent.
>
> (Ibid.)

According to MacKinnon, rape should be defined as sex by compulsion, of which physical force is one form. What standard of culpability she wants to adopt is unstated. Possibly proof of the *actus reus* would be sufficient, making rape a 'strict liability' offense. Most 20th-century theorists have argued against jettisoning the requirement of *mens rea* in serious criminal offenses, pointing out that it is wrong to hold a person responsible for something for which they had no conscious awareness of wrongdoing. Alternatively, MacKinnon might want to focus on the 'compulsion' aspect of the episode and subsume these cases under assault with the requirement for similar mental states.

Susan Estrich (1987) takes a more moderate position on *mens rea* for rape and argues that mistaken belief should exonerate, but only if the belief was objectively reasonable. Nevertheless, Estrich recognizes that it depends upon how we define reasonable. She posits that the reasonable man in the 1980s should be held to the knowledge that 'no means no.' For Estrich the imposition of rape liability for negligent conduct, that is, a man's actions grounded on an unreasonable belief in the woman's consent, promotes deterrence and entails no injustice. The 'key question' for Estrich is what we should expect and demand of men in ambiguous situations. She argues that the law should require a man to understand that 'no means no,' and, if a victim's words are ignored, they should be adequate to secure a conviction of rape.

Making rape subject to the negligence standard has been criticized as it does not require a subjective awareness of wrongdoing, only that the reasonable person would have known. Traditionally crimes committed negligently usually result in significantly reduced amounts of punishment. In the US system of criminal justice, it is supposed that individuals are subject to severe punishments only if their behavior was a product of something that they intended, planned, or at least consciously disregarded the risk of.

An Unfortunate Conjunction

Most statutes define rape as intercourse with force$_L$ *and* without consent. What is the rationale for this definition? One argument is that it assumes a sadomasochistic definition of sex: intercourse with force or coercion can be or become consensual (MacKinnon, 1989). This definition has a history. For instance the Supreme Court of Nebraska said in 1889:

> Voluntary submission by the woman, while she has power to resist, no matter how reluctantly yielded, removes from the act an essential element of the crime of rape ... [I]f the carnal knowledge was with the consent of the woman, no

matter how tardily given, or how much force had therefore
been employed, it is no rape.

Without this view of legitimate forms of sex, why
include both the elements 'with force and without
consent?' This would appear redundant. Reconsidered,
it would seem logical to assume that if force is present it
is because consent is absent. 'Rape cases finding
insufficient evidence of force reveal that acceptable
sex, in the legal perspective, can entail a lot of force.'[7]
And what constitutes an unacceptable level of force is
rarely addressed directly.[8]

Another rationale goes back to the distrust of female
victims. Without the force element, how can we be sure
that they didn't consent and now want to cover up for
their regretted choice? In cases such as these that
motivated the writers of Model Penal Code, we focus
attention on the forcible compulsion and not consent at
all. The current codes require both a showing of
forceful compulsion *and* nonconsent, which leads to
the problems illustrated above. Two strategies present
themselves: We may define rape as sexual activity
without consent and, thereby, give a meaningful
account of consent. This route emphasizes rape as a
crime against sexual autonomy and focuses on a
woman's rightful control over her body and over her
sexual self-determination. An alternative strategy is to
define a range of behaviors which are wrongful because
they are violent, abusive, or in other ways inappropri-
ate. This route focuses on the violent nature of rape.
The latter approach has the virtue of directly focusing
on the behavior of the defendant. Whether his behavior
was wrongful or not, as is the current approach, centers
on what the victim did or failed to do. The focus on the
wrongful behavior of the defendant lends itself nicely to
being subsumed under the law of assault, wherein we
define a range of behavior as wrongful and prohibit
them.

The latter strategy finds sympathizers among feminists, at least some of whom have been skeptical about the law's use of 'consent.' Feminists point to current rape laws' standards for consent, noting that they do little to protect the decisions of women since what counts as having given consent is so minimal as to drain the concept of consent of any moral significance.

Restructured rape law, according to MacKinnon, 'should be defined as sex by compulsion, of which physical force is one form. Lack of consent is redundant and should not be a separate element of the crime' (1989: 245). Rape as sexual compulsion would do a good job of capturing cases where there is physical force or a weapon involved. If an assailant uses physical force or a weapon to secure sex, that fact is sufficient for a rape conviction. Moreover, to see rape as violence is to recognize that sex should be inconsistent with violence. Cases where the violence or threats of violence are evident ought to be clear; it is wrong to use physical force for almost any reason, but especially for compelling sex. There is no excuse for the fact that the current laws have not been more explicit about this proscription.

Nevertheless, the tougher cases for this strategy are the ones where there is no clear evidence of physical force; for example, the threat of physical force was suggested verbally and the size of the aggressor made it credible. Other gray areas are in cases such as *Commonwealth v. Mlinarich*, with no threat of physical violence at all (see p. 47). MacKinnon and others who advocate these changes need a theory of compulsion, one that captures more than actual overwhelming force, but which defines the range of power relationships that might compel a person into sex. We need a theory about which threats, whether explicit or implicit, are sufficient for wrongful compulsion. Agreement converges around threats of grievous bodily harm, but once we move away to threats of lesser harms – threats about, for example, money or jobs – there exists much less agreement that these are forms of compulsion. That is not to mention the issue of whether fraud or deceit is also a kind of compulsion. MacKinnon's approach does a good job in cases where there is evidence of physical compulsion, but lacks effect in other areas.

Reconceptualizing rape as wrongful behavior, whether or not there is consent, was also developed by Donald Dripps (1992), who wanted to focus on the means used to procure sex and distinguish between legitimate and illegitimate means. Dripps introduces a provocative twist by considering sexual services as a commodity owned and controlled by individuals: 'sexual autonomy means freedom from illegitimate pressures to provide [sexual] service.' Consent does not play its current role in the law in Dripps's reconceptualized statute; he drops consent (even as a defense) and defines the wrong entirely by reference to the defendant's conduct and state of mind. Dripps argues for dropping consent as an element of the offense because he holds that nonconsent is only the label we attach to illegitimate causes of conduct. We must grade the pressures to have sex according to their legitimacy: 'from those pressures to have sex that are perfectly moral, to those that are immoral but not criminal, to those that are criminal, to those that constitute crimes of the most serious sort' (p. 1788). It is, claims Dripps, the nature of the pressure or constraint rather than the degree of the constraint. 'Not every constraint on sexual autonomy is illegal or even immoral. Violent constraints will of course be the central concern for the criminal law; nonetheless some nonviolent constraints on sexual autonomy are immoral and should be criminal.' Dripps distinguishes and defines two separate offenses: sexually motivated assault and sexual expropriation. He thereby avoids the problem of underinclusiveness and over-inclusiveness (see p. 70); either the codes define an offense which includes force and thereby leaves out the nonaggravated cases, or the codes might make all offenses hinge on nonconsenual sex (dropping the element of violence), thereby making all the offenses the same in gravity – very serious felonies. Dripps wants to be clear that sexually motivated assault is significantly worse than sexual expropriation: 'I believe that violence is more dangerous and more culpable than an unwelcome sex act, I propose a modest penalty for expropriation.'

In Dripps's view, since so much hinges on the legitimacy or illegitimacy of the pressure put on the victim, it is surprising that he does not provide clear criteria for making the distinction. The notion of some pressures being immoral is also raised and yet left unarticulated. Some pressures, in Dripps's theory, are illegitimate and immoral and yet not criminal. Dripps states that illegitimacy is not implied by constraints, but by whether those constraints are legitimate or illegitimate. He does explicitly reject one positive account for the legitimacy of consent, that is, the view that sexual consent be based upon 'mutuality,' where mutuality should be tested by 'whether the target would have initiated the encounter if she had been given the choice.' He argues that 'complex relationships' involve lots of constraints on choices that are legitimate and that these often fail the standard of mutuality. Dripps gives an example of a relationship where the woman trades sex for financial security, friendship, and to ensure that her husband will not be in 'a predictable snit' (fit of pique) for days after. For him this is a legitimate bargain with legitimate constraints on it. The fact that the agents are in unequal bargaining positions does not bother Dripps since 'All human cooperation, sexual and otherwise, is caused by unequal, and from the individual standpoint, arbitrary, pressures.' But surely, some of those inequalities are a source of illegitimacy.

Dripps's account is inadequate. The woman who acquiesces to sex with her husband so he doesn't beat her or her children may be in a complex relationship, but surely the constraints on her choice are not legitimate. The boss who puts the stipulation on his secretary's continued employment that she be sexually available for him constitutes an illegitimate constraint on her choice. What constitutes a 'complex relationship' for purposes of telling us when the constraints are legitimate is not made clear. Since Dripps does not want to reify consent independently, but rather wants to discuss the legitimacy and illegitimacy of constraints on individuals, we cannot talk about which constraints undermine consent and which do not. Furthermore, he thinks that complex relationships can establish implied authorization, and, since some nonsexual compensation may be at work, the fact that the complainant did not consent or desire the interaction does not indicate whether or not it was a case of sexual expropriation. Even sex with an unconscious person is not necessarily a case of criminal sexual expropriation, since the perpetrator supposes there may be some implied authorization. From Dripps's view we know that many constraints are legitimate, but we don't have a theory for what makes them illegitimate.

One of the most curious exclusions in Dripps's account – curious because of his advocacy of the commodity theory of sexuality – is that misrepresentations or fraud that induce sexual cooperation are not criminal. The reason he cites against the criminalization of sexual fraud is that it would lead to sweeping criminalization of sex, including the recriminalization of adultery. But why is that so terrible given his own theory? It is, indeed, a kind of theft that takes place when individuals secure sexual services through fraud. Given the commodity theory of sexual services there seem to be strong reasons for including fraud. In fact, the attraction that some might have to the commodity theory is that it seems that it would logically entail that appropriation of sex through fraud would be a recognized legal harm – that is, the appropriation of someone's property through fraud – and thereby subject to criminalization. Whereas the common law has allowed individuals to use *any* amount of deception to obtain consent to sexual intercourse and avoid criminal punishment. If a man tells a woman that he is a famous singer in order to induce her to consent to sex, then he is guilty of no offense. If a doctor, or anyone for that matter, were to secure consent to sexual intercourse by falsely claiming that the intercourse would cure an illness, he commits no sexual criminal offense. Even in the case of a man who uses deception to convince a woman that he is her husband and has sexual intercourse with her there are serious disagreements about whether he has committed a criminal offense.[9] Nevertheless, if someone acquires property through trickery or false representation then it would be considered a criminal offense. Dripps argues that sexual autonomy (meaning individual freedom from unwanted sexual invasion) is best analyzed in terms of the commodity theory of sex. And, given his own account, there is no reason why we should exclude fraud from the ways an individual can have property taken illegitimately. Securing valuable services through compulsion, coercion, and fraud are standard instances of criminal offenses.

Though there are advantages to the commodity theory, for example, it could encompass sexual fraud, it does not really advance our understanding of sexual offenses and facilitate a reconceptualization of the criminal law. Interestingly, the old common law sexual offenses were also based on property standards. However, the owner of the sexual property was not the woman herself, but the woman's father or husband. Of course, Dripps is not advocating anything as objectionable as that, and in fact I suggested reasons that would make feminists happy to go along with Dripps on this point. In his view the individual in question owns her body and it is hers to do with as she sees fit. Sexual services are valuable commodities that should be traded for valuable goods in return. Since Dripps suggests that women do not desire sex in the same way as men, women are in a stronger bargaining position vis-à-vis sexual exchanges – they can offer deals on a take it or leave it basis. If men have a stronger desire for sex, women can hold out for a better bundle of goods for each exchange. Since sexual services are owned by the woman in question and sexual expropriation wrongly denies something that is hers, this strategy respects a woman's autonomy over choices in her domain.

The problem with Dripps's account is that sex (outside of prostitution) has very little, if anything, in common with commodities exchanged in the market. Most people do not treat sexual cooperation as an exchange; they don't, for example, look for the highest bidder and work out the terms of the exchange. The very idea, as suggested by Dripps, implies that women are for the most part the sellers of the service and men the buyers. In his view women don't desire sex, or at least not as much as whatever they can exchange for it. The assumptions of this model are far-fetched and paint a distorted and alienated view of sexual relationships, leading one to wonder about the social implications of adopting and encouraging the commodity view. Furthermore, women don't experience rape as a kind of theft, but rather as something much more intrusive, privately shattering, and humiliating. The harms of rape are psychological and emotional rather than merely physical. Steal my car and I wouldn't have those experiences.

Going down the road of excluding consent altogether and focusing on the wrongful behavior of the man will not always capture the cases – the nonviolent acquaintance cases – that I believe the law ought to capture. Many acquaintance rape cases do not have the kind of blatant violence of force that allows us to easily conclude that they were criminally harmful. Also, the absence of consent from the statutes does not make clear that a woman has a right to *choose* whom she wants to have sex with. Without her clear consent, sex with her is wrongful. Consent therefore needs to be central.

What I will propose, to avoid the problems associated with the conjunction of force$_L$ and consent, is that we think in terms of two offenses. One will be aggravated rape where the presence of violence, force, or threats is sufficient for the crime. The other offense focuses on the absence of consent to sexual intercourse.

Conclusion

Feminists have been successful in showing that some legal rules, although they may appear objective in the sense of being neutral between relevant groups, operate to disadvantage women as a group. They have also shown that other legal rules unfairly burden women more than men; moreover, that some rules are not rational for the legitimate ends of the criminal law. After exposing the problems that arise out of the historical treatment of rape, the question arises of how best to reconstruct the rules so that they are not riddled with gender biases, and so that they protect women's autonomy. The legal system is said to be a conservative institution. It should not, nevertheless, be permitted to perpetuate gender stereotypes which seriously diminish the status of women and undermine their sexual autonomy. Criminal law has, according to Stephen Schulhofer, a number of salient characteristics, one of which is that it is 'demanding' – even to persons who find it difficult to comply. In this spirit, the law should always demand that persons respect the bodily integrity and property of others. When 'crossing borders,' agents should be demanded to proceed with caution, ensuring consent is obtained, recognizing the risks involved in the failure to behave cautiously. A second central characteristic of the criminal law is that it is 'judgmental': 'In the event of conviction, it does not forgive. Rather, it condemns, it blames, and it punishes' (Schulhofer, 1990: 112). Schulhofer claims that these are 'male' characteristics and ones which feminists would object to. This is, I think, inaccurate. Feminists would be happy to embrace the characteristics of 'demanding' and 'judgmental.' The point that many feminists have been pressing is that the law has not *demanded enough* of men's behavior toward women and that it has been too ready to excuse, condone, and sympathize with men's behavior.

Notes

1 Debra Rhode illustrates this point by citing that, in many ancient societies, 'the punishment was not directed solely at the aggressor ... In some cultures the victim was required to marry the assailant, and her father was entitled to rape the aggressor's wife or sister.' *Justice and Gender*, 1989, p. 245.

2 'Forcible and Statutory Rape: An Exploration of the Operation and Objectives of the Consent Standard,' *Yale Law Journal*, 62, 1952. This note is cited many times, most recently in comments to the influential *Model Penal Code* published in 1980.

3 The convictions were reversed because of the judge's failure to give consent instructions to the jury.

4 Catherine MacKinnon argues: 'If rape laws existed to enforce women's control over access to their sexuality, as consent defense implies, no would mean no, marital rape would not be a widespread exception, and it would not be effectively legal to rape a prostitute' (1989: 175).

5 The crime of rape centers on penetration. Sexuality is defined in terms of penetration. Feminists have argued that the focus on penetration is a male perspective on sexual violation. The women's view of when they are violated is often different from men's, and yet the male view is determinative.

6   MacKinnon claims: 'The problem is that the injury of rape lies in the meaning of the act to its victim, but for its criminality lies in the meaning of the act to the assailant. Rape is only an injury from a woman's point of view. It is only a crime from the male point of view, explicitly, including that of the accused' (1989: 180).

7   MacKinnon says that 'the level of acceptable force is adjudicated starting just above the level set by what is seen as normal male behavior ... rather than the victim's point of violation' (1989: 173). Generally, outside of sports, we don't allow individuals to consent to violence.

8   Note the South Carolina marital rape case, in which the husband tied his wife to the bed, hit her, and used a knife on her, none of which was sufficient to be ruled unacceptable force. 'Man cleared of Marital Rape,' *Washington Post*, 18 April 1992.

9   States have differed in their treatment of this kind of case; see Joshua Dressler, *Understanding Criminal Law* (New York: Matthew Bender, 1987), p. 526.

Chapter 3

Expanding the Legal Definition of Rape

The scene opens with Nola seeking a reconciliation with Jamie, who is jealous and hurt that Nola persists in remaining intimate with two other men besides him. Nola telephones Jamie, asking him to come over. When Jamie appears at her door, Nola says, 'I need you. Come here, kiss me! Come on!' Nola reaches out affectionately to kiss Jamie. Sullen and defiant, he turns away, first to the right then to the left. Persisting, she places his turned-away face in her hands, bringing him to her lips, and, as he remains impassive, kisses him warmly on the mouth. She says softly, 'I love you. Make love to me.' He responds 'You don't want me to make love to you. You want me to fuck you!' Jamie takes Nola firmly by the shoulders turns her sharply around toward the bed, and while standing behind her, presses her onto all fours on the mattress. He drops his pants and, with a firm hold on her hips, penetrates her. 'Is this the way you like it, huh? Is this the way you like it? Does Greer do it like this? What about Mars? Who else?! Who else?!' He shouts. She exclaims with muffled sobs, 'You're hurting me!'

From Peter Weston's description of Spike Lee's movie
She's Gotta Have It (US, 1986)

I had dated Ted for several months. We met through some mutual friends. I really liked him. He was good-looking and a really neat guy. One evening after going out together for dinner, he invited me to his apartment to listen to some tapes of a band we had talked about at dinner. As we sat on the couch and listened to the music, he became very aggressive. We had 'made out' before but never anything really heavy – mainly hugging and kissing. When he started putting his hands in places I didn't appreciate, I told him so. He acted as if this were a challenge and continued to do what he had been doing. At one point I got up to leave. He

pushed me into his bedroom, threw me down on the bed,
and raped me. When it was over, I was crying and hurting.
His only reply was, 'You know you liked it.'

(Weihe and Richard, 1995: 1)

I thought there would be other people there. I thought it
was just like, 'let's get out of this party.' When we got to
his room and I saw that there was nobody there, I didn't
think I could do anything about it.
We started kissing and then he started taking off my
clothes. I kept telling him to stop and I was crying. I was
scared of him and thought he was going to hurt me ... He
had a hand over my face. I was five two and weighed 110
pounds. I didn't have any choice.
I just wanted to block it out. I felt ashamed because it
happened. I just felt dirty, violated. I thought it was my
fault. It wasn't like he did something to me, it was like I let
him do something to me, so I felt very bad about myself.
[She didn't report the incident to anyone] Who would
believe me? He was a really good football player. No one
would have believed me if I said anything. I wouldn't have
dreamed of saying anything.

(Warshaw, 1994: 30)

None of the above incidents were reported to the police
as rape. Should the criminal law protect against those
activities? Are they rapes? As discussed in the previous
chapter, in some jurisdictions it is not clear that the
events outlined above would satisfy the force element or
the resistance requirement. The fact that a man with
superior strength throws a woman onto a bed or holds
her down on all fours is not considered force is itself
perplexing. But police, prosecutors, and courts have
been reluctant to find rape in these situations, particularly where the parties knew one another. The question
therefore remains: Should these cases be considered
rape? That is, has the law and legal practice been
mistaken in not treating these acquaintance cases as
rape? If so, then we need to reconceptualize rape. The
end of the previous chapter began that process, arguing

that there should be two offenses rather than one. The proposal was to distinguish forceful$_L$ or violent sexual assaults from nonconsenual sex. The former does not look for the absence of consent; force, violence, or even threats of violence are sufficient to make the event criminal. In contrast, the latter offense focuses on the absence of consent, whether or not there is force. In these cases it is the sexual autonomy of the woman that is not being respected by the failure to secure free and informed consent.

As we have seen, for the offense of rape most current penal codes require the assault to be both forceful$_L$ *and* lacking in consent. This conjunction has often led to anomalous and unfair results: lots of force$_L$ but with 'consent' and the rape charge is defeated. And some cases in which the victim's 'consent' was prompted by violence and/or threats are also found not to satisfy the requirements for rape. One such example is in *State v. Lord*, where the accused rapist was acquitted, even though he had threatened the woman with a knife, because the victim's 'provocative dress' was the basis for the judgment that she had 'consented' (see Hazelton, 1991). On the other hand, incidents where there is no consent, as understood by the statutes, and no force$_L$, are also not criminal, and so men in these cases can be considered seducers because they didn't use force.

One possible explanation for the conjunction of the requirements 'without consent' and 'with force' is that there exists a strong reluctance to conceptualize nonviolent, albeit nonconsenual sex particularly with an acquaintance, as genuine rape. This reluctance seems to come from the fact that many people see rape as necessarily a crime of violence, by which they mean it involves more than the force they see as constitutive of sexual intercourse. Therefore they don't see the violence in these situations, which may be due to assumptions like 'sex is good, so it cannot really be a harm,' or at least not a criminal harm. Nevertheless, many feminists have pointed out, aptly put by Robin West: '*From the victim's perspective*, unwanted sexual penetration involves unwanted force, and unwanted force *is* violent—it is physically painful, sometimes resulting in internal tearing and often leaving scars' (West, 1993: 1448). The fear, humiliation, and ongoing trauma of rape, even it unaggravated, makes it a serious harm. My motivation for distinguishing the two offenses is to acknowledge that aggravated rape is a violent crime in the traditional legal sense of violence or force$_L$. Nevertheless nonconsenual sex, even without violence or force$_L$, is also a harm. By separating the offenses we will not confuse them in our own minds, or in the minds of police, prosecutors, judges, or juries. I will say more about this distinction later.

As discussed in the previous chapter, feminists in the 1970s and 1980s provided scathing criticisms of the criminal rape laws, with Susan Brownmiller's groundbreaking work (1976) exposing the fact that the laws were protecting men's interests rather than women's, and reformers arguing that many harms to women were not captured by the criminal laws. As mentioned earlier, there were reforms that dropped the 'utmost resistance' and corroboration requirement, and instituted rape shield laws, among others. But have the laws gone far enough, especially in protecting women from acquaintances who victimize them? I think that they have not. There is debate, however, over whether the criminal law should be expanded to include the range of nonviolent acquaintance rape cases. In calling these cases 'nonviolent,' I am mindful that many acquaintance rapes are violent. The problem is, as I suggested earlier, that the law doesn't often recognize that when a man pushes a woman onto a bed or otherwise uses his superior strength to 'force' her into sex, that it is force$_L$ for the purposes of law. Also the law and the legal system seem to permit a lot more force in sexual relationships when the parties know each other. In support of expanding the concept of rape is the claim that if the criminal law is aimed at protecting individuals from harm, particularly serious harms to autonomy, then it should include these sexual violations since they *are* harms to autonomy. Furthermore, by excluding these harms to women it is natural to ask whether the criminal law is treating women's autonomy rights equal to men's by excluding from criminal protection so much nonconsenual sexual activity, of which women are predominately the victims.

There is a fair amount of agreement about the historical picture that rape laws treated women unfairly, not protecting them from real injury to their sexual autonomy by requiring utmost resistance, corroboration, past sexual history, and so on. It is acknowledged that society did not recognize certain actions as wrongful or as harms to women and thereby failed to protect them. Nevertheless, there is much less consensus about the need for or the direction of reform of current criminal laws. One could acknowledge the historical unfairness of rape laws and agree with many of the early changes, but disagree with extending the coercive arm of the criminal law to nonviolent acquaintance cases. For many the idea that a husband could rape his wife or a man could rape his date is met with disbelief. Illustrating this, when Patricia Bowman charged William Kennedy-Smith with rape in 1991, the *New York Times* had a subheading which read 'For Woman in Florida Rape Inquiry, a Fast Jump Up the Economic Ladder.' The implication from America's most read and respected newspaper was that an untrustworthy Bowman was using the rape charge as a fast route to financial gain. Many people (including the jury) thought: Why would this member of the Kennedy clan, an attractive, eligible, medical student, rape anyone? Sexual interaction without force (as understood in traditional legal terms), particularly when the aggressor is an acquaintance, is not perceived as a harm to the woman. Camille Paglia in *Vamps and Tramps* (1994: 23, 24, 47) asserts what many people believe in saying 'in the absence of physical violence, sexual conduct cannot and must not be legislated from above.'

It is easy to see historical abuses and mistakes as products of sexism – men's interests prevailed over women's, particularly in the legislative and judicial realm. But is the current intransigence to changes that would expand the range of criminal sexual conduct also a product of sexism or is there another explanation? Basically we are asking whether the events in the cases at the beginning of the chapter (among others) are cases of rape. The courts didn't think so. This chapter will therefore address the objections to expanding the conception of rape since I want to argue that the law *should* recognize nonconsenual acquaintance cases as rapes. To recap, the objections concerned: the lack of serious harm in acquaintance rape; that there is no clear line to draw between permissible and impermissible sexual activity once we move beyond forcible sex; serious *mens rea* problems leading to unfairness for defendants, that 'victims' themselves don't always see themselves as such; and the patronizing nature of proposed rape reforms. Looking at the cases of acquaintance rape outlined earlier, for example, some will ask where is the harm, or at least harm that rises to the criminal level. They also will ask how would we distinguish cases like *Rusk, Berkowitz*, and *Mlinarich* from 'ordinary seduction' cases where, admittedly, the woman is reluctant but eventually comes around to consenting to sex. Women after all often do not affirmatively verbally consent to sex, and often admit to using rejection strategies even when they desire sex. Is it then fair to men to hold them liable for rape when the situations themselves are so ambiguous, particularly when men believe (some would say justifiably) that the women's behaviors are consistent with consenting to sex? Is it not patronizing to women, some will ask, to permit them to say later that they did not consent, but at the time were unwilling to speak and let their views be known? In addition to the objections summarized above I will add one from radical feminists who are themselves extremely skeptical about the route to reform rape laws by focusing on consent. After considering the objections, I will explore the context within which the law currently operates and illustrate its effects on the prosecution of rape.

No Serious Harm Objection

The no serious harm objection rests on the fairly widely held beliefs that so-called acquaintance type rapes, particularly without any obvious physical harm over and above the rape itself, are not seriously harmful. In Robin Warshaw's words (1994: xxii), 'Comparing real rape to date rape is like comparing cancer to the common cold,' the reasoning being that sexual inter-course is good, consequently nonconsenual sexual intercourse with someone you know cannot be *that* bad. Obviously some of the pleasure is missing, but it is not wholly a harmful activity. Even the Model Penal Code (see Chapter 2) stated that sexual assault by an acquaintance or someone with whom the victim has previously had sex is 'less severe' a wrong than sexual assault by a stranger. The perpetrators themselves have this view, telling their victims that they really wanted it or they deserved it because of their erotic behavior (Model Penal Code, 1980: 307).

This notion that unaggravated rapes do not seriously harm the victim is tacitly assumed by police and prosecutors, who initially do not see these acts as harmful enough to pursue in the criminal justice system. Susan Estrich (1987: 9) recounts a story told to her by a prosecutor of a woman who came to his office wearing tight jeans and a revealing blouse (relevant facts to him). She told the prosecutor that her ex-boyfriend had raped her. She had gone to his apartment to watch a movie – a porn movie, according to the prosecutor. They moved to the bedroom to be more comfortable. Her boyfriend kissed her and she said 'no,' that she didn't want this, and got up to leave. He, a weightlifter, pulled her back onto his bed and forced himself on her. He did not, however, beat her and she had no bruises. She then ran out and flagged down a police car. The District Attorney did not see this as a case to prosecute as he thought the woman was just trying to use the system 'to harass her ex-boyfriend,' who he said had no criminal record and was not a 'bad guy.' The prosecutor, however, did say that she was a victim of rape. The response of the prosecutor is all too common and, even if such cases do go to trial and a conviction is secured, many are overturned on appeal. As Warshaw says, the myth 'that women lie about rape to "punish" men for broken relationships or win attention for themselves greatly influences police decisions to declare some cases "unfounded"' (1994: 140). Gary LaFree conducted a study of what extra-legal determinants affected police decisions to charge a suspect or not. Among other things he found that detectives were suspicious of acquaintance gang rapes, referring to such cases as 'party rapes' and claiming that they didn't deserve much attention (1981: 582–94)

In his eminent 1984 article Michael Davis argued that rape is not as serious an offense as is often suspected. Through a series of 'thought experiments' he supposes that he shows that unaggravated rape is not even as serious as minor physical assaults. Can the seriousness of a harm be captured by these kinds of 'thought experiments?' In other words, is this an accurate method of ranking the seriousness of harm? I don't think so but, of course, it depends on individual theories of harm. If one theory is based solely on how people score on 'choices of evils' preference rankings, then it logically follows that something is more harmful than something else just because it falls higher up the scale. But I don't think that Davis's method – asking 'Would you rather have your leg crushed or be raped?' – is necessarily the most accurate way to determine rankings of harm, outside of that one view. For example, I might not want something I think will be really painful, like having my fingernail pulled out with pliers, over something, that would ruin my reputation, as Jeffrie Murphy has argued (1994: 217). Murphy supposes that defamation would be a greater harm than losing a fingernail but that because of a reflexive, physiological response to intense pain we would choose the defamation over the nail-pulling. Captives often disclose secrets after being subjected to physical pain with the promise of more to come unless they talk, but those same captives may well believe that the greater harm comes from telling those secrets to the enemy. The fact that women 'go along' with sex in the face of unknown physical pain may also be explained in this way. It is the belief that if they just cooperate they will avoid greater pain or death. Davis's approach to determining harmfulness, therefore, is inadequate once we acknowledge that the fear of pain can make people 'choose' a course of action that is *ceteris paribus* more harmful. However, it still does not follow that acquaintance rapes are serious enough to warrant criminal attention.

Contrary to this common belief about the differences between stranger and acquaintance rape, the research shows that when we compare the impact of both on the lives of the victims, there is *no* difference (Weihe and Richard, 1995). 'Both groups scored similarly on measures of depression, anxiety, quality of subsequent relationships, and sexual satisfaction following their rape.' Victims of acquaintance rape report three areas of their lives that are adversely affected by their attack: their ability to trust others, their ability to be intimate with others, and their ability to deal with the anger resulting from their experience (Ibid., 43ff). These victims often suffer from posttraumatic stress disorder. If we used this empirical evidence about the outcome of acquaintance rape, then we would treat it as a serious harm as these are adverse effects on victims' welfare interests, the kinds of interests that are central to autonomy.

An additional problem with making nonaggravated rape a criminal offense is that, in many US states, rape is punishable as a very serious felony, and those with doubts about the harm involved in date or acquaintance rape argue that acquaintance rape is *not* a serious felony and does not, therefore, deserve severe punishment. Sexual offenses perpetrated with weapons and/or physical abuse or explicit threats often involve physical abuse beyond the rape itself. Both the violence of the assault and the absence of consent constitute distinct harms to the victim (Fairstein, 1994: 158). The idea that rape is one of the worst crimes that can be committed, and as such deserves the severest of penalties, is supported by the terror and the multiplicity of harms inflicted upon the victims of aggravated rape.

My suggestion is that we grant the difference between aggravated and nonaggravated rape and still view nonaggravated rape as serious, albeit not as serious as aggravated rape. Nonaggravated rape consists of violating an individual's autonomy to control their own body and their sexual self-determination. These assaults can be frightening and humiliating experiences. By analytically distinguishing the two offenses we do not make the mistake of undervaluing the terror and extreme physical harm done in the aggravated rape. But we are also left with room to treat acquaintance rape as a crime. Separating the two offenses of aggravated and unaggravated rape permits the law to focus on the unique characteristics of each crime, on the unique wrongs against the victim, and to separate the relevant elements of the offenses.

The focus of aggravated rape should be on the compulsion or force$_L$, the violence of the crime. The focus of unaggravated rape should be on the lack of consent. Note too that, by distinguishing the offenses, in acquaintance rape cases we are looking for the presence of consent as opposed to the presence of force$_L$. Consequently, the focus is shifted: absence of force$_L$ does not entail the presence of consent. By distinguishing the two crimes we acknowledge that not all sexual offenses can be subsumed under the 'sex through forcible compulsion' heading. Forcible compulsion leaves the victim with no choice; for example, when she is clearly physically overpowered by another person. The compelled person has no will at all. Picture someone being dragged down a street with no choice in the direction of movement of his body. A Central Park rape victim who was assaulted by a group of men who held her down, beat, and took turns penetrating her was compelled in the assault. She wasn't threatened, 'Do this or we'll beat you up,' but they circumvented her will entirely and she had no choice in the matter.

We rectify the problem of not seeing nonconsenual acquaintance sex as serious as aggravated rape by acknowledging that it is not as serious. Nevertheless, acknowledging the greater seriousness of aggravated rape does not mean nonconsenual sex is not an offense. By distinguishing the offenses and graduating their seriousness we can preserve the intuition that one is more serious than the other without denying altogether that the lesser, unaggravated rape is still a crime. Convictions for unaggravated rape will also be easier to secure because many people share the feeling that unaggravated rape is different in kind and degree from aggravated rape. Aggravated rape is sexual assault secured by force$_L$ or the threat of violence, which often includes grievous bodily harm. Therefore the aggravated forms of rape deserve more punishment than other forms, and non-aggravated rape deserves less punishment. What we need, however, are statutes which delineate desiderata for these different crimes rather than make it difficult or nearly impossible to see the unaggravated forms as criminal offenses. The current codes suffer from two contradictory ills, the first of which is *underinclusiveness*. By defining sexual offenses in terms of force$_L$ and nonconsent they thereby exclude cases where consent is absent and yet there is no evidence of physical force. They also exclude those cases with force$_L$ and with submission without physical resistance. The second ill is the problem of *over-inclusiveness* – treating every case, whether aggravated or not, as one of the most serious felonies in the criminal code. Overinclusiveness results in juries being unwilling to convict acquaintance rapists, since they do not seem to deserve the severest of penalties. Due to underinclusiveness most rapes are not legally recognized as rapes and hence do not make it into the legal system.

The fact that quid pro quo sexual harassment cases ('Have sex with me or I will fire you') have not been seen as criminal offenses again points to the underlying assumption that these kinds of sexual encounters may be bad, but they are not that bad. Cases where the victim, usually a woman, is threatened with losing her job if she refuses a sexual advance are treated now as civil offenses against the harasser's company. It is important to remember that sexual harassment was not acknowledged legally as an offense at all until feminist theorists, particularly Catherine MacKinnon in the 1970s, argued that it should be treated as a form of legal discrimination. My argument is that we should see quid pro quo harassment as more than just discrimination, but as a criminal harm as well. Similarly, other cases of professionals such as teachers, therapists, physicians, and clergymen abusing their positions to secure sex have not been treated as criminal either.

Although recently, there has been a rash of highly public legal cases against priests, in these cases the victims were underage; therefore the charges were of molestation or statutory rape, and many were civil cases against the Church itself. The reason why cases of quid pro quo harassment, whether by an employer or professor, should not be treated as criminal rape possibly lies in the fact that they have not been seen as cases where there was serious harm to the victim.

The research data show that acquaintance rapes, even though maybe not violent, are still harmful to the victims, who suffer many of the same consequential harms to their welfare as they would have from aggravated nonacquaintance rape. By distinguishing two crimes we avoid the risk of conflating the differences between the types of offenses. To be beaten and raped is worse than to be 'just' raped. One is more serious an offense than the other, but the 'lesser' offense is still serious and the law ought to protect women from it.

Lack of Clear Distinction

Looking at the absence of consent as the sole criterion for the crime of nonaggravated rape might seem promising as a way to reform rape statutes, particularly given the problems with the conjunction of force$_L$ and nonconsent. Nevertheless many argue that there are no clear criteria to distinguish nonaggravated yet nonconsenual intercourse (that should count as rape) from nonaggravated yet non- or not fully consensual intercourse – what the courts have called 'unscrupulous seduction,' 'reluctant submission,' or just regretted intercourse. How then can we distinguish the cases once we move beyond those with physical violence or threats of violence which do provide a clear line of distinction? If the victim is physically overpowered – compelled to have intercourse – there is no doubt that a serious offense worthy of serious penalties has been committed. On the other hand, where there is no overt or obvious physical violence or threat, how can we know whether serious harm has taken place. In the following case Mlinarich had custody of a 14-year-old girl and threatened to return her to a detention home if she refused sex with him. Whether this should be viewed as rape was seriously questioned by the court and led to the defendant's acquittal. The decisive objection was articulated by Judge Wieand:

> If a man takes a destitute widow into his home and provides support for her and her family, such a definition of forcible compulsion ['forcible compulsion' expanded to include any 'compulsion by physical, moral, intellectual means or by the exigencies of the circumstances' (dissenting Judge Spaeth)] will convict him of attempted rape if he threatens to withdraw his support and compel her to leave unless she engages in sexual intercourse. Similarly, a person may be guilty of rape if he or she exhorts sexual favors from another person upon a threat of discharging the other or his or her spouse from a position of employment, or upon a threat of foreclosing the mortgage on the home of the other's parents, or upon a threat of denying a loan application, or upon a threat of disclosing the other's adultery or submission to an abortion. An interpretation of forcible compulsion which employs an ambiguous generic definition of force will create the potential for a veritable parade of threats, express and implied, in support of accusation of rape and attempted rape ... To allow a conviction for rape where the alleged victim has deliberately chosen intercourse in preference to some other unpleasant sensation not amounting to physical injury or violence would be to trivialize the plight of the helpless victim of violent rape.
>
> (*Commonwealth v. Mlinarich*, 1985)

Allowing the range of threats (and possibly some 'coercive' offers) will include too much under the rubric of rape. This can be constructed as a slippery slope argument: First we admit that certain threats, for example, to one's job, are sufficient for 'forcible compulsion,' then it will be admitted that, for example, a proposal made by a millionaire to an impecunious mother to pay for necessary surgery for her child in exchange for sex is forcible compulsion. From there it is an easy slip to view as compulsion proposals that offer goods such as cars, clothes, or trips, in exchange for sex.

This objection looks at cases such as those at the beginning of the chapter and asks how we would distinguish them from others that are structurally very similar, but that have consent. If a man induces a woman to his apartment and, through various non-violent means, gets her to consent to sex, how is that different from other cases? How can we distinguish cases to ensure that when we convict a defendant we are clear of the wrongfulness of his actions? This is the question that many judges have struggled with, most often resolving that they could not draw an adequate line between cases with consent and without consent. This objection is fundamental. Indeed, if we cannot provide a clear distinction then the proposal to distinguish between two offenses would be a nonstarter. However, my belief that we *can* distinguish between permissible and impermissible sexual behavior on grounds of consent will be the basis of the next two chapters, which argue first for a particular conception of consent and then for what undermines consent. I will delay my response to this objection until then.

Mens Rea Objection

This objection, raised most forcefully by Doug Husak and George C. Thomas III, arises from what is to count as the *mens rea* for rape. If we suppose (as we do for most serious felonies) that the offender must have certain beliefs about his actions to be guilty, then a man who believes that the woman he is having sex with is consenting will not be guilty of the crime of rape even if he is mistaken about the consent. Husak and Thomas worry about the procedural fairness to defendants, who, in the absence of physical violence or threats of violence, may 'reasonably' but mistakenly believe that the woman is consenting to sex with him even in the face of verbal refusals and/or other signs of rejection, including physical rejection. Their reasons are based on the social conventions by which women consent to sex. If the law, for example, states unequivocally that a verbal refusal – 'no means no' – is sufficient for rape, the law would be unfair to men since it would be flying in the face of social conventions about consent. Moreover, the objection continues, the criminal law should not shape social conventions by dictating what those conventions should be. This too is a crucial issue in the expansion of rape, and the complexities of *mens rea* will be discussed in detail in Chapter 7.

The Paradox of Acquaintance Rape

This comes from the fact that many so-called victims of these kinds of incidents do not see themselves as rape victims. In the case of Nola in Spike Lee's *She's Gotta Have It* (see p. 59), Peter Westen suggests that moviegoers might feel conflicted about whether Nola was raped, partly because she herself is ambivalent about whether or not she was raped. After the incident Nola confronted Jamie about what happened and calls it 'your near rape of me,' implying a conflicted attitude about the existence of rape. This is borne out by Laurie Bechhofer and Andrea Parrot in *Acquaintance Rape: The Hidden Crime*, who found that victims of coercive sexual relationships with acquaintances do not label their experiences as rape. Similarly, a woman who wrote a letter to journalist Ann Landers (1991) described her nonconsenual sex with her brother-in-law by saying 'I wouldn't exactly call it rape, but it was the next thing to it.' According to a 1985 study in which one in five women reported that they had been forced to have sexual intercourse with a date, most of the women did not think that they had been raped. Another study conducted in the 1990s by Mary Koss also found that many women did not call what happened to them 'rape,' even though it met the statutory guidelines for rape in many jurisdictions (Warshaw, 1994). In a study of 236 respondents

> ... 61% did not define their own experiences as rape. A theme running throughout survivors' comments regarding their rapes was that they did not realize the assault they had experienced as rape until sometime later when they participated in a class, read something about acquaintance rape in the newspaper, or saw a TV program that educated them on the subject.
>
> (Weihe and Richard, 1995: 29)

It is apparent then that many women thought that the law did not consider nonconsenual sex with an acquaintance as rape. There is no paradox here. Even though American states do not statutorily exclude acquaintances – except husbands – they have gauged correctly society's view about such assaults. These are different kinds of cases – where women do not call what happened to them rape and where women are *unsure* whether or not they consented. The latter cases are a problematic category and one that I don't think includes many instances. If the woman was so drunk that she didn't know if she 'consented,' then being drunk would undermine her consent anyway. More likely are the instances where women blame themselves for what happened to them, which is a common reaction to acquaintance rape and possibly one of the most prevalent motivations for victims not going to the police (Warshaw, 1994: 56–58).

Nevertheless, what follows from finding out that 'victims' themselves do not necessarily see that they have suffered a criminal harm? Is that fact itself an argument that the law should not be expanded to include such cases? The fact that these so-called victims do not label their experience 'rape' leads some people to think that the law should not treat it as rape – a criminal offense.

Patronizing to Women Objection

While feminists were pushing for rape reform, another group of critics – for example, Camille Paglia (1992: 57, 70–71), Christine Hoff Sommers (1994), and Katie Roiphe (1993: 67) – argued against change, challenging feminists' conceptualization of rape, and particularly rejecting expansion to include acquaintances. They also questioned the feminists' strategy for advancing women's equality. Critics in this camp argue that feminist views about the pervasiveness of sexual violence and the unintelligibility of consent under the current patriarchal system actually undermine women's progress toward equality, making women out to be incompetent victims who can't take care of themselves on dates, at home, or in the office. They argue that feminists are actually sabotaging women's goals of equality by enfeebling women, by making them out to be victims of men and thereby in need of state protection. Therefore they have challenged proposed changes to rape laws such as the exclusion of force from the criteria. Paglia, Sommers, and Roiphe argue that reformists have vastly inflated the incidence of rape and sexual harassment and maintain that the idea of 'date rape' is a hysterical fiction created by feminists to advance their ideology of the pervasiveness of patriarchy. Paglia also argues that sex often involves an element of risk or danger and that radical feminists want to purge sex of its erotic nature. She further claims that women know or should know the 'risks' of, for example, dressing suggestively and going to a man's apartment. If sex results, women should not then complain to the law about it.

This group of critics has advanced a movement called 'take responsibility,' which advocates that women should take responsibility for making their sexual desires and their interests known. Women should speak up and ensure that their partners know what they want. They should be clear about their sexual boundaries and communicate them to the men around them (Fox-Genovese, 1995; Wolf, 1994; Roiphe, 1993). Additionally women should take responsibility for their choices, including how much alcohol they consume, the company they keep, where they go, and recognize that there are consequences for their choices.

Radical Feminist Objections to Rape Reform

Radical feminists' objections focus on consent. While they agree with other critics that merely expanding the range of cases to include nonconsensual sexual intercourse is inadequate, radical feminists challenge the use of consent at all to determine legal and illegal sex in a society saturated in gender hierarchy. Catherine MacKinnon is especially critical of the genuineness of the law's consent standard and argues: 'If rape laws existed to enforce women's control over access to their sexuality, as the consent defense implies, no would mean no, marital rape would not be a widespread exception, and it would not be effectively legal to rape a prostitute' (1989: 175). She also claims that '[r]ape law takes women's usual response to coercion – acquiescence, the despairing response to hopelessness to unequal odds – and calls that consent' (Ibid., 168). So in a case where the defendant did not threaten the victim on the occasion in question, but in the past *had* subjected her to threats and violent assaults, her crying acquiescence would be taken by most judges as consent.

Because of differential power – socioeconomic, political, and physical – MacKinnon questions whether there can ever be voluntary consent. Even if there was something like a sincere attempt to get consent, the significance of that consent in a society steeped in gender inequality is in doubt. MacKinnon argues that the consent standard of rape statutes assumes a background of equality from which we can judge the legitimacy or illegitimacy of consent. 'The law of rape presents consent as free exercise of sexual choice under conditions of equality of power without exposing the underlying structure of constraint and disparity' (1989: 175). She also contends that failures of consent are seldom without serious consequences, making the likelihood of their freedom doubtful. We might analogize these arguments with those in contracts which are called 'unconsciousable' due to inequality of bargaining power, or even cases of duress where the weaker party's consent is vitiated because of threats of sanctions – either explicit or implicit. Never is it asked, claims MacKinnon, whether, under conditions of male supremacy, the notion of 'consent' to sex is meaningful. MacKinnon argues that, in a society so entrenched in gender inequalities and the eroticism of gender hierarchy, dominance, and sadomasochism, it is difficult (if not impossible) to have genuine consent. Consent presupposes that the agents are, if not equals, at least not in radically disparate bargaining positions and not pressured by various coercive background factors. One way of understanding the meaning of coercive background conditions is to determine what would happen to the agent if they refused consent. Coercive background circumstances would make it unlikely that a person would feel free to refuse without repercussions. So, for example in medical experimentation, using prisoners as research subjects was considered problematic because their circumstances are coercive. The prisoners might correctly believe that their failure to participate in (even dangerous) experiments might result in the refusal of deserved parole or in extra harsh treatment from the prison. MacKinnon argues that, since women are still not equal in society, the inequality in power itself puts women in coercive relationships with men. Consequently, this makes the line between rape and so-called consensual sexual acts difficult to determine.

MacKinnon has two objections here: first that the law is not genuine in its claim about consent; and second that, even if it were, the imbalance of power present in many (most?) gender relationships undermines the legitimacy of consent. An example of the first objection is the 1991 St John's College rape case in which the defense was credible that the victim had *consented* to oral and anal sex with four male students. The case involved a 22-year-old African-American woman who was being driven home by a male 'friend' from the college lacrosse team. After stopping at his home and introducing her to his friends, the 'friend' plied her with so much alcohol that she was unable to stand and became sick. He then stripped off her shirt, forced his penis into her month, and engaged in a number of acts of intercourse. Three of his roommates took turns performing acts of sodomy and fellatio while the victim passed repeatedly in and out of consciousness. The jury accepted that the woman had consented to this 'sexual' treatment on the grounds that she had not explicitly dissented or physically resisted. Cases like this fuel MacKinnon's and other's cynicism about the genuineness of the consent standard in rape law.

MacKinnon argues further that the law makes presumptions about consent depending on the women's relationship with the men in question. Under these presumptions women are not raped by men they know, particularly their husbands. 'The paradigm categories are the virginal daughter and other young girls, with whom all sex is proscribed, and the whorelike wives and prostitutes, with whom no sex is proscribed. Daughters may not consent; wives and prostitutes are assumed to, and cannot but' (1989: 175). Other factors that affect how the law treats a woman's consent pertains to her behavior: did she go to the man's apartment, or to a bar, wear suggestive clothes, drink, use drugs? All these actions make it very difficult for the woman to refuse consent, and for these reasons, MacKinnon and some other feminist theorists are disenchanted with the consent standard for sexual offenses.

The inequality that makes voluntary consent improbable is seen in cases like *Commonwealth v. Mlinarich*, where the defendant used his position of power and authority over his young victim to force her to 'consent' to sex (see p. 47). Other examples, include teachers who 'threaten' female students with failure or low grades if they refuse sexual intercourse, other relationships such as doctor/patient, priest/parishioner where inequality of power can be abused, and the entire range of quid pro quo sexual harassment cases (see p. 70).

Part of this critique is to conceptualize women's subordination, oppression, and harm along a continuum of sexual violence and victimization. '[I]f one were to see sexual behavior as a continuum with rape at one end and sex liberated from sex-role stereotyping at the other, much of what passes as normal heterosexual intercourse would be seen as close to rape' (Russell, 1984: 21). For some radical feminists, all heterosexual sex involves exploitation and only different amounts of harm to women. The radicals' view has implications for rape since drawing a clear line at consent is not justified because consent presupposes general equality of participants and freedom from sanctions for refusal – neither of which, they argue, are present.

Liberal Responses

Before considering the responses to the objections, I would like to think through the political liberal response to expanding the criminal sexual offense. Mainstream liberals, though not necessarily explicitly agreeing with the substantive claims of Paglia, Sommers, and Roiphe, seem to agree with many of their conclusions. Liberals have tended to advance libertarian or libertine views about sexuality, arguing that the government should stay out of consensual sexual behavior and assuming that the notion of consent was unproblematic, at least in the context of sexuality. They tended to welcome the 1960s liberalization of sexual morality, with its wider acceptance of individual sexual expression and experimentation.

Liberals have, particularly in private sexual matters, argued for keeping the government out of personal decisions about sex, leaving decisions about whom to have sex with, what kind of sex to have, and other matters of sexual autonomy to the individual. The liberal tradition has two entrenched principles that contribute to this view of the law's relationship to sexuality. First, liberals have seen issues of sexuality as part of private morality, affecting only the agents involved, and therefore not the legitimate business of the state (Hart, 1996; Mill, 1947). Family life, marriage, and, more recently, 'intimate associations,' were left to this private morality and the 'hands-off' attitude was extended to all sexual relationships. It is an interesting question whether the liberal theoretical arguments of leaving these private relationships alone have in fact worked to support women's sexual autonomy or their equality within these relationships. The answer is, I think, mixed. By not criminalizing extramarital sex or particular sex acts, for instance, women have more sexual options. Nevertheless, shielding private relationships from state regulations has not necessarily, in practice, translated into more control for women of their sexuality. The hands-off approach to private relationships has resulted in the state not pursuing criminal enforcement in issues like domestic violence, rape in marriage, acquaintance rape, and other kinds of abuse and domination in 'consensual' relationships. In practice, a consensual relationship with a person in the past has resulted in the law presuming that whatever goes on in that relationship subsequently is consensual (one way around the rape shield laws is, for example, by revealing past sexual relationships). The hands-off attitude and the shield of privacy means acquaintance rape is met with suspicion or even utter disbelief. More generally, some feminists have been critical of liberal principles of justice that did not extend to the family since those relationships are 'private.' Rawlsian justice, for instance, left issues of the roles, liberties, and organization of the family to the benevolence of the head of household (Pateman, 1988).[1] Within these family relationships women are often subject to domination and other forms of inequality.

The second liberal principle that supports their view about law and sexuality is that only (sexual) acts that are nonconsenual are harmful in the sense of being wrongful and should be criminal (Mill, 1947 and Feinberg, 1984). Sexual relationships that are harmful to the individuals involved are exempt from criminal liability, and for some also from moral censure, if a product of consent. In practice this legal analysis permits assaultive sex acts when there is some semblance of submission to constitute consent, and thereby they are not judged to be criminal. The most degrading assaultive sex acts in these circumstances are thought of as self-regarding, if as with some Millian irony, the agent involved can be construed as consenting. In *On Liberty* (1947) John Stuart Mill argued that individuals know best what is good for them, and that the state can do more harm than good by interfering with their choices even if those choices result in harm. This builds the foundation for the strong antipaternalist position accepted by most liberals. The view construes the criminal law's interest in protecting against harm as mediated by the legal maxim *volenti non fit injuria* – to one who consents no harm is done – (Feinberg, 1986). Wrongful harms are those that someone has not consented to. Consent, then, plays a very important role in the legal picture of sex and, for many, in the moral picture as well. Nevertheless, I think that it is fair to question the liberals' uncritical stance on consent in sexual relationships, as they have been content to adhere to a 'hands-off' policy on sexual relationships with acquaintances and not look too closely at the issue of consent.

Assessing the Objections

Are these compelling objections to expanding the definitions of rape to include acquaintance, nonaggravated, nonconsenual sex? Should we expand our notion of impermissible or criminal sexual activity? Has the criminal law failed to notice significant harms against women? Should the criminal code include a wide array of acquaintance cases where there is no overt force or threats of force? Should rape laws encompass, as radical feminists have argued, an even wider array of sexual relationships, or should criminal prohibitions remain narrowly drawn to include only violent sexuality without consent, or forcible and nonconsenual sex? What role should consent play in sex crimes? Is the notion of consent fairly unproblematic as liberals have assumed? Or is consent to heterosexual relationships in our society with gender inequality much like Hume's claim of the absurdity of suggesting that impressed sailors consent to staying aboard a ship that is out at sea; or like Marx's insistence on the absurdity of the proletariat's 'free' consent to labor contracts under capitalism?

As with many issues, the right answers do not emerge out of some facile slogan on extremes. The anti reformists, Paglia, Sommers, and Roiphe, have raised important questions about the radicals' views about the pervasiveness of violence against women and the continuum of sexual violence. Is it accurate to conceptualize women as always vulnerable and threatened by the men around them, and does that conceptualization leave women seemingly as fragile creatures who cannot speak or take care of themselves? The model is problematic since it apparently portrays all women as powerless victims and all men as sexual predators, which doesn't make women good candidates for autonomy since they are viewed as closer to incompetents in need of protection from the state. Women generally are not incompetent, timid, fragile creatures who don't know their own mind, their own desires, and cannot express themselves. Nevertheless, some women *are*, and some just find themselves in threatening situations that the legal system has not recognized as coercive.

What we have seen is that historical and even current legal rules embody standards that are based on male perceptions or reactions and male expectations of women. The models of behavior and beliefs are derived from male models. These rules fail, therefore, to display the kind of neutrality and fairness that we should expect from the law. Nevertheless, there are often conflicts between short- and long-term solutions. For instance, some women seemingly accept stereotypical gender roles and thereby present themselves as timid, passive, nonconfrontational, and/or afraid of men. If we design laws to protect these women from exploitation and harm are we then sending out the wrong message about women and encouraging women to behave in accordance with those gender stereotypes?

> [Nina asked Larry to drive her home from his house where there had been a birthday party.] He told me he was too tired to drive, that there were extra bedrooms upstairs and would I mind just sleeping over and he'd take me back in [the] morning. Normally I would have been suspicious, but because he knew all the details of my surgery [Nina had undergone major surgery to remove one of her ovaries], I knew that he must realize that sex was out of the question ... [when they went upstairs, Larry demanded sex] He turned into a monster. He grabbed me and yanked down my slacks ... I fought him at first and told him to stop. Then he said I'd better not scream for his roommate because his roommate had the hots for me and knew what was going on and would just join in .... Why didn't I scream for his roommate?
>
> (Warshaw, 1994: 58)

In many such cases it is natural to ask why the woman didn't scream or run or hit back; why she responded passively and became silent or cried. These are all traditional female ways of reacting to frightening situations. Do we want women to continue this behavior when it may be in their long-term interest to give up these stereotypical gender responses. It could be argued that the most effective way of motivating women to give up passive, traditional female behaviors is to penalize those (by not protecting them) who don't give them up. This is one way of interpreting what Roiphe, Paglia, and Sommers are arguing. Similarly Vivian Berger, reviewing Susan Estrich's book *Real Rape*, worried that *too* 'understanding' an attitude toward the [passive women] of the world by the legal system may backfire and ultimately damage the cause of women in general. She argues that we do not want the law patronizing women: 'To treat as victims in a legal sense all of the female victims of life is at some point to cheapen, not celebrate, the rights to self-determination, sexual autonomy, and self- and societal respect of women' (Berger, 1988: 75). Berger worries that Estrich's desire 'to empower women in potentially consensual situations with the weapon of a rape charge may in fact backfire and instead enfeeble them' (Estrich, 1987: 66).

These are real concerns about whether we undermine women's equality and sexual autonomy by having these expanded standards. Even if it were true that it was in the long-term interest of women's equality to exclude the protection of 'traditionally female' victims, wouldn't our failure to protect them from harm now be exploiting them for those overall long-term interests? This strikes me as an objectionable form of using one human being for the benefit of a group. Could we justify to current victims, 'Gee, we recognize that you were harmed by X, but for the greater good of women, we are not going to legally recognize the harm.' Is it the role of the criminal law to direct these kinds of social goals, or to protect individuals from harm by others? If we admit that these offenses involve harms, then is it acceptable to let the perpetrators go free? I don't see that as defensible. The role of the criminal law is to protect against serious harms to autonomy. Consequently, even if it was in the long-term interests of women to be more aggressive and assertive about their desires and interests, it does not follow that we should not protect women currently from nonconsenual sexual interactions. Also, talking about socially engineering gender, do we think it is appropriate for the criminal law to exclude from protection 'traditionally female' styles of behavior? That is a radical suggestion and not one that I would be willing to support.

Ultimately, Estrich may be correct that women will be empowered by the threat of criminal sanctions against those who fail to secure clear consent. This strikes me as right and consistent with most of our criminal code. By providing individuals with the threat that the criminal law will back up their consent or lack thereof, it empowers them. This is not the criminal law saying that there are certain things it has deemed as illegitimate, but rather that the individual gets to choose, and her choice must be respected.

On the other hand, the continuum of violence stance of radical feminists commits us to the view that the difference between rape and permissible nonwrongful sexual relationships is one of degree, not of kind. Their position entails no phenomenological difference between bad sex, unwanted sex, and rape. This is problematic (Henderson, 1993: 56). This analysis belies women's own experiences of the difference between regrettable sex and rape, or wrongful, harmful sex. Bad sex that someone nonetheless consented to might be thought of as unfortunate, and they might even blame themself for their bad judgment. It does not follow that a wrongful harm has been perpetrated. In other circumstances, a woman might judge that the sex was bad where her partner was an egoistical, self-involved lover, making the experience not what she had wanted. These are regrettable sexual experiences but not rape. That is a different judgment from the experience of being forced into sex, that the perpetrator (whether an acquaintance or stranger) disregarded what was said or done and went ahead with penetration – that is a violation of a person. In empirical studies about acquaintance rape, the women were clear that they had not *consented* and felt violated, yet they just did not label it 'rape.' It is important to distinguish these occurrences and, yet, recognize the range of nonconsenual sex violations. The radical feminists are therefore wrong in not acknowledging this line between nonconsensual and merely unwanted or regrettable sex. Interestingly enough, many theorists have equated nonconsenual sex with unwanted sex. Stephen Schulhofer makes this mistake, even naming his 1998 book on rape *Unwanted Sex*. These are clearly different notions, since someone can obviously consent to sex that is unwanted or refuse sex that *is* wanted. There is nothing conceptually incoherent about either of these, which will be discussed further in the next chapter.

No doubt the radicals' claims distort the position of men and women in modern society. Many (maybe most) women have been empowered by the so-called sexual revolution to understand their desires and express them freely with their partners. Many men too have been able to break out of old stereotypical models of gender relationships, finding women with whom they can have intimate relationships based on respect and equality. The construction of all gender relationships on sexual conquest misses the real advances that men and women have made in sexual relationships. Additionally, there is the radical view of women who want heterosexual relationships being conceptualized as laboring under false consciousness since all heterosexual relationships are coercive and thereby harmful. This view patronizes women, suggesting that they have no subtle understanding of the forces in society that structure their preferences. Viewing all heterosexual sex as a product of domination and subjugation distorts the contemporary landscape and leaves women without legitimate models for developing their sexuality. This indictment of all heterosexual relationships is unwarranted and undermines the credibility of other feminists' claims.

On the other hand, the problem with the approach of Paglia, Sommers, Roiphe, and many liberals is that they *underestimate* the amount of sexual coercion in society, the role of patriarchy and gender inequality in sexual coercion, how that coercion is viewed by society, and the role of the law and legal practices in perpetuating the coercion. Abusive relationships, implicit threats of force, and simply greater physical strength are permitted as acceptable methods of securing sex. Many women are still socialized to be passive, to fear men's physical strength, and even to respond to men as authority figures (Warshaw, 1994: 50ff.). Consequently, the fact that women are taught to be passive, to not assert themselves, to be dependent, means that many environments may be coercive or threatening to them. Exacerbating the problem by not backing up women's choices, so that saying 'no' is not treated as nonconsent, the law further encourages the coercive situations in which women find themselves.

Paglia's view (1994) is doubly perplexing, and somewhat confused, since she claims that part of the erotic nature of sexual encounters is that the male partner might become overwhelmed with sexual desire and thoughts of rape. For Paglia, if this rape occurs, the woman has no grounds for complaint since she knew (or should have known) that this could happen. A partner with whom you have consented to sex becoming 'overwhelmed' with desire is exciting and part of the electric, passionate nature of sex. On the other hand, having someone become overwhelmed with sexual desire when you have not consented is not erotic; it is scary and seriously harmful. Accounts by women discussing their experiences of these kinds of situations clearly show that these occurrences are frightening and injurious and have lasting effects on the victims. These are not sexual turn-ons. Paglia's view itself throws women back into another era where they cannot speak up about their own sexual desires – they are not permitted to consent to sex or withhold consent but are left helpless to the desires of men.

Another serious problem with Paglia's approach is that she does not acknowledge that *real* rape can occur with an acquaintance. For her (and Sommers and Rophie) real rape involves violence and someone unknown to the victim. And yet empirical studies show that most women who are raped are raped by men they know (Warshaw, 1994: xi). The classic study was performed by researcher Mary Koss (1988), who found that one in four female college students had experienced rape or attempted rape and 84 percent of them knew their attackers. This study has been severely challenged by the anti-rape reform commentators, who claimed that Koss's definition of rape was too broad; that the study assumed that women took drugs or alcohol only because men gave it to them; and that women were counted as rape victims when they did not call what happened to them rape. In the study only 27 percent of the women thought of themselves as rape victims (Warshaw, 1994: xxi). Koss's work was taken on by a number of theorists, including Neil Gilbert (1991), who argued that it constituted an epidemic of sexual assault. His argument seems to be based on the fact that since acquaintance rapes were rarely reported to police, they could not have happened. The other major attack on Koss's work came from Katie Roiphe (1993), who argued that it was postcoital regret and not rape that the women in the survey were reporting. Interestingly, Roiphe takes the statistic that one in four college women had been the victim of rape or attempted rape since the age of 14 and converts it into sex is, in one in four cases, against your will.

Are the arguments against Koss's work cogent? Her survey did not use the term 'rape' for reasons that should be obvious – namely, that different people have different views about what rape is and, coincidently, many of those views exclude acquaintances from the class of rapists. The survey took the definition that seemed consistent with most statutes in North America, namely, 'unwanted sexual penetration perpetrated by force, threat of harm, or mental or physical inability to give consent (including intoxication)' (Warshaw, 1994: xxiii). This definition does not seem particularly broad and is in line with many of the statutes. But it is not the definition that I would want the law to embody, partly because it is too narrow in requiring force. On the other hand, using the term 'unwanted' is misleading, as since 'unwanted' and 'force' are both necessary conditions it is difficult to see where the objection comes from. However, if anything it is more stringent that it needs to be, as with this definition we get an extremely high incidence of rape.

The objection of women themselves not calling many of these occurrences rape thus begs the question of why the law should treat them as such. There are a couple of responses to this objection. The fact that a person does not realize that something that happened to them satisfies the elements of a criminal offense does not mean that a criminal offense did not occur. In Koss's study 90 percent of the women whose experiences fit the legal definition for rape said that their experience matched one of the following definitions: 'it was some kind of crime, but they didn't know it qualified as rape; it was sexual assault but they didn't know it was a crime' (Warshaw, 1994: xxv). Neil Gilbert's argument that women don't call it rape and don't report it as rape may well result from their (justified) skepticism about the law's response to what happened to them. Women probably well know that they did not consent but question whether the law will consider that sufficient for rape and whether they will be believed by the police, prosecutor and other officials (Weihe and Richard, 1995). Stories of women vilified by the criminal justice system are commonplace, so it should be easy to understand women questioning not their own phenom-enal experiences but rather the law and society's response to them.

Considering the range of cases under discussion, does the fact that the victim knows the assailant preclude that criminal harm was done; and why should it? The focus on stranger rape and violence fails to pick out so many cases without justification. This narrow approach to the definition of rape does not recognize the range of threatening circumstances in which individuals find themselves, and is reminiscent of the days in the not too distant past when spousal abuse was not treated as real assault.

Consider also the argument that acquaintance cases are different due to something like 'contributory negligence' in tort law, where the victim is held to have contributed somewhat to the harm that befell her. In acquaintance cases the victim often put herself in a vulnerable position by getting into the assailant's car, going to his apartment, drinking too much alcohol. Is it fair to say that, since she is responsible for putting herself in these situations, the assailant is not responsible for the outcome? Many victims take on this kind of responsibility, blaming themselves for the man's behavior; and many offenders claim that the women made them do it, by looking sexy or coming to their apartment. This is the approach of the 'take responsibility' movement. It is inadequate, I believe, to say that women should just take responsibility for themselves and absolve men from responsibility for *their* behavior. Even in the tort case of contributory negligence, the wrongdoer is not absolved from responsibility. But the criminal law focuses on the actions or omission of the person stepping over another's boundary or violating another's right. Criminal law does not, except in some rare cases such as provocation for murder, exculpate the wrongdoer for the actions of the victim. A consistent application of the 'take responsibility' approach might return us to excluding spouses from battery because 'she married him' and of not protecting any victims of a harm where they could have made more responsible choices. Householders who do not lock their windows and are burgled are responsible for their bad choice and the law refuses to prosecute the thieves. Moving into a drug-infested neighborhood leads to assaults, thefts, and rape, but oh well, any reasonable person should know that and avoid living there. These are not legitimate responses to harm in criminal law.

Radical feminist views about women's autonomy are not needed to explain why we should expand the criminal law of rape. The present laws do not protect women's sexual autonomy under any theory, even one that relies upon traditional liberal ideas of autonomy. When, for instance, a woman verbally refuses consent, says 'no,' and the law doesn't see that refusal as sufficient to establish nonconsent and thereby sufficient for illegality, the law is not living up to liberal ideas about autonomy. Providing women with the tools to protect their sexual autonomy is not to see them as helpless victims, as Camille Paglia suggests; rather it is to affirm their status as equals. To treat as an equal is to recognize individual autonomous choices, to give them legal effect – something that we don't do, for example, with children or others who do not meet conditions of fully fledged autonomous agents. The problem with contemporary rape law is that it does not recognize autonomous choices of competent adult women. Recognizing that women are vulnerable to sexual assault and that they are singled out on the basis of gender does not commit one to the view that women are helpless victims generally; they are victimized in this particular way and the law currently permits it. The criminal law needs to treat adult women as rational autonomous agents and give legal effect to their consent and protect them when they do not consent.

The Context of the Problem

The anti-rape reform critics' proposals are compelling, since committed liberals and feminists would like to see a world where women experience equal opportunities and power to direct their lives, including their sexuality. Feminists as well as liberals welcomed the changes in sexual mores that came with the so-called sexual revolution, particularly the loosening of rigid control

on women's sexuality. The goal would be for individuals to choose which relationships are most satisfying
for them. Women should be able to speak up for
themselves and make their desires and interests known;
to consent when they want and withhold consent when
they don't. They should not require the state's intervention or protection from unwanted sexual experiences with acquaintances.

With the societal liberalization of sexual attitudes
women have presumably been able to break rigid
stereotypes about appropriate female behavior, and
are now allegedly allowed to acknowledge and express
their sexuality and desires without the social controls
and stigma attached. With the advent of the sexual
revolution women have much more freedom to express
and act upon their sexual desires without fear of being
branded as 'sluts' or 'damaged goods' as in earlier
periods. That is the theory and certainly, to some extent
the practice. Ironically, since the 1960s – when
presumably it became socially acceptable for women
to consent to sexual activity outside marriage and to
explore their sexuality in a manner previously reserved
for men – society has developed contradictory attitudes
about women's sexuality. There still are unrealistic
views about women and sex: *de facto* categorizations of
them as 'good' girls who don't drink in bars, wear
'seductive' clothing, go to men's apartments, or consent
to sex; and 'bad' girls who do these things and then get
what they deserve. These unrealistic views also extend
to suppositions about what women will consent to. In a
case in Arizona (*Arizona Republic*, 1999), the defense
asked the jury to consider whether a 15-year-old girl
with a mental capacity of a five-year-old consented to
sexual activity with 30 males in an abandoned home
over an 18-hour period. One of the defense attorneys
attempting to make plausible the innocence of one of
the defendants, claimed that 'everyone has different
sexual appetites,' implying that the activities were the

experience of a possible sexual appetite that a woman might have and therefore *consent* to these activities to satisfy that appetite! Cases like this are certainly not unique; they leave women to defend *their* behavior in the most unreasonable circumstances since defendants are apparently credible in claiming that women would consent to all manner of bizarre sexual episodes. Why then are such defenses not met with the incredulity and the contempt they deserve? One reason why the law is failing in its handling of consent in rape cases is its absurd conception of what women might consent to; and thereby it continues to protect men's interests at the expense of women's.

Because women *can* (are allowed to) consent to sex, women may have become more vulnerable to rape because perpetrators either genuinely are unaware of plausible conditions for consent or disingenuously feign their belief in the validity of consent because the system apparently rewards defendants with acquittals in such cases. This leaves very little deterrence in the current system. Women are more vulnerable to the consent defense being raised in even the most outrageous circumstances. Where do these attitudes about women's sexual desire and appetites come from? Where do male college students get the idea that it is permissible to ply a woman with drinks and then as a group perform sex acts on her?

Catherine MacKinnon (1989) and Andrea Dworkin (1987) would say that pornography has created and/or reenforced sadomasochistic views of women's desires and sexuality. These views feed men's ideas about women's desires and society at large constructs sexuality based upon views of male domination and female submission – views about male entitlement to sex. The way that we as a society think about sexuality, they argue, leads to much sexual exploitation and abuse of women. The criminal justice system is not immune to these attitudes and, consequently, they find acceptance

of these models. MacKinnon and Dworkin also argue
that we have been socialized erotically to respond to
domination and subjugation: hierarchy is sexualized
and sexual desire is suffused with domination and the
instrumental use of women. Women are objectified by
men for their sexual gratification but, asymmetrically,
women do not objectify men for sex. The argument is
that these attitudes are adopted by both men and
women. Women socialized in a culture can 'volunteer'
or 'consent' to the use or abuse of themselves as objects.
Others have labeled this model of sexuality as a
'conquest model' (Smith, 1999). What the law will
accept as seduction, fraud, or manipulative persuasion
supports the claim that we have a conquest model of sex
relationships – men are the conquerors, women resist
but at some point give in and are conquered. And to this
we can add that 'all is fair in love (sex) and war.'
Sometimes men and women are playing the same game.
Men are aggressive and persistent and women are
passive and resistant to sexual advances. The obvious
problem with this 'game' is that 'no' cannot mean 'no,'
and resistance is interpreted as part of the game.
Women's words then do not have the normal force or
outcome that they would expect (Langton, 1998).

MacKinnon and Dworkin undoubtedly have raised
an important point about the social construction of
sexuality, but one than can, nevertheless, be over-
generalized. There is certainly something to their claims
about current views about sexuality. Exactly how the
sadomasochistic view of sexuality or the conquest
model of sexuality evolved is multifaceted, but it was
definitely encouraged by portrayals in the media,
particularly the pornographic media. Pornography
arguably feeds and reinforces distorted views about
women's desires and 'educates' men about those desires.
The laws themselves embody or at least support, the use
of these myths within the system by, for example,
allowing violent sexual activity to be or to become

'consensual.' In doing so, the law explicitly condones violent sexuality. By requiring both force *and* non-consent means that women's words do not have sufficient perlocutionary impact or the intended effect they would expect in the context of events: saying 'no' does not necessarily have the effect of stopping her 'partner's' advances. The law, rather than rejecting the domination/submission model of sexuality that women like to be forced, so that when they say 'no' they don't mean it, reinforces those views by accepting them as grounds for not prosecuting or for allowing in court that, even though women say 'no,' they don't always mean it. Thus the court will find grounds for consent even with explicit verbal rejections. Conversely, by not seeing forceful sex as inconsistent with permissible sexuality, the law accepts and possibly encourages violent sexuality so that it becomes a question at trial whether a 15-year-old girl consented to have sex with 30 men, leaving her bleeding and unable to walk. Or, as in the St John's case (see p. 154), whether a student consented to anal and oral sex with a number of men while she was intoxicated to the point of unconsciousness. These are supposedly examples of the different 'sexual appetites' of women. But if a woman did 'consent' to anal and oral sex with five men, should that not raise the question of why. People consent to activities because they will get something in return; if nothing else, at least money. Normally, people consent to sexual relationships because they will find it pleasurable or will gain satisfaction through a partner's pleasure. The point is that, without any plausible reason for the sexual activity, there are no grounds for even asking about consent.

Many feminists raise questions about whether liberalization has led to a society in which women have more control over their sexual autonomy (Wolf, 1997). Some feminists have suggested that women are oppressed by the violence and sexual aggression that society allows in the name of sexual freedom. Sexual freedom as interpreted by contemporary courts translates, as we have seen, into an absurdly expansive notion of seduction, as, for example, in the case of a man posing as a talent scout who lured a high school student into his 'temporary studio' with the prospect of helping place her as a model. Using fear and intimidation, he had sex with her (*Goldberg v. State*, 1979); or a man posing as a psychologist conducting a sociological experiment lured a young girl into his 'office' and intimidated her into having sex with him (*People v. Evans*, 1975). Sexual freedom permits what the law calls 'seduction' which, according to the courts, may involve a combination of fraudulent misrepresentation, intimidation, and threats. And the criteria for consent are so weak that they undermine its normative importance. Rape is on the rise, and domination of women persists in many sexual relationships, even where there is purportedly consent. Therefore serious doubts remain about whether women's sexual auton-omy has been advanced through the sexual revolution. If society is truly committed to securing environments where individuals are equally able to live autonomous lives, these forms of sexual control and violence need to be addressed.

On the other hand, women are oppressed by the moralistic controls society places on their sexual expression (Olsen, 1991). For example, US statutory rape laws prohibit any 'act of sexual intercourse accomplished with a female not the wife of the perpetrator, where the female is under the age of 18 years' (Cal. Penal Code, sec. 261.5; West Supp. 1981). This rule not only controls the sexual freedom of young women, but also reinforces sexual stereotypes of men as aggressors and women as passive victims. Frances Olsen argues that 'the restrictive aspects of statutory rape laws are particularly objectionable because they exalt female chastity and treat women as lacking in sexual autonomy' (1991: 307). Further, these laws suggest that young men are not in need of protection and are able to control their sexual autonomy.

Many theorists have seen the question of which sexual relationships to criminalize as one of where social controls should end and sexual freedom begin. Libertines and moralists draw the lines at different extremes – more sexual freedom versus more social control. The problem is that if '[s]exual freedom turns out to be freedom for men to exploit women [and] the burden of social control falls primarily upon women' (Olsen, 1991: 312), then freedom is not being extended equally. The way of framing the issue is misguided. Some forms of restriction entail the expansion of liberty for others: the law restricts the liberty to kill another person and in so doing expands everyone else's freedom to move about without fear that others will kill them. With rape, for example, by restricting male access to sex by requiring a robust consent that is free of force, coercion, and fraud, we would be expanding women's sexual autonomy, and women would have more freedom and control over their sexual lives.

Conclusion

The current vulnerability of women to sexual assault stems at least partly from the fact that the law does not adequately protect their interests, and does not empower them to protect themselves by making their words and actions count. Being treated as an equal means having one's interests respected and protected by the law. The conjunction of the rape law requirements of nonconsent and force means that the law is under-inclusive in picking out harms against women, and thereby is not adequately protecting them against harm. There are many cases which arguably involve a criminal offense, as some of the above illustrate, but which are not picked out by the statutes. Some of the cases involve considerable force or threat of force, which is clearly illegitimate; consequently, there is no further reason to ask about the presence or absence of consent. The mission of the criminal law is to prevent harm against the person; and in cases that involve serious violence or harm to another, *a fortiori*, the law should prohibit such conduct. On the other hand, securing sexual access without genuine consent, even when there is no violence, is also a harm which should concern the criminal law.

The standards for what constitutes consent in current criminal sex codes are so weak as to undermine the moral legitimacy of the consent requirement. Only in the criminal sexual codes do we find a minimalistic theory of consent (Estrich, 1987) exemplified by the cases of Mlinarich, Rusk, or Berkowitz, and Goldberg and Evans. These, the courts argued, were cases where there *was* consent; and they often argue that these cases are examples of seduction. Sexual freedom permits seduction, which, according to the courts, may involve a combination of fraudulent misrepresentation, intimidation, and threats. So-called valid consent includes cases where there is fear, intimidation, fraud, and incapacitation, resulting in a totally bankrupt account of consent.

In general the criminal code is supposed to protect us from serious harms and, certainly since John Stuart Mill (1947), this is its most uncontroversial purpose. Encapsulating the variety of harmful sexual activities should be viewed as part of the core concerns of the criminal law. Current criminal codes fail to adequately protect women from sexual assaults partly because they exclude many harmful sexual assaults, and those the laws do encompass are made difficult to prove. Criminal rape laws have not protected women's negative freedom to refuse unwanted bodily and sexual intrusions. Criminal law normally gives priority to protecting personal negative freedom as opposed to positive freedom, for example, the positive freedom to engage in sexual acts with whomever one wants. Since the laws seem to assume consent in the absence of explicit, emphatic verbal and physical refusal, it looks as if current codes are protecting an individual's positive freedom to have sex. If there is agreement that the criminal law should protect the negative freedom of everyone to avoid unwanted bodily invasions, then the law needs to strengthen the control that individuals have over their own bodies by backing up their control with criminal sanctions.

Note

1   From the manuscript. In the survey of 3187 female college students 15.3 percent had been 'raped;' 11.8 percent were victims of attempted rape; 11.2 percent had experienced sexual coercion; and 14.5 percent had been touched sexually against their will.

Chapter 4
Consent and Autonomy

Every human being of adult years and of sound mind has a right to determine what shall be done with his body.
(*Schloendorff v. Society of New York Hospital*, 1914)

Anglo-American law starts with the premise of thoroughgoing self-determination. It follows that each man is considered to be master of his own body and he may, if he be of sound mind, prohibit the performance of life-saving surgery or other medical treatments.
(*Natanson v. Kline*, 1960)

A grand jury in Austin, Texas failed to indict a man for rape where the victim asked him to wear a condom. Apparently the woman's request somehow implied her consent.
(Milloy, 1992)

Is Consent the Critical Notion?

We have long recognized the right to control what is done to our body. In medicine today, for example, there are elaborate rules and procedures for getting consent from patients and extensive discussion about what is required for consent to be valid for medical procedures and who is competent to consent. Consequently, consent would seem to be the perfect vehicle for protecting sexual autonomy. Before we can say that consent is a necessary condition for treating a person with respect in sexual contexts, we need to know more about the notion of consent. As we have seen, some feminists have been skeptical of the consent standard since it has been so lenient in rape cases that it as has been said sardonically that a corpse could have consented under certain conditions. Considering cases where the law has found consent to sex while the victim was unconscious, drunk or asleep, or threatened with a weapon, the cynicism is warranted.

What accounts for the law's treatment of consent to sex so differently from consent in other areas? The baseline assumption has been that women are consenting to sex until there is significant evidence to the contrary. The default is consent. The assumption itself is puzzling without analogy in law. Most things done to or for another person require consent, even if they are pleasurable or good for a person: without explicit consent to the operation you need to save your life, it is impermissible; without consent to use my car, it is impermissible to use it.[1] Criminal rape laws do not explicitly state that women are presumed to be consenting to sex, rather they imply it in the requirements of physical resistance and the search for verbal refusal. The law looks for explicit signs that would inform the man unequivocally that the woman is not consenting to sex at this time; otherwise he can assume consent. And even some resistance and verbal refusal is insufficient to turn the baseline of consent into nonconsent since courts have accepted the notion that women will sometimes say 'no' when they mean 'yes' and that women often need some physical encouragement, or force, to consent to sex. Consequently, the burden is on the women to say and show that she is *not* consenting – thereby the default is that the woman *is* consenting.[2] 'Such proof wouldn't be needed were the man not allowed to presume as his default position that she was consenting' (Malm, 1996: p. 155). With the exception of feminists, who claim that this presumption of consent is a product of patriarchy since it works in the interests of men's positive sexual autonomy, the reasons for this presumption have not been explored by rape commentators. Are there other reasons that might justify the assumption? Another argument might be based on evidentiary considerations. Since it is so difficult to determine whether a rape was committed, the law requires explicit evidence of nonconsent to establish the offense. This argument, however, is inadequate since the criminal justice system is supposed to protect individuals' sexual autonomy or simply bodily integrity, which would support the default in the other direction – namely, that there is no consent unless there is evidence to prove consent. Why not, for evidentiary reasons, assume the converse – no consent until there are clear signs of affirmative consent? The first problem with the law's approach is not the consent standard, since the law was not focused on consent, but with the *presumption* of consent. Drop the presumption and the law will have to search for *actual* consent.

The question that I want to explore is whether there is a role for consent in our understanding of rape. Is it the critical notion to understanding acquaintance rape in particular? Is consent a useful concept, one that helps distinguish lawful from unlawful conduct? Does it protect autonomy as it purports to do; and, if so, how? As part of this exploration I will consider the different senses and implications of each of these.

The last chapter argued that rejecting consent as an element of the crime of aggragavated rape makes sense when there is physical force or an explicit threat of physical force. The conjunction of force and nonconsent has a pernicious history in the criminal law. The use of violence, including overwhelming compulsion or threats of violence to secure sex, is wrongful and should be sufficient for liability for aggravated rape in law without the need to inquire further about consent. The idea that in the face of force the law holds out the possibility of consent does not protect women's autonomy and is inconsistent with the rest of the criminal code, which does not permit consent to death or physical harm (outside of regulated sports). Violent sexual assaults secured through force include the most terrifying attacks, both physically and psychologically, that can be inflicted on a person. As such they should be treated as among the most serious felonies in the criminal code. This chapter then focuses on nonaggravated or acquaintance rape and the role of consent in its determination.

The Moral Importance of Consent

The liberal theory supposes that what fully autonomous rational agents consent to is worthy of respect. There are nevertheless a number of details that need spelling out before we accept that asking for and getting consent are critical factors in protecting autonomy. What exactly is consent? Under what conditions has a person consented? On the other hand, what is missing in situations where sexual intercourse has taken place without consent? If, as we saw above, the standards for what counts as consent are so weak, then demanding consent will not function as a precondition for respect. Consequently, detailing the essential conditions for consent in particular contexts is crucial for it to be the protector of autonomy.

Consent, I will argue, figures centrally in unaggravated rape, providing the key to understanding the moral wrongfulness and seriousness of this form of sexual assault. Consent is important because we value autonomy, and consent provides individuals with a certain kind of power over their 'territory.' In order for consent to provide a serious moral demarcation, one that protects and promotes autonomy, the requirements for what *constitutes* consent must be fairly stringent. How should we think about the moral status and force of consent? Autonomous persons can be analogized to sovereign nations that may rightfully control their borders. The law, in a manner of speaking, backs up agents' rights to control their own borders by requiring consent to cross those borders. Valuing autonomy is valuing the self-governing person. Autonomous agents are left to identify their own interests, make choices that fit into larger life plans, and make decisions about their own good. One way that we respect autonomous agents is by leaving them room for choice and respecting the choices they make. From the moral point of view, concern about autonomy and self-determination is represented by guaranteeing agents control over their domain through their power of consent. Consent can play this role only if there are fairly rigid standards about what counts as consent. Indeed, if consent is inferred from the mere fact of silence or submission through intimidation or implicit threats, then consent does not provide individuals with a significant weapon with which to police their boundaries. Consent is important because by protecting personal autonomy it allows individuals to control important issues in their lives by changing their rights and responsibilities. Before consent we have duties not to interfere with, take, or touch another's body or property; after consent the structure of duties has changed over the subject of consent. After Mary consents to sex with John, John no longer has a duty not to touch Mary sexually. Mary's consent makes it permissible for John to have sex with Mary. The fact that consent transforms relationships gives it moral importance.

Consent is also the mechanism by which we treat each other as equals, by asking for consent before crossing another's border or taking what is rightfully theirs, whether it is their property or their body. Asking someone for consent for a sexual relationship is a prerequisite for treating them as an equal. This works because not asking a person for consent to sex treats their wishes or choices as unimportant, that is, as if they were inferior. The case of Berkowitz (see p. 2)

illustrates the point as the defendant, seeing himself as
superior to his victim, did not need her consent or did
not need to worry about her consent. Equally wrong,
and probably closer to the truth in this case, is that it
was not important for him to find out whether her
protests were 'real' since his desires were what was
important. The same lack of respect for the individual
is illustrated in other cases where consent was
neglected. Consider, for example, the Tuskegee,
Alabama, experiments in which the researchers failed
to seek consent from the subject African-American
men afflicted with syphilis because they believed that
the men were not as important as the research itself
(Pence, 2003). Or consider even more benign medical
treatments where the doctor fails to get consent since
he supposes that he 'knows better' than his patient. It
is insulting when physicians act paternalistically
towards us and treat us as if we were children,
inferiors incapable of understanding and making
decisions for our own good. Failure to ask for consent
from a person for something that is rightfully part of
their domain harms their status as an equal. Getting
consent from the agent for access to their body for a
sexual relationship is minimally required to show
respect for that person. Failure to seek and secure (a
woman's) consent before proceeding with sex is to see
the other person as a tool or instrument for one's own
gratification, or to see them, in Kantian terms, only as
a means rather than as an end-in-herself. White slave
owners treated their female slaves as sexual tools –
consent was not required for sexual access since the
masters did not see the women as autonomous agents
worthy of respect. The man feels entitled, superior,
and thereby does not need consent because women (or
a particular woman) are inferior to him, not equals
from whom he needs permission to gain access. Failure
to secure consent, particularly over significant matters
such as sexual access, is a harm to a person's worth or

value as a fully fledged equal moral agent. The act of overriding the victim's consent conveys the message that she is not entitled to the same status or respect as the aggressor.

Similarly, asking some third person, Bob, for consent to do something to Mary is also a harm to her. That is, unless Mary has extended Bob that right, as in granting 'power of attorney' then Mary is harmed by the failure to get consent from her. Although the failure to get consent is in itself a harm, depending on the topic of consent – consent to use my car, operate on me, have sex with me – the level of seriousness, and consequently the level of harm differs. Failure to get consent to use some trivial item of mine or to use my property to reach the beach harms me, but in a minor way. In contrast, sexual access that is not consented to is a significant harm.

I have argued that asking a person for consent is necessary, but is it all that is required for the resulting activity to be respectful to that person, or is the substance of 'what is consented to' also relevant to whether the action treats the person as equal and autonomous. In other words, when someone apparently consents to something exploitative, degrading, or demeaning, does it provide us with a moral objection to that form of sexual conduct? Alternatively, is a failure of the conditions of consent necessary and sufficient to render the conduct morally objectionable? Would the fact that an individual apparently consented to an act of degradation naturally make us ask whether it could be a product of rational autonomy that is required for meaningful consent? Here I want to explore the concern first raised by John Stuart Mill (1947) about the distorted preferences of men and women derived from a society still in the grips of patriarchy.

A brief caveat is in order about the notion of men getting consent from women for sex. Why, we might

ask, is it not the other way around, or the partners
mutually asking for consent? This conception paints a
picture of the man as the active seeker of sex and the
woman the passive granter of sexual access to her body.
This is unfortunate for a number of reasons, not least
because it is a distortion of the facts. It portrays women
as not interested in sex, which distorts the true picture
of women's sexual identity, desires, and plans. It is
partly a product of current social views about female
sexuality that we get this picture of the sexually active,
aggressive male and the passive disinterested female.
There is a lot of discussion about male sexual desire in
the media and in culture generally and little attention on
female sexual desire, the assumption being that women
have little sexual desire to discuss. What is interesting
about this view of female sexuality, which seems to
have endured through the 'sexual revolution,' is how it
sharply contradicts most of Western history's view
about female sexuality. The view, up to the 19th
century was that women were more carnal, more sexual
than men. Included in this view was the idea that men
were the victims of women's sexual prowess, lured into
sex by women. This is not the place to develop which
view of male/female sexuality is 'correct,' but rather to
note that our views about sexuality are shaped by
societal myths/stories that may find little or no
foundation in the psychology or biology of males and
females. Nevertheless, a liberal society should encourage individuals to develop and express their own
sexual autonomy within certain constraints, for example, with no harm to others, and, if possible, tear down
artificial views that might hamper the development of
one's own sexuality. We might wonder if these myths –
in either extreme – have alienated women from their
own sexual desires and sexual autonomy, leaving them
straightjacketed in societal norms about proper female
sexuality.

Protecting Sexual Autonomy in the Criminal Law

Competent adults should have control over their bodies and with whom they engage in sexual activity, and the law is generally supposed to protect individuals' bodies from nonconsensual touching, movement, or penetration. Saying they have control means that at least they can prevent others from accessing their body without their consent. Conversely, saying that a person (that is, a woman) has control over her body and sexuality is to say that she *can* give permission to someone seeking a sexual relationship with her, as controlling one's sexual life is not just about having the negative power of withholding consent. Historically, women did not have control of their sexuality either way – they were not allowed to refuse the person who controlled their sexuality and they were not allowed to have sex with persons of their choosing. Saying that autonomous agents have control means that they will not be penalized for granting or failing to grant consent. Sexual autonomy means the right to determine one's own sexual life, including the right to choose celibacy, for example for religious reasons; in other words, the right not to exercise one's sexual capacities. Conversely, individuals can exercise their sexual capacities for a variety of reasons, including intimacy, sexual pleasure alone, as a favor, or for money.

We should therefore distinguish between positive and negative sexual autonomy. Positive autonomy includes the freedom to seek out opportunities, choose partners, engage in sexual activities that are mutually fulfilling, and also to choose the sexual orientation that suits. Interests in controlling reproduction are also included in a robust notion of sexual autonomy. These positive liberties are limited only by the sovereign right of others to refuse consent. Arguably, the state should not block the pursuit of positive sexual autonomy except where the exercising of power violates another's negative sexual autonomy. So for example, criminal codes that make it an offense to secure an abortion or to use contraception stifle individuals' positive sexual autonomy without the justification of harm to others (on the assumption that a fetus is not a person with protectable rights) and are thereby unwarranted. Similarly, criminal laws against homosexuality are illegitimate since they stifle sexual autonomy without the justification of preventing harm to others. The criminal law to support sexual autonomy should stay away from most areas of sexuality except those involving harm to others – infractions of negative autonomy.

The criminal law protects important autonomy interests, particularly about being *free from* certain invasions. This is not unique to sexual autonomy since it is normally the law's role to protect us from certain interferences from others. The law is not designed to help people secure sexual access any more than it protects other aspects of positive autonomy. For the state to protect individual positive sexual autonomy would entail securing for them more opportunities for sex and access to more sexual partners. Securing positive sexual autonomy would undoubtedly be objectionable since it would require the government to force some people to have sex with others with whom they have not consented. The criminal law exists to protect negative sexual autonomy, meaning that individuals should be free from unwanted sexual access and have control over their sexual borders.

Who Has Sexual Autonomy?

Like many liberties, those that make up sexual autonomy are reserved for competent adult agents. The age at which someone is deemed an adult is most often perceived as a legal matter, but there are of course other issues, for example, religious traditions to consider. The law decides at what age someone can legally consent to sex or to a medical procedure; it also decides at what age they can decide which parent to live with, and when they can join the armed services. There are legitimate concerns about where adulthood ought to be drawn in regard to particular issues. For example, many US statutory rape laws declare that all females under 18 are *not* competent to consent, but the same rule does not always apply to males under 18. Does such differential treatment unduly restrict the autonomy of teenage girls or does it not adequately protect teenage boys? Young children, on the other hand, cannot consent to sex because they do not have sexual autonomy – the ability to consent or withhold consent to sex. But that is not to say that they do not have any rights over their bodies. Children can be sexually victimized but it is not because their sexual autonomy is overridden.

The issue of when someone is competent to consent to sex is a significant one. Illustrating the difficulties is the question of whether the retarded or mentally ill are competent to consent to sex. Do we want to say that no one who is retarded is competent to consent to sex; and does that blanket prohibition deny them an important human good? On the other hand, there are plenty of cases of retarded people being sexually mistreated, exploited, and harmed. So how do we resolve the question of competency? Retardation and mental illness are not all or nothing states; there are different degrees of retardation and mental illness. There will be clear cases at either end of the continuum where we would judge the person to be competent or incompetent. A retarded adult with the mental abilities of a three-year-old clearly cannot make rational judgments about the nature of actions or their consequences. On the other hand, a high-functioning retarded adult living on their own or in a group home may well be able to determine the nature and consequences of their actions. We will want to be alerted to the fact that retarded people, even high-functioning ones, will be more susceptible to being exploited or deceived. Competency to consent will be taken up in more detail in the following chapter.

What is Consent?

We have said that consent is essential to showing respect for autonomous agents and treating them as equals. But what exactly is consent – its ontological status (Malm, 1996)? There are a number of ways of construing the nature and effect of consent. One common understanding is that a person 'authorizes' another to act in an area which is part of their domain, for example, giving power of attorney. Consent gives permission or authorizes someone to do something or take something from the consenter, where the consenter has legitimate control over that thing. Another way of thinking about consent is of giving permission to cross a personal boundary: 'Any act that crosses the boundaries of a sovereign person's zone of autonomy requires that person's 'permission', otherwise it is wrongful' (Feinberg, 1986: 177). Consent is always given to the actions or proposals of others. Since we have the right to control what is done to our bodies, medical professionals who want to perform certain procedures on us must seek our prior permission: Surgery without consent is battery. Political philosophers have argued that we consent to living under the laws of a nation (the actions of the officials), and we can give someone permission to use our house, car, or land. We cannot, however, give someone permission to use something that is not rightfully ours; we cannot give permission to use someone else's house, car, or bicycle. Consent gives permission or authorization to do what would otherwise be prohibited. That permission or authorization provides a new reason for acting. In other words, consent gives John a new reason for acting that he didn't have before Mary consented. That new reason for acting, I shall argue, is a moral reason since consent is morally transformative.

Consent transforms existing moral and legal relationships often making what was impermissible, permissible. This conception of consent consequently must be normative since it changes existing rights and obligations. Consenting is not the same as merely willing or wanting or other kinds of mental states or attitudes because these have no power to change the normative universe, which is why I cannot 'consent' to someone using another person's property. I can say the words, but they do not transform the moral and legal universe; they are a sham like counterfeit money. In the case of rape, as in a number of other areas, consent turns a criminal act into a noncriminal one. Consent can turn battery into surgery, murder into voluntary euthanasia, rape into intercourse, theft into donation, kidnaping into a vacation. It thereby performs a kind of 'moral magic' on relationships (Hurd, 1996). The reason that we focus on consent is because it has this power to transform relationships, to change the impermissible into the permissible – an ability that consenting shares with promising.

To ensure autonomy, consent must be voluntary and deliberate since its 'understood purpose is to change the structure of rights of the parties involved and to generate obligations for the consenters' (Simmons, 1979: 76). The consenter, then must satisfy certain prerequisites to be able to act voluntarily and deliberately. Consent should also be distinguished from mere voluntary actions. Individuals must have the capacity to judge the object of consent. They must not be so high on drugs or alcohol that it impairs their judgment, or emotionally distraught to the extent that they cannot judge the quality and consequences of the activities to which they have consented. In other words, they must

understand what they are consenting to. The quality or
nature of the act must not be misrepresented or falsified.
Finally the person must be above the age of consent at
which the law deems them capable of appreciating the
character of the proposal and understanding the
ramifications of their actions. This is stipulated by law
and forms the demarcation between when a person is
assumed to have the capacity of judgment pertaining to
serious questions in life and when they do not. The
factors that undermine consent will be discussed in the
next chapter. Minimally consent must satisfy these
requirements.

The Ontology of Consent: Different Conceptions

There is a lot of confusion over consent, particularly in
rape cases, because there is a variety of ideas of consent
at work in law and in the vernacular generally. Some
are descriptive only, either of the requisite attitude or
mental state or of an action or performance. For
instance, the claim 'She consented, saying "Yes I'll do
it" after he pulled out the gun' describes consenting
behavior. Other theories are descriptive and normative
and give either an attitudinal or mental state account or
a performative account as the descriptive part. 'Consent' is, unfortunately, also used in a confusing number
of ways by courts, legislatures, and commentators –
even in the same jurisdiction. This is troubling because
what counts as consent, what the force of that consent
is, and when it would be reasonable to believe that a
person has consented, hinge on particular understandings of consent. As many statutes specify that one
essential element of the offense of rape is 'sexual
intercourse without consent,' how consent is construed
is important to whether that element of the crime is
satisfied. I will argue that consent is normative and
performative, *an illocutionary act* (Austin, 1962).

There are two major accounts of the nature of consent: the attitudinal and the performative. In the attitudinal account, consent is analyzed as consisting of any one of a number of private states of mind or attitudes on the part of the consenter, ranging from a mental 'choice' to willingness, grudging acquiescence, or even submission. Performative consent is analyzed as 'something that is *given* or *withheld* by a person through what is said or done in a particular set of circumstances' (Baker, 1988: 233). The performative account is often also perceived as normative; the act of consenting is regarded as normatively significant in that it consists of giving permission, that is, 'conferring a right on another to do something which otherwise that other person would have an obligation not to do' (Ibid., p. 232).

Both the attitudinal and the performative accounts of consent describe the behavior or experiences (mental states) of the individual. In that sense they are obviously both descriptive concepts. We could however conceive of consent as a descriptive concept only, with no necessary normative implication, as with the claim above that 'she consented with a gun to her head.' The normative judgment then would be entirely separate from the description of the conditions for consent. The locutions 'invalid consent,' 'unlawful consent,' or 'illegitimate consent' are used in this way. The implication is that there was (descriptively) consent – the person said 'yes,' acted in particular ways, had the appropriate mental attitudes – but we judged it not to be valid or legitimate consent. Many courts have adopted this view, and one, for instance, stated that 'Consent to intercourse induced by fear is no consent' (*State v. Davis*, 1973). The statement sounds paradoxical, but not if we understand that this is one of several meanings of consent. The first 'consent' means descriptively consented, whereas the second 'consent' has moral and legal force – it has the *moral magic* to transform the relationship. Statutory rape often involves cases where the female descriptively consents but, since she is under age, her consent is not valid, and hence it is an instance of rape.

Giving a descriptive account or even using 'consent' descriptively only and then following it with a normative judgment confuses the normative work that we reserve for consent. Consent is not mere acceptance of or submission to a proposal, but carries with it a certain seal of approval. If consent signifies a change in legal or moral relationships, then it must have normative significance. Consent changes the normative judgments pertaining to the acts in question, so that something might look like consent, but if it is flawed in some way – the person is hypnotized, drunk, or threatened – then they have not consented, even though they said 'yes.' I think that it is conceptually clear to reserve 'consent' for cases that succeed in changing moral and legal relationships. It would then not just be a matter of acceptance or submission, with no normative judgment entailed. Consent then should be distinguished from mere *acquiescence* or *submission*, which many courts and commentators in rape cases have allowed to count as consent. One reason that this is misguided is that assent in such cases may well be in the face of threats of various kinds. Another reason is that mere submission or acquiescence do not carry the normative dimension: we have simply a description of a person's mental attitude and/or behavior. Whatever account of consent we adopt, it should be conceived of as a normative concept that transforms moral and legal relationships.

The Attitudinal or Mental State View

Is consent a kind of mental state that one *has*, a kind of willing or desire for something, or is consent mainly something one *does*? If consent is more akin to willing, a private mental state, then its existence might be inferred from behavior; but the behavior is *not* necessary for the existence of consent. In the attitudinal account the consenter is logically privileged because consent is solely a private state of mind. Many US jurisdictions such as Michigan, Florida, and California and some commentators have assumed the mentalistic conception of consent. For example, the Model Penal Code claims that when the court is inquiring into the defense of consent in rape cases it 'is an inquiry into the victim's subjective state of mind' (see Chapter 2). Michigan says that a woman's 'subjective consent' and not her external manifestations of acquiescence is what is important to the defense of consent; Florida discusses the victim's 'subjective state of mind' of the victim, while California's focus is on what the victim 'subjectively' *feels* as opposed to what she objectively *does* (*People v. Hale; Coley v. State; People v. Barnes*). The Canadian courts have also adopted the attitudinal or subjective approach, stating that 'since consent is a state of mind, any test designed to determine a purely subjective matter should also be subjective.' The English courts as well quite explicitly accepted the state of mind approach in *Regina v. Malone* (1998), where the defendant had sex with a 16-year-old intoxicated girl without her consent. She was going in and out of consciousness when she realized that Malone was having intercourse with her. She wanted to resist but was too inebriated to do anything. In appealing against his conviction, the defendant claimed that consent for rape was something that was 'demonstrated' or 'communicated' and not merely a subjective state of mind. Thus by failing to demonstrate her consent she had consented to sex with him. The Court of Appeal argued that, for purposes of law, consent is a 'state of mind' and not something that must be 'demonstrated' or 'communicated.'

For the subjective account of consent certain conditions must be present for someone to be capable of consent. First they must be conscious, that is, not asleep or unconscious, as a person who is asleep cannot make judgments or think rationally (or indeed consciously think at all). Only cognitive abilities are required, not the capacity to act voluntarily. The person must also have certain cognitive abilities that must not be impaired by alcohol or drugs, since these can affect individuals' ability to make judgments even about their own desires. For example, after too much drinking one might eat too much even though one's considered subjective desire is to diet. The capacity to consent minimally means that the individual must understand the nature of the situation and the consequences of the proposed course of action. The problem with impaired judgment from alcohol or drugs (or emotional impairment) is that the severity of the impairment is clearly on a continuum: many people can function as well after one or two drinks as after no alcohol. They can subjectively form mental states clearly and consent to the proposals of others with full knowledge and understanding of what they are doing. At the other extreme individuals can drink so much as to totally incapacitate themselves, to radically obstruct their ability to have intelligible mental states. Consequently, they fail to satisfy the requisite conditions for consent. It is important to remember, however, that these abilities and capacities are on a continuum. Whenever we talk about mental capacities and voluntary actions we need to be aware that there are forces, pressures, and cognitive defects that affect all our choices and actions: rarely does an individual act 'fully' voluntarily in the sense that there are no pressures or influences on his will. The question is when are there too many. Consent is all or nothing, that is, either a person consents to something or not; but acts and choices can be more or less voluntary. We are interested in the threshold of voluntariness, when an act or choice is voluntary enough to be a true reflection of a person's autonomy.

In many cases, the courts focus on what the woman desired and whether her words or deeds adequately conveyed her *desires*, suggesting that consent is a mental state, a kind of desire. But why pay attention to desires unless it is presupposed that consent is a kind of desire? This perception of consent as desire is also apparent when the courts and commentators cite empirical evidence which supposedly shows that women sometimes desire sexual intercourse even though they say 'no' in a particular encounter. The woman's desire for sex is thus evidence for her consent. For these theorists, consent is a kind of subjective desire that one has. (This even includes Schulhofer's account (1998), which relies upon what women desire as opposed to what they do).

One problem with such a view is that we can and do often desire something yet refuse to consent to it. For example, imagine committed lovers who desire to have sex with one another and yet refuse to consent to sex because they believe in celibacy before marriage. There is nothing counterintuitive or paradoxical about claiming that one's desires do not entail one's consent. In fact this is what is so striking about the above analysis of consent. It is not difficult to imagine cases where the two diverge, and yet the courts and many commentators regularly conflate the two. Simply equating consent and desire cannot be correct. Heading off this concern, Heidi Hurd has defended a form of the attitudinal account that differs from the mere mental state of desiring something.

> Suppose that a woman desires sex with a married man. Suppose that she harbors this desire even as he achieves penetration. Does the fact that she desires intercourse constitute consent to it? While this appears plausible, one can certainly imagine her desiring intercourse while not consenting to it. We often refuse what we want. We often choose in opposition to our desires. If it is her choice to engage in intercourse not the sheer fact that she desires to

do so that constitutes consent to intercourse, then one must conclude that consent is equivalent not to desire as such but to the execution of desire, namely, to choice.

(1996: 126)

Hurd argues that consenting to x is a subjective state of *choosing* x, and that there is a distinction between subjective desires and subjective desires that turn into a choice (but not an action). But what exactly is the difference between them if they are both mental states? The notion of desire itself is ambiguous, as Harry Frankfurt pointed out. He distinguished different levels of desires: we can have desires about our desires, for example, I can have a meta-level desire that I don't desire to eat chocolate cake. Hurd needs to tell us what kind of desire constitutes the desire to choose x which is consent. How do we distinguish the desire to have sex with x and the desire not to consent to sex with x? Is it just the firm conviction, the mental state, to opt for x or is it something more? The mental state view needs to explain how to distinguish 'mental choices' from mere desire, even Frankfurt's meta-desires.

In the attitudinal account, behavioral or verbal signs are merely *indications* of the person's mental state, that is, the consent; they are not the consent itself. There is no objective behavior that is necessary or sufficient for consent and, since we have no epistemological access to a person's private mental states, consent can be very difficult to judge according to this concept. Actions that are construed as co-operative and thereby desiring sexual activity are not themselves consent (in Hurd's view mere desire for something is not sufficient or necessary for consent); they are evidence from which consent is inferred.

The attitudinal concept could explain well what is going on in *People v. Burnham* (1985). Rebecca Burnham's husband beat her severely until she agreed, under threat of further beating, to stand on the street in front of their house and entice motorists to have sex with her while her husband Victor photographed her. Although Rebecca feared physical injury from Victor, she feigned expressions of desire to the motorists. Obviously Rebecca's mental state was not one of consent but just the opposite and yet her behavior seemed to token consent.

What are the arguments in favor of the attitudinal or mentalistic account? Heidi Hurd (1996) argues that 'if autonomy resides in the ability to will the alteration of moral rights and duties, and if consent is normatively significant precisely because it constitutes an expression of autonomy' then consent must constitute the 'exercise of the will.' The focus of consent needs to make reference to the person's conscious choice or will. Hurd is on to important aspects of consent, namely, that it originates from the person and is a deliberate product of their will. It doesn't just happen to the person and they cannot accidently consent. It is volitional, and for that reason it changes the moral and legal landscape.

Another argument in favor of the mentalistic account that may provide the reasons behind the courts' analysis is that verbal expressions of consent are neither necessary nor sufficient for consent. Saying 'I consent' could be in response to a coercive threat or a result of gross misrepresentation; consequently, we cannot take verbal consent to be sufficient for consent (Brett, 1998: 69). 'Yes' may not mean yes. A 'yes' as a result of a threat is not consent. A 'yes' that results from a misrepresentation causing someone to have a false belief about what they are consenting to is not consent. On the other hand, the person does not have to say 'I consent' to consent, as verbal expressions of consent are not necessary for genuine consent. Many sexual interactions take place without verbal expressions of consent and yet we do not suppose that all these interactions are 'without consent.' If there is consent in these cases without verbal expressions, then the consent is not identical to the verbal expression. The mentalistic account does not require a verbal expression of consent.

For Hurd and others attracted to the subjective account, someone who is unable to express any consent, either verbally or behaviorally, could still consent to sexual relations. For example, if Mary, a quadriplegic deaf-mute, subjectively wills to have sex with John, is John, in the absence of any objective indications of her consent, justified in proceeding to have sexual relations with her? According to the mentalistic view of consent he is. Hurd (1996, 137) suggests that to deny the mentalistic approach will deprive those 'who have lost their physical autonomy of the only power left to them—namely, their ability to exercise moral magic through subjective will ... ' This is a strange argument since John has no reason to believe that he is not committing a crime, a serious harm to Mary. Imagine in the medical case that we permitted doctors to perform surgery on patients in this state, that a physician just believed that a deaf-mute quadriplegic is consenting to surgery. Even Hurd cannot endure the consequence that John would escape legal culpability for penetrating Mary in this case since he has no reason to suppose that she is consenting. But as 'a moral matter' he would be acting justifiably.

Besides this bizarre outcome of the mentalistic account, there are a number of reasons why this view of consent fails. The most important reason is the role that consent is to play in the world, namely to publically transform legal and moral relationships. Consent can only have this transformative impact if it is *communicated* from one party to another. Communicating consent gives John a justification for changing his reasons for action. By saying or doing certain things in an appropriate context, we communicate our consent, those words or acts are tokens of consent. Mental states or attitudes alone cannot communicate to another person, consequently they alone cannot give another justification for changing their reasons for acting. With Mary's mental states alone, John has no reason to infer that there is a transformation in the rights and obligations in their relationship. Consent as a mental state does not do the work that we morally and legally want done. As Joel Feinberg argues, the inadequacy of the mentalistic approach is that John does not have 'any direct insight into [Mary's] mental states ... the question of his responsibility must be settled by reference to presence or absence of ... authorization by [Mary], not what [Mary's] secret desires or hopes might have been' (1986: 173). There is a necessary communicative element. The communication of consent is what protects autonomy. I will argue that the performative account can accommodate important insights of the mental approach, for example the fact that consent is a product of a person's will – it is given intentionally, without the pitfalls of the mentalistic approach.

The Performative Account

In my opinion the performative account provides a better analysis of consent by removing it from the realm of subjective feelings and attitudes and making it public. Consent would not make legal sense as a demarcation between the legally permissible and impermissible if it were merely a function of a person's mental attitudes, with no epistemological access necessary on the part of the person receiving consent for its presence. If consent is performative then it is an act that one does. Nevertheless, consent is a performative that signifies a mental state.

Since consent is something that one does, beliefs about what a woman 'really wanted' cannot support a reasonable belief that she consented. Consent as a public act is not necessarily related to what someone wants. There is quite a lot of confusion between notions of consent and what is desired or wanted. Stephen Schulhofer named his 1998 book on rape *Unwanted Sex*, implying that nonconsensual sex is the same as unwanted sex. This is confused since one can consent to something unwanted. These are distinct concepts. Imagine, for instance, that you have cancer and don't want chemotherapy; nevertheless, you consent to the procedure. Conversely, you can withhold consent to something even though you want to do it. The woman who wants to be a virgin bride but nevertheless very much desires sex with her boyfriend will refuse consent to something that she wants very much. What she wants to do and what she will consent to are different. This confusion is very serious since what women are claimed to want or desire is used alone as grounds for their consent. This will be discussed further in Chapter 7.

In the interpersonal cases where disputes arise about the presence of consent, the performative account bars a person from claiming that, no matter what they said and did, in the absence of fraud and coercion, they did not consent in their mind. What a person says and does, and the circumstances surrounding the words and actions, are extremely important to this concept of consent, in which having a positive inner attitude toward the consented to action is neither necessary nor sufficient for consent. It is, however, necessary to have the *intention* to consent: the performative account is not merely about consent as behavior, action, words, or gestures; the actor must intend that they be taken as consent.

Since consent is something that is done there is nothing unintelligible, according to the performative account, about the fact that 'it can be given on one occasion but withheld on another similar occasion, even in relation to a similar kind of action' (Baker, 1988: 233). Hence, determining whether consent was present in a particular context will depend on what a person said and did in the context and on the particular set of circumstances. Saying 'I consent' in a context of explicit and/or implicit threats means there is no consent.

To understand the performative account we should turn to the work of John Austin who explained that we can do things with words – what he called 'speech acts.' For example, when a bride or groom says 'I do' at the appropriate time they have changed, transformed their relationship – they are married. Their words in that context succeed in making a transformation in their relationship that can only occur given certain conventions. The marriage convention in the USA is such that saying 'I do' by particular people (a bride and groom who are not already married) in front of a particular person (a member of the clergy or a judge) will succeed in marrying the individuals. Performatives are conventional. They require conventions to interpret words, acts, or gestures that have particular meanings in particular contexts defined by conventions of society.

The mentalistic account was supported by the fact that verbal expressions are not necessary or sufficient for consent. But doesn't this fact undermine the performative account? Speech acts are not only performed with words: the performative of a bid at an auction can be done by certain behaviors such as scratching one's nose or head or raising one's hand.

> In very many cases it may be possible to perform an act of the very same kind *not* by uttering words, whether written or spoken, but in some other way. For example, I may in some places effect a marriage by cohabiting, or may bet with a totalizer machine by putting a coin in a slot.
> (Austin, 1962: 8)

We can consent by using words, saying 'I consent to *x*,' or through actions, nodding one's head in the appropriate circumstance, or by failing to say anything in a circumstance when silence is understood to be consent. This is often called 'tacit consent.' Nevertheless, we only understand these other ways of performing speech acts within particular conventions. Insults are performative and provide good examples of the range of ways of insulting other people and how those ways are conventional. There are verbal expressions, for example, 'You idiot,' actions like 'giving someone the finger,' and there are inactions that can insult, such as failing to shake someone's hand. These are obviously conventional since they differ from culture to culture, and what is considered an insult in one culture might be a sign of respect in another, for example, burping after a meal.

John Austin's performative analysis of language acknowledges three types of speech acts: locutionary, illocutionary, and perlocutionary. Locutionary is merely the act of saying something, for example, 'I do.' Illocutionary is what someone does in saying something; in saying 'I do' at a wedding one gets married. Perlocutionary is what you bring about by saying what you say; by saying 'I do' she made him very happy. The performative analysis of consenting is as an illocutionary act: one does something by consenting – one authorizes, gives permission, transforms moral and legal relationships. One does not require a particular locution such as 'I consent' to do it.

How someone performs the illocutionary act of consenting depends on what they are consenting to. For example, consent for a medical procedure has become extremely formalized: it is specified what the patient must be told; what benefits and risks must be discussed; what alternatives must be presented; what kind of mental and emotional state the patient must be in, and what capacities they must have. The conventions surrounding medical consent have changed, motivated interests in protecting patients' autonomy by ensuring that they really understand what they are consenting to and how their consent will alter their future options. In the case of sex we have not required the formal machinery of signed forms that has become customary in the medical arena to token consent. Note however that Antioch College in Ohio recently instituted a much more formalized sexual consent procedure requiring explicit consent to each escalation of sexual interaction. The rules were an attempt to avoid the confusion in conventions to sexual consent that lead to genuine mistakes and thereby to date rapes. Many criticized their attempts at reforming the conventions surrounding sexual consent, saying they would undermine the sexual experience. Yet the fact that they are changing certain sexual conventions is not an argument against them, particularly when the goal is (as in medicine) to more fully protect autonomy.

However, conventions do exist for sexual consent but they rarely involve an explicit 'Yes, I would like to consent to sex with you.' How then should consent to sex be understood? There are performatives that are understood as consenting to sex, for example, a couple who have been out on several dates and now find themselves at John's apartment kissing on the couch. As the kissing and petting escalates, Mary's unbuttoning her blouse or John's clothes is token consent to a sexual relationship. With any performative we cannot stop at merely describing the behavior without discussing the circumstances in which it is done. For example, saying 'I do' outside of a wedding doesn't mean that you are married; neither does saying 'I do' in front of someone who doesn't have the legal power to marry or saying 'I do' when you are already married. Saying 'I do' when you have gun to your head will void the act of marriage.

There are a number of what Austin called 'infelicity conditions,' or conditions that define when words or actions fail or misfire in performing a particular speech act like consenting. For example, if, earlier in the evening, John had threatened to kill Mary if she didn't act enthusiastically about a sexual relationship with him, then her enthusiastic sexual actions would not constitute consent. This is analogous to Rebecca Burnham, whose husband threatened to beat her if she didn't solicit motorists for sex (see p. 33). The women's behavior alone indicates consent but the wider context tells us that there is no consent. As another example, if John broke into Mary's house while she was sleeping and initiated sexual relations with her pretending to be her husband Mary, only half awake, responded to his advances, her actions would not constitute consent to sex since she was deceived about the nature of the activity (she believed she was consenting to sex with her husband).

Infelicities are ways things can be or go wrong such that one will not have consented if one or more of these conditions pertain. There are two general kinds of infelicities: those that affect someone's capacity to consent – they were unconscious, asleep, insane, high on drugs, drunk, or under the legal age of consent – and abuses of the procedure of consenting, such as coercion and fraud. We may want to examine other abuses, for example, those concerning the relationship of the actors and how that relationship unduly undermines the act of consenting as these abusive relationship cases may themselves reduce to coercion or fraud. The next chapter discusses procedural abuses in more detail. Merely saying particular words or doing particular actions are not sufficient to token consent, as the circumstances in which they were done are essential to the performative to determine whether it was successful or not.

We have seen that performatives do not have to be verbal and that they can be behavioral (and sometimes involve the absence of behavior in a particular context). Neither should performatives merely be associated with verbal or behavioral expression. The person must *intend* to consent. The person must have a certain mental state to consent, namely to intend their acts or words to be consenting. Some commentators have assumed a performative account that includes only the objective features of the case, what someone said or did, as the consent. Consequently, these theorists have supposed that there is another category, the so-called 'hybrid view' that includes both performance and mental state. The solely 'objective' or behavioral view is misguided (and not faithful to Austin's view, which is not itself an argument against it). The person who is hypnotized and then told to say and do certain things that objectively 'look' like consent does not consent. The hypnotized person does not authorize John's acting differently toward her. The hypnotized person does not give permission to have sex with her. There is a separate question that is often confused with the question of consent, namely the question of whether a reasonable person would believe she was consenting – the *mens rea* of the actor. This will be discussed in detail later but, briefly, the circumstance will determine whether it was reasonable for John to believe she was consenting. If he is at a hypnotism exhibition and he knows that there are a number of subjects roaming about who have been hypnotized, then it would not be reasonable for him to believe that an unknown woman who was sexually responding to him was consenting. Outside such a bizarre context it probably would be reasonable for John to believe that a woman was consenting to sex if she removed her clothes and his clothes, and fondled him, and there were no other reasons to think that she was not acting as herself. The central objection to the behavior-only view is that it does not hinge on autonomous will, as someone could unwittingly or mistakenly consent by performing the requisite behavior. Consent does not then satisfy its more important role of expressing and protecting the autonomous will of the actor.

Tacit Consent

Conceiving of consent as performative and normatively significant means that it does not follow from the fact that consent was not withheld that it was given. If the agent does not consent, does nothing, or explicitly refuses consent – 'No, I don't want to' – there is no consent. John Locke (1980) agreed with this analysis and said that consent is an 'act ... whereby [among other things] anyone unites his person, which was before free, to any commonwealth.' Consent can be given, however, in some cases without explicitly saying 'I consent' and Locke's famous discussion on tacit consent has set the stage for later discussions. The argument is that silence or inaction, in some circumstances, express consent. A. John Simmons gives an example of a meeting in which the chair announces: 'There will be a meeting of the board at which attendance will be mandatory next Tuesday at 8:00, rather than at our usual Thursday time. Any objections?' (1979: 79–80). There is silence for a period and then the chair notes that everyone agreed (or consented) to the revised time. Consent to the proposal is given by the failure to speak up when given the opportunity. But silence can only be taken as a sign of consent under circumstances meeting very specific constraints. The actors must know that by not saying anything they are expressing consent and they must know the substance of what they are consenting to, that is they must not be deceived about what they are consenting to. They must intend to consent by their silence. They must be given a reasonable amount of time to respond and put forth their protests. They must not be acting under coercion, that is, they must be able to withhold consent without fear of reprisal. And finally, the means of dissent must be reasonably easy to perform. The following example shows when the means for indicating dissent are not reasonably easy to preform and the consequences of dissent are detrimental to the potential dissenter. The chair in our previous example now says: 'Anyone with an objection to my proposal will kindly so indicate by lopping off his arm at the elbow' (Simmons, 1979: 81). A more appropriate example for our topic would be that the consequence of not consenting to sex is a beating.

When the relevant constraints for tacit consent are met, and hence when a person's behavior should be construed as consent, can be problematic. David Hume raised concerns about Locke's argument that, by residing in a country, persons tacitly consent to its government. Hume points out:

> Can we seriously say, that a poor peasant or partizan has a free choice to leave his country, when he knows no foreign language or manners, and lives from day to day, by the small wages which he acquires. We may as well assert that a man, by remaining in a vessel, freely consents to the dominion of the master; though he was carried on board while asleep, and must leap into the ocean, and perish, the moment he leaves her.
>
> (1965: 263)

Similar worries might be raised about tacit consent in other areas. Joel Feinberg uses the notion of 'symbolically appropriate' behavior as a sign of consent, suggesting that certain behaviors in specified contexts are universally recognized as expressing consent. Feinberg views the following case as one where consent is clear.

> A and B have sexual relations ... As preliminary caresses are exchanged A finds at each successive stage enthusiastic encouragement from B, who is all coos and smiles, though no words are exchanged, and no permission requested. After the fact he [A] would be rightly astonished at the suggestion that he had acted without B's consent. To fail to dissent when there is every opportunity to do so, while behaving in appropriately cooperative ways, is universally understood in such contexts to express consent.
>
> (1986, 184)

Though no explicit question was asked and no explicit answer given, Feinberg claims that consent in this circumstance was actually expressed, not by 'silence but by symbolically appropriate conduct in the circumstances.' The notion of 'symbolically appropriate' behavior as a sign of consent needs to be questioned seriously in sexual encounters, given the number of 'misperceptions.' Ellen Goodman, in a newspaper column discussing the alleged rape by Senator Kennedy's nephew William Kennedy Smith, asks 'How is it possible that there is such a perceptual gap about "consent" for sex?' The woman in this case claimed that she was raped and Kennedy Smith claimed they had consensual sex. One or the other might, of course, be lying. Nevertheless, what often happens is that there is a difference in perceptions about the same situation. Goodman claims 'The man will portray steamy sexual intercourse in the grass with just a spicy soupçon of rough stuff. The woman will describe sexual assault and a piercing violation of her will.' The man doesn't believe that he has used 'force,' nor does he believe than the woman resisted enough or more than what would be common with 'normal seduction.' He believes that she acted in 'symbolically appropriate' ways. The problem, as Goodman points out, with this difference of perception (when it exists) is that the state is left with the burden of proof that the victim was violated. Just saying so is not sufficient. The courts and public claim in many of the nonaggravated cases that the woman is lying or deceiving herself; there was no rape.[3]

Sometimes 'symbolically appropriate' behavior can be radically redescribed in different circumstances.[4] In Feinberg's example B might be extremely afraid of A, concerned that if she doesn't 'go along' A will hurt her; perhaps because on a previous occasion A hurt or threatened B. It may well be doubted that B had 'every opportunity' to dissent if every opportunity means an opportunity without fear of reprisals. If A and B had a long-term caring relationship, then the scenario described by Feinberg could appropriately be one in which consent was expressed. On the other hand, if A and B had just met and A had made frightening comments to B, then that same behavior would not necessarily express consent. Consent secured through behavior under one description cannot merely be transferred to that behavior under another description. At least legally, in areas where it is known that misunderstandings are prevalent, it is not unfair to require that agents do not rely upon 'symbolically appropriate' behavior for consent. When a serious wrong is committed if behavior is misinterpreted – as in rape cases – it is proper to require agents to go beyond symbolically appropriate behavior to ensure that consent is given.[5]

The Range of Consent

If I consent to a physician removing my appendix, then unless I withdraw consent she is at liberty to carry out that single procedure (she no longer has a duty not to take out my appendix). She cannot decide, while she is 'in there,' to remove one of my kidneys – even if it might be in my interest. The exception to this would be in a life-threatening emergency. I have given up my right to complain if she removes my appendix (unless it is done negligently). I might later regret consenting to the surgery and decide that I no longer want the surgery performed, but that does not change the fact of my earlier consent to the operation. In sexual relationships, as in other relationships, there can be misunderstandings about what a person is consenting to. You might consent to some sexual activities that you consider 'normal' such as coitus or oral sex, but not include consent to be tied up and beaten as part of a sexual encounter. Consent to sex is somewhat referentially opaque, 'Sure, I consent to do *that*.' (Of course in most cases there will not even be such a statement, but rather tacit consent, viz, certain behavior that tokens consent). In most instances it will be understood what 'that' refers to since the parties will know each other and share similar ideas about sexuality. Problems arise when the parties do not know each other well. Imagine the case where one party says that she is interested in sadomasochistic sexual practices, which for her means spanking, dressing in leather, and acting out dominance and submission roles; yet the other party understands sadomasochism as referring to very different, much more violent activities. Consider the case of *People v. Jovanovich* (1999), in which the New York supreme court upheld a lower appellate court decision that consent can be a defense to violent assault and battery occurring within the context of a sadomasochistic encounter. The case involved a male postgraduate at Columbia who was sentenced to 15 years in prison for kidnaping, assaulting, and sexually abusing a female Barnard College student. The two New York students had met online and frequently discussed in e-mails their mutual interest in sadomasochism. The victim admitted in an e-mail to being in such a relationship with another man, and described in intimate detail her sadomasochistic fantasies, which included being tortured. At trial the victim testified that when the two met in person for the first time, she voluntarily went to Jovanovich's apartment and agreed to be tied to a futon as part of a sexual encounter. But she also testified that she never consented to being tortured for 20 hours. Jovanovich poured candle wax on her, bit her, shoved an object into her rectum, and refused to release her even after she invoked a 'safe word' which meant 'stop.' Neighbors testified that they heard screams coming from the apartment and friends corroborated her injuries. The defendant claimed that this was all part of a consensual sadomasochistic encounter. Recognizing that consent to sex can be referentially opaque exposes the consent seeker to liability for rape for failing to obtain consent to some sexual activity that was not part of the consent giver's understanding of what she was consenting to. The burden lies with the person seeking consent to clarify that there is consent, particularly when involved in sadomasochistic practices.

Taking sexual autonomy seriously means that when there are (or may be) doubts about the content of what is being consented to, the seeker of consent should clarify the parameters of what is being agreed to and not make assumptions about what the other person believes they are consenting to. Sadomasochistic relationships pose particularly difficult issues because masochists are not supposed to get what they want or consent to – actions are supposed to be imposed against their will. I will return to the difficulties raised with sadomasochistic relationships in Chapter 8.

Although consent can change a wrongful act into a permissible one, we need to be careful about what other inferences we draw from consensual relationships. Consent does not make all actions morally permissible. It does, to a large extent in a society committed to liberal principles, provide an argument for decriminalizing those acts that are a product of consent. It does then make legally permissible the acts of John when Mary consents. It provides an excuse for John when it was reasonable to believe that Mary was consenting. Nevertheless, it is important to mention that, from a moral point of view, not everything that a person would consent to should morally be done. Nor should a person do something to another person just because they consented to it. A noncontroversial case illustrating this is a patient consenting to medically futile surgery. The surgery is not excused by saying that the patient consented. In a later chapter I will discuss the difference between what the criminal law ought to permit and what is morally permissible, for example whether all things are considered morally acceptable in all sexual relationships where there is consent.

Notes

1 There is an exception in cases of long-term relationships, but even here we need to be careful how we understand the exception. For example, I may take my husband's vehicle without his explicit consent on a particular occasion if I need it. I assume that there is a baseline of consent to use his vehicle if I need it and he doesn't. Now if we are separated then the fact that he is my husband shouldn't be grounds for the assumption of consent. The marital exception to rape was based upon the assumption that the partners were always consenting to sex. That assumption was not warranted since the marriage license does not eradicate sexual autonomy, whereas marriage may well generate assumptions about other things within our power to consent.

2 Heidi Malm's comments on Stephen Schulhofer's *Unwanted Sex* at the American Philosophical Association's Central Division meetings, Chicago Ill., April 2000.

3 There may be some cases in which the accuser lied (the FBI estimate 2 to 4 percent), but that is true of other crimes as well.

4 At auctions certain gestures are taken to signify assent to particular prices. In many instances, individuals new to auctions have been misinterpreted as acting in these symbolically appropriate ways.

5 Something like this is done in contract law with the Statute of Frauds, which does not recognize certain agreements, for example, verbal contracts for real estate exchanges, because of the problems of misunderstanding that arise from those circumstances.

Chapter 5

Factors Undermining Consent: Incapacitation

Four men in a bar carry a drunken woman from the restroom to a booth in the bar where they undress and each engages in intercourse with her. At the men's rape trial, their lawyer's argued that 'if the woman had consumed enough alcohol to be helpless, ... then she could not be sure that she had not consented to sex.' The jury acquitted them.

(*New York Times*, 26 March 1996, at A17)

Up to this point I have been arguing that rape should include cases where there is no physical force, but where there is an absence of consent. I now want to investigate what undermines consent. When is it that 'yes' does not mean yes, that is, when does it not change the normative relationship? We have already established that nonconsenual sexual activity is harmful and should be criminalized regardless of the relationship between offender and victim and regardless of how much or little force is present. This means that in cases where there is no consent, and that includes cases where the person says 'no' or engages in some rejection strategy such as 'turning cold,' the criminal law should understand that there is no consent (Koss, 1988: 12). If there is no performative act of consent then there is no consent on the performative model. Either there is a performative token of consent or not. When there is rejection there is no consent, but when there is no response at all, the proper inference is *no consent*. For instance, if the groom does not say 'I do' at the wedding he will not be married; if the patient at the hospital does not sign the consent form, she has not consented. Failure to consent, even without rejection, should be understood as nonconsent. But of interest here is when there appears to be consent and yet there are factors about the consentor or the circumstances that undermine the legitimacy of the consent. Appearances, as is often said, can be deceiving. For example, when someone says 'yes' in response to a threat to their life, there is no normative consent, no normative transition of the relationship. That's the easy case. But what about submitting to threats of other kinds of harm – not necessarily physical? Are they sufficient to undermine consent? Certain kinds of deception also undermine consent as well, but which? If you do not understand the content of what you are consenting to, you do not have the appropriate mental state for consent. How much do you have to understand or how much deception is consistent with consent?

In the next chapter, I will consider the issues of coercion and deception. But before that I will explore the conditions under which a person is considered incapacitated; conditions about the agent herself that makes her incapable of consent. Some individuals are always incapacitated, perhaps because of their mental functioning level, and others are merely temporarily incapacitated because, for example, they are drunk or unconscious. Nevertheless, the issue is never that simple and, consequently, we must ask what level of mental functioning a person needs to be capable of sexual consent. Generally, if incapacitated, the person's actions do not morally transform a relationship. Being incapacitated normally means that one cannot form the mental states necessary for consent. However, the incapacitated person can often still perform the physical act of consenting. If a person lacks the mental and emotional functioning to understand the nature and quality of what they would presumably be consenting to, then they are incapable of consent. As we know, a minimum prerequisite of consent is that the person is conscious. Beyond consciousness, a person needs the capacity to make judgments about the consented to activity, to understand its consequences and its social meaning. Many individuals who lack mental abilities because of retardation or mental illness do not comprehend the meanings and consequences of sexual relationships and consequently are incapable of consent. What constitutes incapacity such that, even though the person may have apparently consented, the consent is not valid due to incapacity?

When Does 'Yes' Not Mean Yes?

When does apparent consent or a token of consent not constitute consent? Certain behaviors that descriptively look like consent do not constitute consent unless certain conditions are present. Consider again the hypnotized person who says 'I consent to x' under the direction of the hypnotist. What he does in saying 'I consent' has no normative significance; it is not consent, even though it might look like it. Consent is undermined by one of two general kinds of infelicities: first, internal conditions that affect the actor's capacity to consent – being too young, asleep, unconscious, drunk, or high on drugs. There are a number of internal incapacities which I will discuss below. The other kind of infelicity are abuses of the procedure of consent, of which coercion and fraud are the clearest examples. Notice that sometimes these categories are blurred, for example, some actors may have idiosyncratic fears such as agoraphobia, and consequently can be coerced by a threat that would not 'normally' have that coercive effect. Similarly, someone who is mentally retarded, an internal condition, is more likely to believe something that a 'normal' adult would not, and thereby would be more vulnerable to fraud. Before I turn to these infelicities of consent, I will recap on the essential features of consent generally.

As we know from Chapter 4, consent must be voluntary, that is to say that the action was done intentionally in the absence of external and internal conditions that would undermine free rational action. In other words, the actor has accurate information about what she is doing, is in control, and acts deliberately. The actor must be able to form intentions and be at liberty to act according to their intentions. An epileptic seizure, for example, is not a voluntary action on the part of the person, but a movement of his body outside of his control. There is, nevertheless, a continuum of voluntariness, ranging from what might be called fully voluntary actions to completely involuntary actions. A fully voluntary choice would be one in which someone had plenty of time to reflect on their choices and the outcomes, totally without pressure from within (obsessive desires or addictions, for example) or from without (there is no gun to their head). Perhaps most choices fall short of the fully voluntary; they are made in more hasty and pressured situations (Feinberg, 1986: 99ff.), but nevertheless we consider them voluntary. The impulsive choice of eating cheesecake may well be voluntary even though the choice runs counter to my considered preference, which is to diet. This is a kind of weakness of will, but we would not conclude that the choice was not voluntary (and therefore I don't have to pay for the dessert). If I was not coerced or deceived about the choice, nor was I drunk or high on drugs, then in this kind of case we would say that it was voluntary. Is the 'choice' of a longtime addict to inject heroin voluntary, or the alcoholic's choice to have a drink? Alcoholism is called a disease, implying that it is not in the actor's control. What about adults who were abused as children and who now abuse their own children; are their acts voluntary? There are plenty of difficult cases that are contestable as to whether they are voluntary.

Once we recognize that voluntariness is not an all-or-nothing concept – that there can be more or less voluntary actions, and that there are contested cases where it is disputable whether the person's action was voluntary – it makes sense to ask whether there are grounds for having different standards depending on the context and what is at stake. Since very few actions are what might be called 'perfectly voluntary choices' we have to decide when a choice is *sufficiently* voluntary to count as voluntary. This will depend on what the action is and on its context. For the purposes of criminal wrongdoing we make different judgments depending on the crime, the level of culpability, and the social purposes advanced for making it criminal. For example, for first degree murder US laws require that the person act intentionally with knowledge of what he was doing, and yet for vehicular homicide the agent could be extremely drunk and charged with that offense. A drunken defendant's claim that he drove his car involuntarily into the pedestrians will not be met with sympathy by police and prosecutors, even though that same drunk might be able to void a contract he signed because he was intoxicated at the time. For purposes of contract law his action was not voluntary enough to bind him. For civil and criminal law the standards of voluntariness may be different, and even within criminal law standards can vary according to the nature of the offense, the level of culpability, and the social purposes advanced by treating it as voluntary or not. For the purposes of deciding whether someone's choice of dessert was voluntary we will accept a much lower threshold for voluntariness than if we are deciding whether they voluntarily signed a will. We have different standards for voluntariness for different contexts. The choice of dessert is rarely going to elicit questions about its voluntariness because so little is at stake. Increase the importance of the subject of choice and our scrutiny of choice or consent intensifies. Consent for medical treatment involves very important welfare interests and consequently serious harm by defective consent. Hence we require more in terms of the person's capacity and scrutinize the external conditions in which consent was given.

It is often claimed that sexual consent is different from other kinds of consent since it occurs in a context unique from, for example, that in which consent to a medical procedure is given. Sexual consent is usually given in private, and is emotionally and sensually charged. It is not the context for deliberative discussions about the merits and demerits of the proposal. What has been inferred from the private, emotional context in which sexual consent is given is that we should thereby significantly *lower* the standards and conditions of voluntariness for consent[1] since it is difficult to ask for high standards of voluntariness in the sexual context. The problem with weakening standards is that we then run a higher risk of harm from getting consent wrong or from false positives: we make it more likely that women will in fact not be consenting when men and the law take them as consenting. It will be women, not men, who run that higher risk with lower standards of sexual consent. Without some compelling reason to force women to shoulder the higher risk of harm to them, the law should maintain standards of voluntariness that ensure validity of the consent.

That compelling reason for weakened standards for sexual consent might be to maximize sex, as more permissible sexual contacts occur when standards for voluntariness are lower. How sexual consent is conceptualized depends on whether we are more interested in maximizing sexual access or protecting against nonconsensual sexual access. If the former, then the bar for consent would be lower than in other arenas. According to theorists like Camille Paglia, part of the thrill for women is that the men they are with might become overwhelmed with sexual desire and rape them. So asking for more rigid standards of sexual consent will take the fun out of sex, an idea I repudiated earlier (see p. 86). Sex is fun if it is consensual, otherwise it is not fun. When discussing sexual consent it makes sense to worry more about the implications of false positives rather than false negatives since consenting to some act or practice gives permission to change the status quo of the consenter. False positives, where there really wasn't consent, illegitimately make that change. We need to ask what the effect on your interests would be if the choice was not voluntary and you did not give permission but the consentee proceeded as if you had? When the outcome of false positives is very serious, we strengthen the conditions for consent. Some choices are trivial and getting them wrong is trivial, with little effect on your welfare. But change the context and make the false positive the choice to have a 'Do Not Resuscitate' order, and the consequences to autonomy are devastating. For the patient who wants to be put on a ventilator in the Intensive Care Unit, getting her request wrong is serious indeed since it would lead to her death. In some activities we worry more about false positives than false negatives and thereby make standards to consent more stringent, medical consent being a good example of this. If the patient is not made aware of the alternative therapies, does not know the side effects, the risks, and so on, the consent to the treatment is not valid. The physician runs the risk of an assault and battery charge, not to mention malpractice, for acting on defective consent. We should only be willing to risk false positives in situations where a mistake does not involve grave harm to the nonconsenting agent. One way of mitigating against serious harm is if the consented-to activity is easily reversible. Given that having non-consenual sex is serious and that it has adverse effects on a person's interests at the time and well into the future, false positives should be guarded against. False negatives are normally not so serious since they keep the individual at their initial baseline, *ex ante*. In the sexual case, the person asking for consent is not permitted to proceed with sex. In such cases, if it is a false negative the consentor has the opportunity to clarify consent. False negatives are less serious since it is always possible to say 'I really do consent to x.' On the other hand, false positives that are acted on – that is, the agents have (nonconsensual) sex – are not reversible (Koss, 1988).

Most activities for which consent is required are fairly serious, and talk of consent versus mere choice signals a heightened seriousness of the activity. Something that is ours to control, our body, property, legal powers, is being given up when we consent. Standards of consent require that there be contextual variations in the levels of voluntariness required for the validity of consent (Feinberg, 1986: 261ff.). For instance, consent to be a medical research subject has come under intense scrutiny in recent years. In that context standards are very high, requiring detailed information about the risks, disclosure about any therapeutic benefits, constraints about compensation that can be offered in exchange for consent. How do we determine what the standards should be in the various contexts? How stringent the standards ought to be is a function of the seriousness of the violation of a person's domain, the level of harm from a failure of consent. This approach would argue for heightened standards for sexual offenses since the harm of nonconsensual sexual activity is grave.

Internal Constraints: Alcohol

Normally we do not let others exploit an incapacitated person and use that person's condition to their own advantage. The fact that a victim was drunk or high on drugs should naturally lead to the conclusion that she was not consenting, as she was incapable of voluntary consent. Showing that the woman was incapacitated should establish the element of the *actus reus*, 'without consent.' Consent is the vehicle through which individuals autonomously direct major parts of their lives. Poor choices or choices which fail to conform to a person's good are often made without one's full faculties. Hence consent granted at those times is not legitimate.

Alcohol poses a significant problem for consent to sex since men and women use it to 'get into the mood' for legitimate sexual interactions. Generally alcohol is used as a relaxant and as a social lubricant. The presence of alcohol or other mood-altering drugs is not itself sufficient to undermine a person's consent. Nevertheless, most instances of acquaintance rape, particularly on college campuses, occur when one or both of the participants have been drinking. According to Mary Koss's study 75 percent of the men and 55 percent of the women reported that they had consumed drugs or alcohol prior to the attack (Warshaw, 1994: 44). Alcohol and drugs can disinhibit male aggression and women's ability to resist assault. It is interesting that evidence from a number of studies shows that men use alcohol as an excuse for aggressive sexual behavior (George and Norris, 1991). Men also believe that alcohol reduces women's sexual inhibitions and, consequently, they will use alcohol to make women more sexually compliant. In one study 75 percent of college men reported attempting to use alcohol or drugs to secure sex from an unwilling woman (Mosher and Anderson, 1986). The lack of resistance by the women in acquaintance rape cases comes up again and again in the defense arguments as a method of undermining women's claim of rape. The victim's lack of resistance in the St. John's College case (see p. 79) was used as evidence for her consent. The defense argued that if she wasn't consenting to the men's behavior, why didn't she resist (although she did verbally resist). This case illustrates the role alcohol plays in acquaintance rape cases. The defense argued that the victim got drunk intentionally to cast off her inhibitions, suggesting that she had consented. Her denial, when she hadn't resisted, made the defense question her credibility. The defense also used the fact that she remembered some details of the assault (but not all) to argue that she was not too drunk to consent, as the prosecution asserted. The defense strategy put this victim in a paradoxical situation that: 'she was sober enough to have effectively resisted had she so wished, or that she was so drunk her testimony lacked credibility' (Kramer, 1994: p. 134).

Another relevant factor in acquaintance rape cases particularly involving college students is the jury's perception that these are 'nice boys' and that conviction for rape would 'ruin [the defendants'] lives' (Fried, 1991). As prosecutor Linda Fairstein has pointed out:

> Jurors in acquaintance rape cases are inordinately swayed by the physical appearance of the man on trial ... I have now heard hundreds of times—especially when middle-class, professional defendants stand up in the courtroom—the murmurs of prospective jurors or public onlookers saying, 'I can't believe it—he doesn't *look* like a rapist.' Or 'He doesn't look like he'd have to *force* someone to have sex with him.'
>
> (1993: 135)

There is also a double standard about perceptions of male and female drinking: intoxicated women are viewed as shouldering a greater responsibility for being raped than the men who rape them. The admonition is 'She got what she deserved' by drinking so much in the presence of men, and 'She must have wanted it' and got drunk to get it. Women who drink are perceived to be more promiscuous, more available, and they are perceived by men to be easier to get sex from since alcohol depresses reaction time and loosens their inhibitions. There are two messages here: that the women want more sex and that it is easier to get sex from them, whether they want it or not. On the other hand, men tend to be excused from alcohol-related sexual aggression. Men who had used alcohol were judged less blameworthy for sexual crimes than men who had not (Richardson and Campbell, 1982).

In a similar case at Florida State University (FSU) 'Allison' was systematically given a large amount of alcohol in order that a number of male students could have sex with her. After the assault she was dumped in front of another college building, where she was discovered unconscious and with a 'life-threatening' blood alcohol content of .349 (Oltarsh sentencing proceedings, 16 May 1990). Allison was still in a semi-comatose condition five hours after she was found. Amazingly, the defense argued that she had consented. The attorney argued at the preliminary hearing that the 'victim has an affinity for group sex and consented on the night in question.' (How does someone with an affinity for something have that satisfied if she is unconscious? If I have an affinity for Cabernet and it is poured down my throat while sedated, my affinity will not be quenched.) The fact that when she was found she had 'slut,' 'bitch,' and 'whore' written on her thighs with grease paint, and that her wrists and ankles were reddened and her body covered with abrasions and scratches, did not undermine the defense's argument that she had consented.

Allison was not capable of consent and the defendants worked at getting her into that state of incapacity. Many such gang rape cases illustrate, as discussed earlier, that the public and the courts are willing to give credence to women consenting to these sexual episodes where their interests and pleasure are not at all a focus. Why would Sandra, the victim in the St. John's case, consent to having one man stick his penis in her mouth while another hits her face with his? Why would Allison consent to having sex with several men in the shower when she was too drunk to even stand on her own? What are these women getting out of these relationships that might give any credence to their consenting? People normally consent to sexual relationships that they will find pleasurable. In these cases, there was no apparent reason for consent.

There are, of course, borderline cases of a person being too incapacitated to consent, and it is difficult to state in abstract terms when a person has had too much to drink or is too high on drugs to consent. But we can start with the clear cases like St. John's College and FSU and say that a person who is passing in and out of consciousness is too drunk to consent. A person who cannot carry on normal functions – stand up, drive a car, carry on a conversation – is too inebriated to consent to sex. The women's incapacitated condition alone should have made the defendants' consent defense a nonstarter. Whenever a woman is incapacitated to the point where she cannot physically resist, again that should not be taken as a sign of consent – which it frequently has. As argued earlier, lack of physical resistance should never be used as a sign of consent.

Consider another case from Massachusetts in which a male doctor offered to make a house call to treat a female hospital technician for her back pain. At her house the physician injected her with 5–10 mg of Valium to relax her muscles. She became '[v]ery groggy, very out of it, very heavy ... like I couldn't move my arms or my legs,' and then she lost consciousness. Upon regaining consciousness, she found herself undressed and the physician undressed beside her, fondling her and starting sexual intercourse. She reported that she drifted in and out of consciousness and was physically helpless. Her state of mind precluded consent (*Commonwealth v. Helfant*, 1986). These are conditions internal to the actor. Although in both of the above cases the defendants intentionally either plied the victim with drinks to get her drunk or injected her with enough medication to induce incapacitation, both were done so as to make the women compliant to sex. But, even if the defendants had not been the instigators of their victims' incapacitation, taking advantage of a person in that condition would amount to nonaggravated rape. It is not necessary for the defendant to create the conditions; exploiting someone who is incapacitated is enough.

> Anne, a 17-year-old fresher at Stanford University, came to Thomas's room where he encouraged her to play 'drink Blackjack.' She ended up drinking eight peppermint schnapps. After consuming the alcohol, Anne didn't feel well and lay down on the bed. Thomas began to kiss and undress her. Anne told him to stop but he disregarded her protests. Anne was too intoxicated to physically resist and felt threatened by Thomas's size and his actions. Thomas was not charged with rape, but only statutory rape, which rendered the issue of consent irrelevant.
>
> (*State v. Thomas*, 1991)

The cases discussed above are fairly extreme, but what about a simple case like the one between Anne and Thomas? Anne voluntarily engaged in a card game that entailed her drinking a shot of alcohol each time she lost. Over a very short space of time, this inexperienced drinker had consumed a massive quantity of alcohol. But this was not a case of Dutch courage; in this case Anne repeatedly asked Thomas if he was trying to get her drunk to have sex with her, and said that she was not interested. Even when she was drunk and ill, she told him after his advances that she didn't want to have sex with him. Under the performative account of consent, that alone should have been sufficient for nonconsent as Anne's drunken state does not undermine her refusals of consent. This then is not a case of a person presumably saying 'yes' and of us wondering whether the consent was valid. In this case, she said 'no.' The defense assumed that the fact that the woman voluntarily drank the alcohol implied her consent to sex. In the other cases as well, it appears that the focus is on the voluntariness of the drinking: consent to drinking is assumed to entail consent to sex.

The law has often treated voluntary intoxication differently from involuntary intoxication in rape cases; but should it? In determining whether someone is a victim of other sorts of crime when drunk or high, does it matter whether the person got drunk voluntarily or was slipped the alcohol (or other substance)? Obviously, getting someone inebriated in order to take advantage of them is wrong. In other areas of the criminal law just taking advantage is wrong.

It has been said that there is a kind of inconsistency about not holding the drunken victim responsible for her drunkenness and what it leads to, while the drunken defendant is held criminally responsible for his behavior. Heidi Hurd states that:

> On pain of condescension, we should be loath to suggest that the conditions of responsibility vary among actors, so that the drunken man who has sex with a woman he knows is not consenting is responsible for rape, while the drunken woman who invites sex is not sufficiently responsible to make such sex consensual.
>
> (1996, 141)

Hurd is arguing that if we are going to hold people who are drunk responsible for their criminal behavior, then we should treat women's consent as valid when they are in the same state. There is no symmetry between the two in other areas of the law. For instance, the drunk who leaves his car unlocked with the keys in the ignition does not give permission for someone to take his car, even if he tells them they can have it. Drunks who are admitted into hospital emergency rooms are not competent to consent to surgery. We treat the two issues of responsibility differently.

A better argument looks to the conditions for consent, the requirements for consent versus the requirements for responsibility for criminal wrongdoing, such as rape or murder. Actors can have the relevant intentions as specified in the criminal law for conviction for rape or murder even if they are drunk: because the mental state required for responsibility for those crimes is minimal. The criminal law's mission is to deter wrongdoing; consequently, we set the bar low on required mental states for intentional wrongdoing. Criminal offenses involve harming some third party who has no control over what the offender does. In the consent case, A can avoid the effects of B's drunken consent by not having sex with her. Consequently it is not unfair to shift the burden of responsibility to A. On the other hand, we require (or should require) much more robust capacities and mental states for valid *consent* for which one is responsible. Consent, remember, transforms moral relationships and permits actions that otherwise would be criminal. With consent we have the incentive to make the threshold of responsibility high enough to ensure that the consent truly does emanate from the person. With criminal wrongdoing the offender violates someone else's rights, so we want to deter that behavior and give potential offenders incentives not to get into a position where they might offend, that is, violate our rights. There is no analogous concern on the other side. If men knew that by getting drunk and engaging in nonconsenual sex they would be responsible for rape, they would have a strong incentive to avoid that behavior.

Counselors advising college women, for example, about how to avoid date rape would tell them to avoid intoxication not because they are then blameworthy for their victimization, but as a matter of prudence. Female students would be less likely to be victims of acquaintance rape if they did not, among other things, drink to intoxication. Saying that they would be less likely to be victims of a crime is not to say that they are blameworthy for the victimization. The police regularly give advice on lessening the chances of being a crime victim; they do not, however, suggest that once you are a victim you are to blame for it. Could not the same be said about women's intoxication? That is, that intoxicated consent is always valid and thereby women couldn't argue that they were drunk and therefore could not have consented. Such a practice would give women an incentive to avoid alcohol. On the flip side it would provide men with an even greater incentive to ply women with alcohol since women would bear all the responsible for what anyone else did to them when drunk. Even if we had the caveat that only voluntarily intoxicated women would be responsible, the line between voluntary and involuntary drinking is a difficult one to establish. In both the FSU and the St. John's College cases I would see them as involuntary drinking, but that judgment is controversial. In the FSU case the victim showed up having already drunk quite a bit of alcohol and one of the defendants then proceeded to strongly encourage her to continue drinking. In the St. John's College case the woman was a very inexperienced drinker and the men berated her to continue drinking.

The other problem with making women responsible for inebriated consent is that it would be horribly out of line with the law's treatment of consent in other areas. Imagine the physician who said 'She was intoxicated but consented to the surgery,' or the thief who claims that 'He was blind drunk and gave me his car.' Treating drunken consent as valid also undermines the values that consent is meant to preserve. The reason we require consent is because we think that individuals should control important issues in their lives. We do not give them control over those important aspects of their lives if they can validly consent when drunk or high on drugs, if we accept consent that is not thoughtful and concerned, without impairment of one's mental abilities.

Mental Illness and Retardation

It is an unfortunate fact that many retarded and mentally ill people are subject to sexual exploitation and abuse. The problem faced by liberal theorists is whether to say that no one with 'subnormal' mental abilities, with a below average IQ, is capable of sexual consent. Would we want to say that *all* mentally ill people cannot consent to sex? Wouldn't such a sweeping rule unjustifiably deny all those with mental retardation and mentally illness the right to sexual autonomy by not permitting them to affirmatively choose to have a sexual relationship? That kind of sweeping paternalism is repugnant to liberals. In cases of very low mental functioning we may well be justified in finding them always incapable of making sexual choices. Such persons, even though they are physically mature, have the mental abilities of young children. They do not have the ability to reason and make judgments about important issues in their lives, and project into the future what the consequences of a choice will be. Nevertheless, mental retardation lies on a continuum, with many people at the other extreme.

Consider the following case from New Jersey in 1989 involving 'Betty Harris,' a mentally retarded 17-year-old (In re. B.G.). Her 'friend' and neighbor Christopher Archer, aged 18, enticed her into a dark basement with 13 young male athletes from Glen Ridge High School, located in the elite and affluent suburb of Glen Ridge. Christopher had told Betty that, if she entered the basement, she could have a date later that night with his older brother, Paul. Betty recounted that the scenario

was 'romantic because he [Christopher] had his arm
around me' and she had a long-time attraction to Paul.
Soon after entering the basement, Betty was positioned
on a couch where the men asked her to remove her
clothes and, among other things, perform oral sex on a
number of them. They inserted into her vagina a
broomstick covered with a plastic bag and Vaseline.
After masturbating her with the broomstick, they
inserted and masturbated her with a similarly coated
bat and then with an old dowel. Betty testified that,
although all the objects 'hurt' her, she never attempted
to leave the basement and never asked the men to stop.
Rather, the men laughed and cheered, calling Betty a
'whore' and discussing how far the objects could go into
her body. Two of the men then sucked Betty's breasts
and requested that she masturbate six of the other men,
which she did. Finally, the men told Betty that she could
leave the basement, but that she could not tell anyone
what had happened because her mother would find out
and Betty would be expelled from school, all of which
Betty believed.

Under certain accounts of rape, this incident would
not qualify as rape since the men did not threaten Betty
with bodily harm or use force; nor did she resist.
Without threats, force, or resistance it might appear as
if it is not rape. Betty's presence in the basement and her
going along with the sexual activities without resistance
makes it look like she consented. The defendants,
needless to say, argued on this basis that she had
consented since she did remove her clothes and didn't
resist. What we need to consider with retarded people is
their level of understanding and ability to make
judgments, particularly about consenting to sex
(Denno, 1997). Beyond saying that no retarded person
can consent to sex, which is to deny them any sexual
autonomy, we need to ask questions about their
particular mental capacities and knowledge. If there is
no understanding about the nature of sex, its meaning

in society, and its consequences, then that person cannot consent to sex. On the other hand, if a retarded person does possess sufficient intellectual, emotional, and social resources to make the judgment to have a sexual interaction with another person, then we do not want the state to deny them the right to exercise their sexual autonomy. The retarded person has to know more than just about the physical nature of the sex act. As some jurisdictions require:

> An appreciation of how it will be regarded in the frame-work of the societal environmental and taboos to which a person will be exposed may be far more important … In order to have a meaningful understanding of sex, it is necessary to appreciate many ramifications: emotional intimacy between partners, pregnancy, possible disease, and death. It is not necessary to understand all of these concepts in order to establish that the mentally retarded person had the capacity to consent, but they are elements used to determine whether the person had a meaningful understanding of the nature and consequences of sexual intercourse. This appraisal also encompasses an inquiry into the moral quality of the act—'the nature of stigma, the ostracism or other noncriminal sanctions which society levies for conduct it labels only as immoral.' Therefore, a basic understanding of the mechanics of sexual intercourse alone is not equated with the understanding of the nature and consequences of sex.
> (Pollack, Harcsztark, McGrath and Cavanaugh, 2000)

We do not have all the details of Betty's mental abilities, but because this event involved a number of defendants who violated her with objects and otherwise exploited her lack of knowledge and judgment, we can determine that she did not have the capacity to consent. We do not need to adopt an overly romantic view about sexual interactions to claim that what went on in the Glen View case was not consensual sex. Rather, it was a group of men exploiting this girl's mental incapacities for their own sexual gratification.

Applying the criteria presented above, consider the Alaskan case of 'T.Y.J.', a 25-year-old woman who was having sex with Kenneth Jackson. Their relationship came to the attention of the authorities when it was discovered that T.Y.J. was pregnant as her mental abilities were that of a child at kindergarten. Though she held a job, she could not do simple arithmetic and could only write her name and only read her own address and certain 'survival words.' Her understanding of sex was limited to a 'rudimentary awareness of the mechanics of sexual intercourse' and she 'was aware that babies came from "sex".' Nevertheless T.Y.J.:

> Did not understand birth control, how to prevent pregnancy, or what sexually transmitted diseases are or how to prevent them. She did not know the meaning of words such as IUD, condom, rubber, syphilis, gonorrhea, or AIDS. Apart from her awareness that pregnancy resulted in the birth of a baby, she did not understand any of the practical consequences or potential complications of pregnancy.
>
> *(Jackson v. State,* 1995)

Here is another case where the victim physically tokened consent to sex, but, given her gross lack of understanding of what she was consenting to (except the physical nature), the correct inference is that she did not consent. She performed the action of consenting but she did not have enough mental, emotional, social, and intellectual abilities to form the requisite mental states to consent to sex.

The difficulty with retarded people is recognizing that many do have the intellectual, emotional, and social abilities to consent to sex, and designing rules and procedures so that the legal system does not foreclose all their sexual relationships. Retarded persons are vulnerable to sexual exploitation but, in our attempt to deter exploitation and harm to them, we do not want to close off the possibility of their leading human lives, including sexual relationships with others. This will be a difficult task but, by recognizing first that many higher-functioning retarded people can and do have complicated 'legitimate' sexual feelings that ought to be respected, we need to be vigilant about the unscrupulous taking advantage of them.

Age

Young children are incompetent to consent to sex. They do not possess cognitive and emotional capabilities to understand the physical, psychological, emotional, and social aspects of sex and sexual relationships. That is not to say that they do not have sexual feelings and sensations from a very young age (Levin, 2002), but sexual arousal in children does not mean that they can fully comprehend the significance of sexual intercourse with another person.

Young children are vulnerable to adults since they see them as authority figures and believe that adults have their interests at heart or, conversely, that adults wield powerful sanctions over them. The current rule presumes that all individuals under the age of consent – in most American states this is 18 years old – are incapable of consent. No judgment about the particular situation is made; merely being under that age is sufficient for nonconsent, which works well for young children. We can trace age-of-consent laws back to late 13th-century Britain when the boundary between childhood and adulthood was drawn (Brownmiller, 1976: 29). These laws, which say it is crime to have any sexual contact with a person under 18 years old, whether exploitative or not, deny individuals under 18 sexual autonomy. Minors cannot say 'yes' or 'no' to a sexual relationship.

As stated above, this rule makes good sense for children who don't have the cognitive and emotional capacities and understanding for sexual consent. All liberties presuppose certain capacities, but something as robust as sexual autonomy requires the individual to have quite sophisticated abilities and understandings to make choices consistent with their well-being. Do the same issues about exploiting young children apply to older adolescents, who often certainly understand the mechanics of sex and the consequences of sexual interactions? They lack sexual experience and may lack emotional maturity, but are developing it at this stage of life. In what sense do they lack the mental ability to consent to sex or withhold consent to sex? Many more states are willing to treat teenager offenders in the criminal justice system as adults, arguing that they have the cognitive abilities to commit crimes with the same intentions as adults, appreciate the nature of wrongdoing, and cannot be rehabilitated because they are no longer malleable, as is assumed of most juvenile offenders. Sexual consent requires more than the mere intentions that are required for wrongdoing, but it is insulting to assume that all older teenagers cannot make those sexual judgments. Anne, the victim from Stanford (see p. 151), was affronted by the fact that the District Attorney chose to charge the offender with statutory rape rather than actual rape as the statutory rape charge could have been brought whether or not she had consented. Anne wanted it acknowledged that she *did not consent.*

The victims of statutory rape are almost always female. In 1981 the Supreme Court upheld the constitutionality of a California case criminalizing sex with female minors but not male minors (*Michael M. v. Superior Court of Sonoma County*). The court's argument relied upon the greater risks to females from pregnancy; it did not argue that the laws echo and reflect the social myth that females are not supposed to desire sex, and, therefore, virginal girls would never consent to sex. Whereas the opposite is true for boys –

they are supposed to always want sex, be indiscriminate about whom they have sex with, and have no repercussions afterwards. Another problem with these statutory rape laws is that they don't distinguish between very different types of cases. For example, if two 16-year-olds are having 'consensual sex' it is treated the same as a 40-year-old man having sex with a 13-year-old girl. The latter relationship, between a much older, experienced man and a very young woman, might make us suspect advantage taking and at least diminished capacity for consent due to the influence that adults have over adolescents. On the other hand the two 16-year-olds don't have those structural problems – 16-year-old girls do not see 16-year-old boys as authority figures as persons who have sanctions over them, although they could have other problems. None of this is to suggest that female minors are not victims of rape. They are in great numbers, and teenage girls are particularly susceptible to acquaintance rape. They are more gullible and more easily swayed by others' promises or statements proffered to intimidate or deceive. But totally denying the sexual autonomy of older teenage girls treats them as incompetents when in fact they may be perfectly capable of making these choices. It disavows their sexuality (even in the face of a culture promoting it) and is, therefore, disrespectful of them as developing, autonomous agents.

Obviously, we need some demarcation for the law between being a child and being an adult, but my argument is that the line may be too high. Eighteen-year-olds are often quite mature and sophisticated and many of those individuals choose to have sexual relationships. Statutory rape laws deny all adolescents from making sexual choices. In those cases, even without a complaining witness, the man could be convicted of a serious felony. Nevertheless, teenagers are susceptible to unique kinds of exploitation because of their inexperience and vulnerability to adult influences.

Note

1   The private nature of sexual consent is somewhat unique but the emotional nature of the context may not be. Medical consent, for example, is often asked for when the patient or proxy is anxious and emotional. Being told that your life is at risk is upsetting to say the least, and can cloud your judgment. Therefore you may not accurately assess the risks of the medical procedures that are being suggested. And yet, even with these barriers we suppose that it is important to require stringent standards on the voluntariness of the consent.

Chapter 6
External Constraints

A high school senior's principal threatens to block her graduation if she refuses his ongoing sexual advances.

(State v. Thomson, 1990)

Raymond Mitchell, labeled the 'Fantasy Man' by the press would telephone women, pretend to be their boyfriend, and tell them that he had a fantasy about having sex with a blindfolded woman. He would convince them to leave their doors unlocked and wait in bed blindfolded. His further instructions were that they should not touch him during sex.

(State of Tennessee v. Mitchell, 1999)

My analysis of consent – granting permission to do that which would otherwise be impermissible – requires that consent be given without the presence of external constraints such as coercion or deception. So-called consent received through coercion or deception does not entail permission to act. Consent to sex is normatively significant since it is the method by which we grant others a right to cross our intimate borders. Only if the consent given meets certain standards do the newly formed relationships secured through consent come into existence. The *appearance* of consent is not sufficient until the circumstances under which consent was allegedly given are scrutinized; in other words, a 'yes' does not always mean 'yes.' The hypnotized person who says the words 'I consent' does not consent to anything. Consider again the 14-year-old girl who allegedly consented to sex after she was threatened with return to a detention home by her foster father (see

Is It Rape?

p. 44). Was that genuine consent or was it coerced by the threat? Would we say that consent under those circumstances is not genuine, but counterfeit? Cooperative behavior should not, in all cases, be taken as expressing consent.

Coercion

With both deception and coercion there exists a continuum of possible cases. With coercion they range from clear cases of threats to one's life, physical well-being, or livelihood, to the less clear cases of threats about college grades or threats regarding benefits such as promotions. What makes a proposal coercive? For the reconceptualized unaggravated rape rules, we need to know when there is sufficient coercive pressure to undermine the legitimacy of consent. In other words, we need to know when a 'yes' or a consent token is not legitimate because of coercive pressure.

In *Louisiana v. Powell* (1983) the victim accepted the defendant's offer to drive her home. Instead he took her to a secluded location and slapped her several times to intimidate her into submitting to sexual intercourse. The victim didn't resist, went along with his demand, and removed her clothes and had sex with him. The Louisiana Court of Appeals reversed his conviction because the physical harms with which he threatened her were less than death or 'great and immediate bodily harm.'

Threats of bodily harm are obviously cases of serious evils, so that a person who is forced to choose between bodily harm and unwanted sexual assault might submit to the latter under coercive pressure. Economic threats to financial well-being, for example, are more difficult to judge. An employer using the threat of the loss of a woman's job in exchange for sex may very well be coercive, particularly when he knows that she needs the job and cannot risk its loss. Until recently (before the 1970s there was no clear legal offense) these cases have been treated as sexual harassment, as private rather than criminal harm. And yet if they involve coercion, then they would be nonconsensual sexual activity under the model presented here – a criminal wrong. In at least some of these cases, it is clear that the victim has no viable alternative but to acquiesce since the loss of her job would constitute a serious, undeserved evil (her employer could even ensure that she would not be employed in that field elsewhere). Hence the coercive pressure is great, making it likely that her choice was less than fully voluntary.

Coercive threats present a person with two unsavory alternatives, usually in the form: 'Do this evil thing or I will do this even worse evil to you.' The criminal law itself involves coercive threats to individuals in the form: 'Do x (where x is following the dictates of the law) or you will suffer a penalty.' For individuals who don't want to do x, and yet they see the option of noncompliance as the greater of evils, they are coerced into doing x. The coercive nature of the criminal law is justified to prevent harm that would result from criminal wrongdoing. On the other hand, when one person A coerces another person B to do their bidding, B acts involuntarily and A has wronged B. When the coercive threat is successful the victim 'chooses' the lesser of the evils to avoid the threatened harmful consequences of noncompliance. In other words, coercion is thought to pressure the victim into choosing compliance with the threat. The amount of coercive pressure put upon an individual by various threats differs, and when exactly that pressure is *enough* to undermine someone's will is a tricky question. Coercion is said to undermine the ability to act voluntarily. Since the choice was forced by outside pressure, we do not treat that choice as emanating from a person's will. Coercion, however, never extinguishes choice as compulsion does. The awful choice in the 1982 movie *Sophie's Choice*, where the Nazi says to Sophie: 'Choose one of your children to die or they will both die' still provided her with a choice. Because she was put in a situation that forced her to choose between these two alternatives, the choice is not voluntary. Compulsion, on the other hand, literally takes away choice by physically forcing the victim down the path the aggressor wants. Physically holding a woman down with superior weight and strength and penetrating her is compulsion. Physically dragging a person is compulsion. Where compulsion and coercion get mixed is when the victim does not, for example, scream or attempt to physically resist the compulsion, because she interprets that there is an implicit threat – 'Don't resist because it is no use given my superior strength and weight, and if you do an even greater evil may befall you.' The presence of compulsion leads the victim to read in a coercive threat. Many victims in acquaintance rape cases are compelled, with the man's superior strength and weight, with this implicit threat interpreted by the victim who is frightened when the aggressor forces himself on her. I think that it is reasonable to interpret many acquaintance rape cases as involving the victim 'reading in' the threat of something worse if she does not go along, and yet it is surprising how many of these kinds of cases the courts have met with incredulity, as if a man who greatly outweighs a woman could not compel her to have sex and suggest the threat of physical abuse. Coercion involves the following conditions:

1. A makes a threat to B that he will cause or fail to prevent some consequence that B finds unwelcome unless B complies with the demand; and
2. A intends to force B's compliance with the threat; and

3. A's threat is credible to B, she believes that A has the power and is willing to carry out the threat; and

4. Unless he is bluffing, A has actively intervened in B's option-network to acquire control of the relevant option-switches; in particular he can close tight the conjunctive option that consists of B's noncompliance with the demand *and* B's avoidance of the threatened unwelcome consequences; and

5. B understands the proposal and is frightened by it, and at least partly to avoid an unwelcome projected consequence, complies with A's demand' (Feinberg, 1986: 198).

The coercer A has control over B's immediate future and can force her to act in the way he wants through the threat of unwelcome consequences. Threats of death and grievous bodily harm are obviously serious unwelcome consequences, so that a person who is forced to choose between death or serious bodily harm and sexual assault might submit to the latter under coercive pressure. Threats of lesser physical harm or threats to one's livelihood move along the continuum but still may be sufficient to undermine an individual's ability to act freely and, thereby, undermine 'consent.' Judgments about which threats undermine our ability to choose freely are partly a function of our judgments about the seriousness of the threatened consequences, which range from the serious, 'I will beat you up' to the not so serious, 'I'll be really peeved.' Projected consequences that are not very serious do not normally coerce. What is 'not very serious' is difficult to state in abstract terms because seriousness may depend upon the particularities of the person being threatened. Threatening to put a spider on the shoulder of a person you know has a mortal fear of them may put extreme coercive pressure on them. The rest of us may not understand their sense of dread but we can acknowledge that such a proposal could be coercive to those people. 'In a certain sense' Feinberg reminds us, 'it is B's own subjective characteristics, values and preferences peculiar to him, that determine how coercive the pressure is' (1986: 199). The threatened unwelcome consequence is part of the assessment, but also its seriousness in relation to the demand. The threatened consequence of noncompliance must be worse than the unwelcomeness of compliance. Both alternatives must be unsavory otherwise we would not call it coercion (this is the genesis of the expression 'stuck between a rock and a hard place').

In the standard account of coercion, the focus is on unwelcome threats that force the actor to choose between two unwelcome options. For instance, where the defendant said to his victim on an isolated country road 'Either have sex with me now or I'll beat you up and then have sex with you anyway,' the defendant intended to force her to comply with his desires by threatening even worse consequences for noncompliance. The victim was afraid of the projected evil consequences and complied with his demands to avoid them. Clearly, this is a coercive threat. Many cases obviously involve threats, consequently the victim who accedes to such threats has not consented. But what about cases where it is not so clear that the proposal is a threat rather than an offer? In determining whether something is a threat the emphasis has been on losses relative to a baseline. Thus a proposal is coercive to someone only if it projects consequences 'worse than' what normally happens to that person, as in the classic gunman case in which the victim is threatened 'Your money or your life.' The general distinction between making a person 'worse off' or 'better off' relative to their baseline is illustrated in the following cases:

1. Ms Pecunious is approached by a gunman who says, 'Have sex with me or I will shoot your baby.'

2. Ms Impecunious has a baby who will die without an operation. Alas she has no money and no way of getting any to pay for the surgery. A lecherous millionaire proposes to her: 'If you agree to become my mistress, I will pay for the operation for your baby' (Feinberg, 1986: 229ff.).

The standard approach to these kinds of examples is to say that the first is a threat and the second is an offer. In the first, the gunman threatens to make the mother 'worse off' than she would be in 'the normal course of events.' Her normal course of events is that her baby is alive and she does not have to have sex with the man. Whereas in the second case, the millionaire proposes to make her 'better off' since in the normal course of events her baby will die given she has no way to pay for the surgery. Threats make you 'worse off' than in the normal course of events and offers propose to make you 'better off.' Offers open up a new (welcome) option that you did not have before, whereas threats close an option that you had before. We generally therefore like to get offers.

One problem with the standard account of coercion is that there are different ways of understanding 'the normal course of events.' The normal course of events can be understood descriptively as what would have happened in the same circumstances without the proposal, or a more richly hypothetical test of what statistically would happen minus the entire episode. Normative analyses of the normal course of events look to what the victim has a right to expect to happen or what morally ought to happen. The normative baselines are open to substantive moral arguments about what one has a right to expect or what moral consequences should follow. Depending on one's moral outlook – utilitarian, Kantian, contractarian, libertarian – one will understand the moral baseline in very different ways. Beyond disputes about what morality requires, normative approaches are problematic since, in those accounts, what makes them coercive is that the proposer threatens to do what he has no right to do. How do we then account for the police officer who yells to the fleeing felon: 'Stop or I'll shoot'? That is a coercive threat, but the police officer has a right to shoot a felon who poses a danger. Normative analyses of the normal course of events will not account for all these instances of justified coercion.

Let us consider another pair of cases. In the first Mary's boat sinks on a deserted lake after John earlier intentionally drilled holes in it. John comes out and proposes that he will rescue Mary if she has sex with him. In the second case, Jill's boat capsizes on a deserted lake and she is approached by Tom in a boat, proposing to save her in exchange for sex. Both women are faced with evils: drown or have sex with unscrupulous John or Tom. Are the proposals threats or offers? Mary faces drowning now that her boat has sunk, but she is only in that predicament because of John's intervention. Is not rescue/drowning her normal course of events? But the fact she faces these options is the result of John's doing; consequently, we should consider what usually happens when she goes out on the lake in her boat – namely, that no one drills holes in her boat putting her at risk of harm. John's malevolent handiwork has made her normal course of events worse that they would be otherwise. Consequently, he is threatening her: 'Submit to sex with me or I'll leave you here to drown (after putting you in the situation where you would drown).'

On the other hand, is Jill's normal course of events that she would drown? If so, Tom's proposal is an offer to make her better off. In this case, the proposer did not create the evil consequence of drowning but only uses it to his advantage. Under one descriptive interpretation of the normal course of events, we consider what would happen in the same circumstances but without Tom's proposal, which Feinberg called the *talis qualis* test for 'exactly as it is' but for the unwelcome consequence. In that case we take what would have happened *otherwise*. Under this analysis, Tom would have saved Jill without condition. That makes it a threat. Another descriptive understanding of 'normal course of events' is more hypothetical: what would have happened if Tom hadn't come onto the scene at all? In this case, since Jill was on a deserted lake she would have drowned; consequently, Tom's proposal is an offer to make her better off than her normal course of events. In the normative account, Tom should offer an unconditional rescue, hence it is a threat. Nevertheless, in the normative analysis that says that no one has a right to be rescued, it would come out as an offer! The normative accounts are, as mentioned above, open to differences in interpretation too. How then do we decide which interpretation of the normal course of events is best? Consider another under-standing of the normal course of events, which construes it as what the person has an 'epistemic right' to expect (Feinberg, 1986: 226). In Jill's case we would ask what she would expect from someone in a boat who has the ability to rescue her. In this case she would expect that someone to rescue her. We expect (unless we are in pirate-infested waters) that someone who comes upon us drowning will offer an unconditional rescue. In this interpretation the proposal is a threat to make her worse off than the normal course of events. This view relies on norms of expectability that are often based on moral norms, but it is because we expect and rely upon them that it makes sense to use them in determining whether a particular proposal is a threat or an offer. We consider what the recipient of the proposal has an (epistemic) right to expect based on their experience and general practice. And there may well be situations where the morally right thing to do is not what would be expected; we do not expect pirates to make unconditional rescues, for example. This inter-pretation is compelling since if the proposal radically diverges from what a person expects, they then justifiably take it as a threat. We live with practices in our community which build expectations about others' behavior, and when their behavior deviates from those normal expectations it is distressingly unwelcome.

Let us consider again the proposal made by Mlinarich to his foster daughter: 'Have sex with me or I'll return you to the detention home.' What is the normal course of events for this 14-year-old child? Does the adolescent have a right to stay at Mlinarich's house so that his proposal to send her back to the detention home is an evil, making her worse off than the normal course of events? In the normative account, clearly she has a moral right to expect that her foster father will not condition her staying in his home on sexual acquiescence. In a libertarian normative view, Mlinarich has no duty to care for this adolescent; therefore, his projected consequence of returning her to the detention home is moral. If we ask what would happen in the exact circumstances without the projected consequence, or consider the set of circumstances with the entire episode subtracted, the proposal comes out as a threat to make her worse off than normal. In the analysis that I favor, we ask what is to be expected normally in these circumstances, namely that children can expect that they will not be asked to have sexual relationships as a condition of their staying in a foster home. Foster children can expect their foster parents to act in their interests and not use them to advance the foster parent's sexual interests. That makes this proposal a threat, which I think is the common sense answer.

Now let us consider the following cases. In the first, an employer is about to fire his employee because of her poor work performance, but then proposes not to fire her if she will engage in sexual activity with him. In the second case, the employee was not going to lose her job otherwise, but her employer uses the threat of firing in exchange for sex. Like our earlier examples, involve both of these choices between evils that the proposers use to secure compliance. In the first case, the proposal not to fire the employee if she will engage in sexual activity is a benefit since it proposes to make her better off from her normal course of events, in this case that she will lose her job for work-related reasons. In the second case, the employee does not expect to lose her job for performance-related reasons, consequently, this proposes to make her worse off than normal. Therefore, it is a coercive threat. The student in *State v. Thomson* whose principal conditioned her graduating on having sex with him, would be worse off than normal since, hypothetically, she could expect to receive her diploma without having sex with her teacher. She does not expect to receive her diploma unconditionally as certain conditions are part of her legitimate expectations, for example, achieving a certain level of academic merit, while others are not.

In the following example a man says to his girlfriend: 'Have sex with me or I'll break up with you.' She views his options as a choice between evils. She would like to continue a platonic relationship with him (she may have religious reasons for her preference to wait until marriage), but his proposal does not leave that option open to her anymore. Is this a coercive threat that would undermine her consent for the purposes of the criminal law, or is it an offer: 'I'll stay with you if you have sex with me.' It sounds more like a threat: 'Do this or else.' But this is where looks can be deceiving; under the normative analysis it is moral for him to demand this as a condition of their relationship, especially in an era when it is fairly common for couples to have sex before marriage. What about the epistemic right analysis and community expectations? Conditioning their relationship on having sex could be expected (at some point) and if the woman does not accept the condition she will be left with the consequence of their relationship breaking up. She may not like the condition, but her disapproval would not make it coercive any more than his dislike for her putting a condition of their continued relationship that he helps her with the cleaning.

On the other hand, in *Commonwealth v. Biggs* (1983), the defendant threatened his 17-year-old daughter, saying that it was her religious obligation to comply with his sexual demands, that if she didn't she would suffer God's punishment and her father would subject her to public humiliation. Fathers generally do not condition anything on the sexual compliance of their children. Children expect that their parents will not project evil consequences to secure sexual relationships with them. This case illustrates the subjective nature of many evils. This girl believed and was afraid of her father's projected unwelcome consequences, namely, that failure to submit to him would have devastating religious repercussions and she would be publicly humiliated. She saw these as such evils but thought that submitting to sex with her father was the lesser of the two. For many people the threat 'Have sex with me or God will get you' would be inert, having no coercive pressure at all. But it is cases like this that should make us resist the temptation to conclude that the level of the seriousness of the evils can always be determined objectively. With an objective model, we might likely exclude the threat involving the projected evil 'God will get you,' and yet here that threatened evil was sufficient to secure compliance; and the girl's father knew that it would have a coercive effect on her.

Whether a proposal is a threat or an offer is based on the recipient's expectations in the particular circumstances. There are certain unwelcome consequences as conditions of compliance, particularly for sex, that certain individuals, given their roles or professions, should not make and therefore making them constitutes a threat. For example, fathers are not expected to condition anything on the sexual compliance of their children, so even proposals that look like offers of benefit operate like threats when made to their children. For a father to try to offer his children rewards in exchange for sex would be a threat because it is such unexpected (not to mention immoral) behavior. Parents have tremendous power and influence over their children and children are not going to view any proposal that involves sex as a welcome opportunity. The pressure of such proposals would be great and, consequently, they should be seen as undermining the legitimacy of consent for criminal rape statutes. On the other hand, a boyfriend telling his girlfriend that he will only continue in their relationship if she has sex with him does not involve his threatening anything that is radically unexpected. Making threats may not be a nice way of treating her, but it does not propose anything illegitimate.

Judgments about coercion, then, turn partly on our normative ideas about what conditions it is appropriate or expected to put on another person. To a large extent, that depends on the relationship of the agents. Parents or legal guardians cannot threaten evil consequences in exchange for sex with their children or wards *under any circumstances*, unlike the case above of the boyfriend threatening to leave his girlfriend if she didn't have sex with him. Other relationships where it is coercive for the proposer to attempt to exchange sex to avoid an evil are those between teachers or principals and their students. The principal who threatened the student with not graduating if she did not submit to him is conditioning her graduation on sexual compliance. But what about the teacher who proposes giving a student a better than deserved grade; is that not an offer to make her better off than she would have been in the normal course of events, and thereby not coercive? Because of the expectations of the relationship, teachers' proposals to students allegedly to make them better off in exchange for sex become threats as the

so-called offer could reasonably be understood to entail
an implicit threat – 'Have sex with me or I'll give you a
grade you don't deserve.' Teachers at any level are not
expected in the community to condition avoiding an
evil or attaining a benefit on students having sex with
them. Students have legitimate expectations that their
teachers will not use their position of authority to
secure sexual relationships. Consequently, any proposal
to secure sexual compliance from them can justifiably
be understood as coercive. As we have seen, other roles
that establish expectations about sexual relationships
are those of employees and employers; employees do
not expect their bosses to make sex a *condition* of
continued employment. It is a similar case with prison
guards and prisoners.

Proposals for sex by persons in particular roles or
professions to persons in their care or charge are
coercive because of their authority and power while in
that role. Particular professions or roles engender
certain expectations by individuals in their charge and
by society generally. Lifeguards are expected to provide
unconditional rescue for drowning swimmers. Consequently, a lifeguard's proposal to save you for a price is
a threat not to save you. Likewise, firefighters and
police within their professional duties are expected to
do certain things for citizens without on-the-spot
compensation, and particularly not in exchange for
sex. Aid workers are not expected to use their position
of authority and power over the vulnerable to secure
sexual compliance, hence any who propose: 'I will give
you food in exchange for sex' can be understood as
threatening to withhold food unless they get sexual
compliance. We, as the users of their services and the
citizenry at large, have legitimate expectations that
persons who are granted certain power and authority
will not use it to advance their sexual interests.

What about the clergy, therapists, doctors, and others
with whom we might find ourselves in vulnerable

relationships? Can the minister therapist, or doctor who has been counseling or treating a distraught woman propose that he will only continue if she has sex with him? All of these relationships can put a person in a particularly vulnerable position. Revealing all your deepest secrets, only to have that dependency and trust exploited by someone who is professionally in a fiduciary relationship with you is certainly exploitative, but is it coercive. Since we have expectations that professionals such as therapists and the clergy will not condition professional relationships on sexual compliance, these proposals become threats to bring about unwelcome consequences. A patient's relationship to her therapist is one of terrible exposure and vulnerability; we often tell them our deepest fears, embarrassments, and disappointments. Having that trust exploited while in their care by using it to secure a sexual relationship is itself threatening. The patient might well worry, 'If I don't go along with his wishes, then he might expose my secrets.' Or she might be so 'under his influence' that she believes whatever he says must be good for her. In those cases he is exploiting her emotional dependence on him. This may be more analogous to the mixed cases discussed at the beginning of the chapter, as someone with diminished capacity because of emotional dependence is easier to coerce by someone who knows her fears and plays upon them. Mental healthcare professionals who use their power over patients to advance their own sexual interests undermine society's expectations of them. We place unusual amounts of trust and power with certain professionals and we expect them not to abuse it. We grant members of certain professions privileges and powers not generally held by individuals in society at large. We also place in them heightened trust with certain kinds of personal information because we expect that they will handle it in a professional way with our best interests in mind. Consequently, when those same professionals attempt to secure sexual relationships with people in their charge, they abuse the trust and privileges invested in them.

Nevertheless, not all threats are coercive and we need to establish whether some offers are coercive. 'Have sex with me or I'll take your book' may come out as a threat in any analysis, even the normative ones, and yet we would not want to say (barring exceptional circumstances) that it is coercive. What is threatened, proposing to make the victim 'worse off' here is not *that evil* and, consequently, we do not think such a threat would pressure anyone to do something they viewed as an evil. Some threats, though intended to be coercive, do not have the coercive effect on the victim, while other threats are not even meant to be coercive, for example, because they are said in jest. Hence, not all threats are coercive. On the other hand, can some offers be coercive? As we have seen, whether something is a threat or an offer depends on the recipient's expectations of the proposal, whether it is worse or better than what is customary. A serious objection to this approach to determining coercion is that, under this analysis, those who are already badly off become difficult or impossible to coerce because they are already facing undeserved evils; they are in desperate situations. Imagine the Nazi officer who says to the concentration camp prisoner that if she has sex with him, she will not be executed along with everyone else. She cannot expect much in the concentration camp, consequently this proposal makes her 'better off' than she could expect. In the case of the lecherous millionaire and the impecunious mother facing the death of her child without the surgery, what can the poor expect; what generally happens when people with the means find people without the means to pay for surgery? The poor cannot expect the rich to pay for their treatment, so consequently this looks like an offer. In the paradigm where the proposer says 'Your money or your life,' he has created the evil consequence that his victim will lose her life. He has manipulated and closed off her options to make all choices other than his preferred one ineligible. Many theorists make a lot of whether the proposer has created the evil or merely used background circumstances to his advantage. Should we do so? The creator of evil may be worse because he has done more wrong than the opportunistic proposer, but can't they both be methods of coercing another? Note that there are circumstances where the proposer did not create the evil consequence, like the opportunistic rescuer, but he diverges from what would normally be expected to happen. If offers never coerce, then the least well off in society become the least susceptible to coercion, since their baselines are so terrible to begin with. That implication seems counterintuitive. Certainly the least well off are open to exploitation through their vulnerable circumstances, which leads, at least some of the time, to their being coerced. This is certainly the intuition behind protecting prisoners and vulnerable populations, for example, people in developing nations, from being research subjects amid the worry that they can be coerced more easily, partly because of their vulnerability and miserable normal course of events. Whereas, an evil faced by a criminal – say, a prison term – might be expected in view of his past actions. A plea bargain becomes an offer of a benefit, rather than a choice between evils, given his miserable, but expected and deserved, baseline. The criminal should expect to go to jail for a certain amount of time and, consequently, sees the plea bargain as an offer.

Threats are more commonly associated with coercion than offers, but we may want to leave room for when individuals are in such desperate circumstances that they may be vulnerable to coercion. Going back to our examples of Ms Pecunious and Ms Impecunious (see p. 73), with Ms Impecunious the proposer is able to secure compliance only because of his victim's weak bargaining position or her desperate situation. He uses the evil state of affairs regarding the baby's preventable death in the same way as the gunman, viz., as his guarantee to get compliance. In both cases the intention of the proposer and the effect on the victim is the same – she is faced with the same alternatives, one an unthinkable disaster. Given that, should we have different judgments about these two cases? For purposes of contractual consent, we will say that the victim acted under duress. But should the lecherous millionaire be held liable for rape? Ms Impecunious has great pressure put on her to accept his proposal to become his mistress to avoid the death of her baby. She is forced to choose between two evils, one of which is an unimaginable tragedy; the lecher knows that she has only one eligible choice and he uses that to extort the choice. The millionaire did not create the world in which the woman's baby needs an operation and she doesn't have the money to pay for it. The problem in this case is that millionaires are not expected to pay for treatment for the poor, but neither are they expected to use the misery of others for their own sexual advantage. If, however, this millionaire had used this as an opportunity to offer the woman a job we would think very differently about the case. Sex is different and we should look at proposals to secure it differently.

At least in some rape cases, the threatened evil is not spelled out by the aggressor, who uses the ambiguity of the circumstance and his greater differential power to his advantage. Analogously, confronted with three big men in an alley saying: 'Give us your wallet or else,' we do not have to spell out the exact evil that will occur upon refusing to infer that the transfer of the wallet was not voluntary. When a woman is isolated and one large man has gravely intimidated her this could constitute threatened serious harm upon failure to submit. If the proposer makes a credible threat to bring about or allow to occur an undeserved evil to the victim, the threatened evil involves something serious, and the victim complies because of fear of the threatened evil, then it is likely that the victim acted under coercion. There is obviously much more that should be said about coercive pressure, but our interest here, however, has been to show that a 'yes' does not always constitute consent, particularly in the presence of explicit or implicit threats.

Deception

Besides compulsion and coercion, deception is the other primary method of undermining the legitimacy of consent. If Mary agreed to John's proposal only because she was tricked or deceived by John, then John should be criminally liable for the harm to Mary. As we know, consent must be voluntary and informed to have the force of changing moral relationships: It is not enough to get another person to utter the words, 'I do' or 'I consent.' Deception or fraud, similarly to coercion, affects the voluntariness of an agent's action. Fraud *causes* the person to falsely believe something about what they are consenting to. Cases of fraud also lie on a continuum, ranging from the most flagrant cases that render a person's choice totally nonvoluntary, to cases where the person is deceived about some minor aspect of the activity, thereby only slightly reducing the voluntariness of the consent. Therefore we need to determine when the deception is enough to undermine voluntariness for the purposes of the criminal law of rape.

In the current rape laws fraud or deception has been broken into two distinct types: What is consented to is called fraud *in factum*, where the alleged consentor B believes she is consenting to act x and the proposer A does act y. The consentor is deceived about what she is consenting to. For example, B thinks that she is signing a contract to purchase a new car when the contract, as A knows, is for a boat. The second type is called fraud *in the inducement*, meaning that the proposer A deceives B to make her consent to his proposal – A tells B that he is a famous fashion photographer and will help her get into the fashion industry if she sleeps with him. In all other criminal codes, except the area of sexual offenses, this difference in types of fraud does not exclude the deceiver from criminal liability. Indeed, in transfer of property cases – theft by deceit – fraud *in the inducement* utterly *vitiates* consent. 'Theft by fraud … is now universally recognized, that taking another's property with his fraudulently induced 'consent' is no different in principle from taking it when there is no expression of consent at all' (Feinberg, 1986: 287). Fraud *in factum*, however, constitutes rape while fraud *in the inducement* does not. Why is sexual consent treated so differently from property cases? Is there something about sexual cases, as opposed to property cases, that makes fraud *in the inducement* acceptable?

There have been a number of cases involving doctors who asked for consent to do a gynecological examination – the doctor told the patient that he was inserting an instrument into her vagina but instead inserted his penis (see, for example, *McNair v. State*, 1992). The patient consented to something other than what was done. These were cases of fraud *in factum* because the facts of what was consented to were misrepresented. On the other hand, in *Boro v. Superior Court* (1985), for example, a doctor told his patient that she had a life-threatening illness which could be cured by the insertion of a serum through sexual intercourse. She was induced to consent to sex by the threat of this terminal illness. This case was held to be fraud *in the inducement*, and hence there was no criminal wrongdoing. Is there a rational justification for the differential treatment of these cases, such that one is the serious crime of rape and the other is not? Arguably, in both cases the victim is traumatized, humiliated, frightened, and harmed. Why treat fraud cases in the sexual arena differently from those in areas like property? The distinction itself is not that clear, either. For instance in the commercial case, A tells B that his (barren) cow is not barren, knowing that B wants to breed the cow. Telling B about the cow's breeding potential induces her to consent to purchasing the cow, and yet what B thinks she is consenting to is the purchase of a fertile cow. Is this a case of fraud *in factum* or *in the inducement*?

With *in factum* cases the victim does not consent at all to what is done; instead she consents to something else entirely. In these cases it is clear that no consent to sex was secured. The victim's mental state, which is necessary for the act of consenting, is for x and the proposer knows that it is y. On the other hand, the argument goes, in cases of fraud *in the inducement* the victim consents to what the proposer does, but for fraudulently mistaken reasons. The criminal law does not require ideal rational voluntary choices, as we have noted before, since very few of our choices might pass that test. Nevertheless, if we think that there are degrees of voluntariness, false beliefs – particularly about important matters about the substance of what one is consenting to that have a causal impact on your choice – radically reduce the voluntariness of consent. Since one's beliefs about what one is consenting to are wrong, and those beliefs were created or encouraged by the proposer, one's consent is invalid.

Nevertheless, the problem with fraud *in the inducement* is that exaggeration and puffery are part and parcel of romantic or sexual relationships. People make themselves sound and appear better in order to impress their partner and entice them into sex. Men drive more expensive cars than they can afford and women wear push-up bras to entice and influence men's choices. Jane Larson claims the prelude to sexual relationships involves: 'Exaggerated praise, playful suggestions, efforts to impress, and promises intended to reassure and trigger emotions (but not to be strictly believed) are all part of the ritual of escalating erotic fascination that makes up a "seduction" in the colloquial sense' (1993: 449). Exaggerating one's physical attributes and puffing up other characteristics may induce another to like one more, to see one as more attractive, and ultimately induce another to consent to sex. The predicament with fraud *in the inducement* is that of drawing lines between behavior which is part of normal seduction and the kind of fraud that would undermine consent. Is there a difference in the kind of minor deception and exaggeration in which all potential lovers engage and the type of extreme deception in *Boro v. Superior Court*, in which the fraudulently induced beliefs *wholly* determined the victim's consent to sex? This seems different in kind from telling your partner that you earn more than you do, or that you are the boss of the company when in fact you are not. In *Boro* the patient consented to sexual intercourse, but only as a form of therapy, necessary, she thought, to avoid death. She would not have consented to sexual intercourse otherwise. The deception about her medical condition and the sexual intercourse as a form of therapy formed the exclusive reason for her consenting to sex. *Boro* is a difficult case, and may not thereby be a very good one for understanding fraud. In this and similar cases the proposer made the victim believe that she would die if she did not go along with his plan; consequently, it functions like a coercive threat. Cases like this remind us that the ways of undermining voluntariness for consent can be used together: The consequences that the proposer projects are unwelcome to the victim – she will die without treatment or she will have painful and life-threatening surgery – and yet the projected consequences are contrived. But the fact that they are contrived does not diminish in her deceived mind their power to frighten her.

One way to defeat the *in factum/in the inducement* distinction is to build more into the description of what is consented to, thereby making all *in the inducement* cases into *in factum*. In *Boro*, she consented to 'sexual intercourse as a form of medical therapy for a life-threatening disease.' This move changes fraud *in the inducement* to a case of fraud *in factum*. Packing more into the description of what was consented to handles another raft of troubling cases involving a man deceiving a sleeping woman into believing she is having sex with her husband or boyfriend, only for the woman to wake up and discover that the man caressing her and engaging in sex with her is not her husband or lover. The courts have often analyzed these cases as fraud *in the inducement*, arguing that the women consented to sex even through the fraud. In a case of a twin brother impersonating his twin in order to have sex with his girlfriend, a New York court held that 'In general, in the absence of a statute, where a woman is capable of consenting and does consent to sexual intercourse, a man is not guilty of rape even thought he obtained the consent through fraud or surprise' (*People v. Hough*, 1994). Are these impersonation cases fraud *in factum* or *in the inducement*? Did she 'consent' to sexual intercourse but was misled into believing it was with her husband, making it fraud *in the inducement*? Or did she consent to sex with her husband but *not* with this other person, hence fraud *in factum*? If, as suggested, we build more into the description of what is consented to, then we turn these *in the inducement* cases into fraud *in factum*. She consented to 'sex with her husband.' In those cases where the central material element of what is consented to is misrepresented, arguably fraud *in the inducement* can be changed to fraud *in factum*.

Feinberg argues that fraud *in factum* cases are wholly involuntary – there is no consent at all – whereas *in the inducement* cases lie on a continuum: some instances substantially reduce voluntariness, others do not. So, for example, Feinberg uses a case of a doctor obtaining sexual intercourse with a patient by promising a large cash payment and then paying in counterfeit money or not paying at all. 'This would be a case of fraud *in the inducement*, but it would not reduce the voluntariness of the consent sufficiently to support a rape prosecution, or even a charge of "theft for services."' (1984: 295). He goes on: 'The fact that a woman is willing to have sex for money implies that the sexual episode in itself is not a clear harm to her when she is not paid.' Feinberg's analysis is faulty because it does not follow that the sexual episode was not a clear harm. If Mary is a doctor and someone secures her medical services by fraudulently telling her that he will pay her for services, but he later does not, surely she is harmed by not being paid. The fact that she is willing to sell her services does not show that she is not harmed when she does not receive the promised money. Feinberg means that any woman who is willing to sell her sexuality cannot place the same value on it as others who are not willing to do so. This doesn't necessarily follow either. In Feinberg's example, the woman could be in desperate need of money and reluctantly agree to sell sex to survive. The proposal then has a coercive effect on her. She views the proposal of sex for money as an evil but a lesser one than her alternatives. The fraud that induced her to have sex will make her feel additionally violated. But, even if she is a prostitute who does this all the time, not being paid for something that you were expecting to get paid for is a harm. Admittedly, in the prostitute's case, fraudulently securing sexual services is more like a commercial harm or theft as opposed to a sexual offense. But, as it stands now in the criminal law, having your property or service secured fraudulently is more easily treated as a crime than having your body and sexual life secured through fraud.

It is worth speculating on the reasons for the law's unsympathetic reaction to victims of sexual fraud. Often what is at work is the suggestion that if these women are so gullible, naive, and stupid, then they get what they deserve when they consent to fraudulent claims. This suggestion is strange since one might suppose that the naive and gullible are exactly the people we want the criminal law to protect (the strong don't need its protection). Why should the law allow unscrupulous exploiters to prey upon such individuals? Another possible reason for the law's reluctance to admit fraud *in the inducement* is a view about the motives of the defrauded person. Cases where, for example, the deceiver pretends to be someone famous, or deceives his victim into believing that she will get a job or promotion, arguably seem unworthy of legal concern. No one doubts that the victim actually was led to believe something that was false and had sex because of that belief. Take the case of Oscar Kendall, who impersonated the famous fashion photographer Richard Avedon, enticed a number of women in to vulnerable locations such as hotel rooms, and then forcibly assaulted them. These women were fraudulently caused to believe that Kendall was someone else. The general lack of sympathy in these cases is because it is believed that the women acted out of ignoble motives – the desire to get into the fashion industry, to have sex with famous people, and to exchange sex for an employment opportunity. The assessment shifts to the female victim and not to the actions and intentions of the proposer, even though his motives and actions are not without fault – intentionally leading another to believe something which is false in order to secure consent to sex. That behavior is wrongful and results in harm. Neither the ignobility of the motives nor the naivety of the agent stops the criminal law from protecting against other harms perpetrated by defrauding exploiters who, for example take advantage of people's greed. The criminal law still protects those who are defrauded, even if it is a result of their own stupidity and/or greed or some other vice. Protecting the sexual autonomy rights of women may require the range of deception to be extended to defeating voluntary consent.

This *caveat amator* approach in the sexual arena is aberrational in that the harms that result from sexual fraud are often serious. Finding out after the fact that you were tricked into having sex is frightening, humiliating, and can undermine future relationships. It might be reasonable for the law to take a *laissez-faire* approach when the harms resulting from fraudulent interaction are minimal. So, for example, fraud perpetrated at a flea market for an artifact costing $20 would not get the same amount to legal attention as fraud in a case of medical treatment because the harm from the medical case is much more serious. Conversely, in areas where the harm that will result from fraud is serious, the law should not (and does not in most instances) take a *laissez-faire* approach. Sexual intercourse fraudulently secured, as in any nonconsensual sexual relationship, is a humiliating, frightening invasion of a central part of a person's life.

Translating fraud *in the inducement* into fraud *in factum* still will not solve the problem since, if we build too much into the description of all consent, we make any minor deception a case of fraud. The man who falsely says that he owns a golden retriever, resulting in the woman believing she is consenting to 'sex with a man who owns a golden retriever' not 'sex with a pit bull owner,' would be a case of fraud *in factum*. Likewise the man who is led to believe that his partner is a Playboy bunny and not a striptease dancer would be defrauded since he believed that he was having 'sex with a Playboy bunny.' What is wrong with fraud is that it *causes* a person to consent to something that they would not otherwise consent to. Sometimes the misrepresented characteristic is not something that would affect the person's consent: they would have consented knowing she was a stripteaser or that he didn't own a golden retriever. So fraud is presumably only wrong when it does not have this causal affect, which seems right for rape liability. On the other hand, it is still morally wrong to lie and misrepresent yourself even if it does not have a causal impact on consent. But, even when it does have this outcome, do we want to say that all deceptions result in liability for rape? Does the man who falsely professes love for his partner constitute a case of criminal fraud? How about a promise of marriage as an inducement to sex? How do we distinguish normal, expected exaggeration and pro- mises from unlawful fraud? Here too I think that we can appeal to expectations in a potential sexual relationship. As Jane Larson (1993) suggested potential lovers expect exaggeration, playful promises, and flattery as part of the erotic prelude to sex. Saying that you are more successful than you are, promising to see her on a regular basis, adulating her every characteristic, constitute the playful banter that indivi- duals expect. However, when a woman or a man asks their partner if they have HIV and they say they do not when in fact they do, that is not expected behavior. That is a direct lie that would affect whether or not one would choose to have a sexual relationship with a person. The fact that he is a store clerk instead of a lawyer would not necessarily have that effect. Having sex with someone who masquerades as your husband involves misrepresenting an essential characteristic of who you are consenting to, not a minor aspect of the character of the consented to activity. Having sex with an imposter is not going to result in indifference on the part of the victim. On the other hand, finding out that your lover is not exactly the person you thought – he does not have a Harvard degree, does not come from a famous family, and is not rich – will not be met with such disbelief and deep sense of harm. Even this is not enough since, if someone so systematically deceived you about all aspects of their past and present identity, I think that deception too would rise to the level of criminal fraud. Such a case would far exceed our expectations about normal embellishments in romantic relationships.

The sleeping victim cases discussed earlier should be seen as cases of incompetence, not fraud because the sleeping (that is, unconscious) person is incapable of consent since they cannot subjectively form the mental state that is required along with the action of consent. The fact that they physically respond to the sexual caresses should no more be understood as tokening consent than the sleepwalker should be understood as taking his 'daily constitutional.' These cases should be analyzed in the same way as any concerning someone who is incompetent to consent. What about the spouse who initiates a sexual episode – is that nonconsenusal? Spouses (but not estranged spouses) and long-term lovers who are in caring relationships can and do make assumptions about their partner's consent.

Conclusion

The determination of consent requires consideration of both the internal and external features of the choice situation. Failures of consent occur because of external features: the person was coerced or defrauded into the choice by the person 'asking' for consent. The background circumstances themselves also can be coercive if the person is desperate and the proposer uses that desperation to their advantage. Alternatively, there can be failures of consent because of internal constraints on the consentor, that she was drunk, on drugs, insane, too young, and so on. Focusing merely on the words that were said or not said as evidence of consent means that one can fail to pick out the background conditions within which the individual is making the 'choice,' or fail to notice crucial features about the consentor's ability to give consent, or fail to account for the actions or words of the proposer and their effects on the consent-giver. Consent is vitiated by external factors such as coercion and fraud and also by internal factors that incapacitate a person. The fact that a victim was drunk or high on drugs should naturally lead to the conclusion that she was not consenting, as she was incapable of voluntary consent. Showing that the woman was incapacitated should establish the element of the *actus reus* 'without consent.' Consent is the vehicle through which individuals autonomously direct major parts of their lives; poor choices, or choices which fail to conform to a person's good, often result when choosing without one's full faculties. Hence consent granted at those times should not be held as legitimate. It should be noted that normally we do not let others exploit an incapacitated person and take advantage of their condition.

Nevertheless, if the law wants to protect women's sexual autonomy then not only should it look for the defeaters of consent – external and internal conditions that would undermine consent – but it should also require positive signs of consent. Consent to a sexual encounter should not be inferred from the failure to refuse; the law needs to look for positive signs of assent to the proposal. Threatening actions or gestures on the part of the man should undermine the credibility of consent, but additionally the fact finder should look for signs of consent from the woman, what she said and did, not negatively but positively. Antioch College's proposal that students wanting to engage in sexual conduct must give their partner consent to sex was ridiculed in the media as taking the spontaneity out of sex, making it too analytical, too 'unsexy.' These criticisms are unwarranted and rely upon an unflattering view of women, that they are not supposed to want sex and must be pressured into it – the sadomasochistic view or the conquest model. If not based on those models, would it be thought unsexy and unspontaneous to have parties to a sexual encounter positively agree to have sex with one another? It is these traditional stereotypes that encourage and foster in women conflicting attitudes about their sexual desires and stifle their sexual autonomy. Until we have standards that require women to be honest and open about their sexual preferences and require their partners to be clear about the women's willingness and excitement about the sexual encounter, we will continue to run the risks of women being forced into sex and men possibly unwittingly engaging in nonconsensual sex. If the cultural and legal norms permit women to enter into sexual relationships without positive expressions of consent, then men continue to believe that it is permissible to proceed without those signs. Requiring women to acknowledge and express their desires about sex encourages autonomy by requiring individuals to be informed about their desires, express their desires, and be accountable for those desires.

Rape statutes should spell out as essential elements of the offense that there was no freely given affirmative consent to the sexual acts. The statutes should specify exactly what is meant by 'consent', thereby not leaving its interpretation to the discretion of judges and juries. The offense is committed knowingly, then, whenever the accused fails to secure affirmative consent. In the cases examined, all the defendants *knew* that the victim had never affirmatively expressed consent, *a fortiori* each defendant knew he was raping his victim. Explicitly stating in the statutes what counts as consent makes 'mistake' defenses, which defeat the *mens rea* requirement, much more difficult to claim. Under the present system mistakes about consent are more readily accepted because of the way in which consent is construed; namely, that lack of physical resistance is a sign of consent, or passive submission or consent to previous relationships are signs of consent. In practice, mistake defenses are often resolved on the basis of what particular jurors believe it was reasonable for the defendant to believe. If a juror believes that 'no' means 'yes' then he or she will believe that it was reasonable for the defendant to believe that the plaintiff was consenting, hence the juror will vote to acquit on grounds of reasonable mistake. Or, if a juror believes that women often feign reluctance and disinterest, then again that juror will understand these as signs of consent. Leaving the question of mistake about consent up to juries will likely turn on individual jurors' perceptions, often based on outmoded and detrimental stereotypes, about women. However, with the analysis proposed here, how can the defendant claim that he was mistaken when he disregarded what the victim said, or failed to take care and discover whether she was consenting? How, indeed, can he claim to be mistaken when in fact she did not affirmatively express consent?

Chapter 7

I Thought She Consented: The *Mens Rea* of Rape

Leak was furious at his wife for refusing to give him money that he asked for while drunk, and so told his friend Cogan that she liked to have sex with other men in front of him but would act like she didn't want sex. Although Mrs Leak was sobbing while Cogan was having sex with her, Cogan claimed that he believed she was consenting. The jury thought that Cogan honestly believed that she was consenting, although they thought that it was not a reasonable belief.

(*Regina v. Cogan*, 1975)

Consent is the gatekeeper for protecting individuals' autonomy. Consent plays a particularly important role in protecting sexual autonomy. I have tried to show that, to play this role, the conditions for consent must be sufficiently robust and informed by our understanding of voluntariness and the various ways in which it can be undermined. We need to acknowledge the seriousness of the harm that results when consent is lacking in sex, in other words, that nonconsenual sex is a serious harm even without physical force. The enriched conception of consent to sex that we have developed is a story about the ontology of consent – an account of what consent is. Asking what consent is, is essentially to consider consent from the perspective of the consentor. When someone has consented to sex, it requires that we spell out the conditions for sexual consent from the perspective of that person.

But rape, like other serious felonies, requires a particular mental state about the crime committed. Establishing the *actus reus* of rape, namely, sex without consent, is not sufficient for conviction for rape. Guilt for the crime of rape, along with most serious crimes, requires the defendant to have a specific mental state, or *mens rea*, which refers to what he actually believed or understood at the time of the crime. For rape, the defendant must have believed that his victim was not consenting or that she might not be consenting. Here we are considering what the man believed about the woman's consent. So if the offender claims that he *believed* she was consenting while admitting that, in fact, she was not he was *mistaken* about her consent and therefore will not have the *mens rea* for the crime of rape. The question for the jury is: Do they believe – beyond reasonable doubt – that the defendant knew that the woman was not consenting or that she might not be consenting? The jury's attention becomes focused on what the defendant believed or what he thought the victim meant by what she said or did. The question here is when does a mistake about consent exculpate or make the defendant not liable for the crime of rape.

The reason why we require more than a prohibited action in criminal law, that is, why we require a mental state as well as the prohibited action, is because we believe that it is unjust and possibly inefficacious to punish a person without it. H.L.A. Hart said: 'All civilized penal systems make liability to punishment for at any rate serious crime dependent not merely on the fact that the person to be punished has done the outward act of a crime, but on his having done it in a certain state of frame of mind or will' (1968: 114). For retributivists who justify punishment on the basis of moral guilt, the right mental state is necessary for the person to be at fault; and utilitarians often argue that a person cannot be deterred from something of which he has no mental awareness, so, therefore, punishment would be futile (Bentham).[1] The state of mind that must be shown for any crime can vary, and there are four levels of culpability: purpose, knowledge, recklessness, and negligence. The first three are generally acknowledged as mental states that warrant criminal liability, although the lesser mental state of, for example, recklessness, might warrant a lesser punishment than knowledge. Negligence is controversial and many argue that it should never be sufficient for criminal liability. Acting negligently in regard to a material element of a criminal offense means that the accused *should be aware* of a substantial risk of harm from his conduct but he is *not* aware of it. We will discuss negligence below when examining unreasonable mistake. Accepting that unreasonable mistakes excuse or exculpate means that negligence is not sufficient for criminal liability (Archard, 1999).

What then are the beliefs about consent that might exclude liability for rape? In some cases a woman may protest, either verbally or physically, and yet the defendant will claim that he believed she was consenting. Do the stereotypes about women, for instance, that 'no' means yes and that women require some force, provide justification for defendants' claims that they lack the *mens rea* for the crime of rape? Standard *mens rea* doctrine may not apply since, as MacKinnon (1989) has pointed out, it is in the interest of men to remain oblivious to women's desires, signs, and sensibilities. The law, she says, 'allows one person's conditioned unconsciousness to contraindicate another's violation.' Is MacKinnon correct about her assessment of the mistake defense? One approach to forestall the most egregious of self-absorbed and possibly self-deceiving men about the consent of women would seem to be to require that their beliefs about consent be *reasonable*. Consequently, not *any* belief would be accepted, no matter how unreasonably based upon insensitivity and self-delusion. The defendant's claim about belief in consent must be tested against what the reasonable person would believe about consent in the context. Unreasonable beliefs about consent will not, then, exculpate.

Unreasonable Beliefs about Consent

Before considering the reasonable belief standard, let us examine the highly controversial argument for accepting unreasonable beliefs about sexual consent as exculpatory. Let us consider the landmark appeal case of *Regina v. Morgan* (1976), held in Britain's House of Lords (Curley, 1995). In 1975 Morgan, a senior noncommissioned officer in the RAF (Royal Air Force), invited his three drinking partners (who were his subordinates) to have sex with his wife, claiming that she liked 'kinky' sex and would feign refusal but in fact welcomed the intercourse. The four men dragged Mrs Morgan from the room where she was sleeping to a room with a double bed. They held her down while each took turns having intercourse with her. Throughout, she protested vigorously, both physically and verbally, including screaming to her children to call the police. Morgan, because he was her husband, could not be charged with rape, but was charged with aiding and abetting rape. The other three men were charged with rape. Relying upon what Morgan had told them, they argued at trial that they thought she had consented and, consequently, could not be convicted of rape since they did not have the *mens rea* for rape. The trial judge in his instruction to the jury added that the belief about consent to exculpate had to be reasonable; that is, 'such a belief as a reasonable man would entertain if he applied his mind and thought about the matter.' The defendants were subsequently convicted. They appealed, claiming that the judge had erred in giving that instruction to the jury. They argued that any belief in consent, as long as it was honestly held, would be incompatible with the intention to commit rape. The House of Lords accepted the argument that unreasonable beliefs would exculpate; in other words, that any belief about the woman's consent, no matter how objectively unreasonable, would establish that the defendant was without fault, and hence could not be convicted of the crime of rape.

Many people saw serious problems with this ruling, as it permits a defendant to be acquitted of rape just in case he believes a woman is consenting, no matter what his reasons are for believing it. Those in favor were theorists such as Glanville Williams (1975), who argued that not permitting unreasonable mistakes to exculpate is to convict a man for being stupid. 'To convict the stupid man would be to convict him for ... honest conduct which may be the best that this man can do but that does not come up to the standard of the so-called reasonable man.' Rape is an extremely serious offense from which the criminal law should protect individuals. Rape is very difficult to prosecute under any circumstances, so permitting unreasonable mistakes to excuse would make prosecution even more difficult. In cases where the defendant claims he was mistaken about consent and the mistake is unreasonable, the individual acted on a false belief about a very serious issue that would result in a significant harm to another person. The fact that the mistake was unreasonable means that the agent acted not merely without evidence, but contrary to what any other person who was paying attention to the features of the situation would find reasonable to do. The woman was screaming to her children to call the police. E.M. Curley argued soon after this decision that the court was wrong in viewing this as a negligence case and should have seen the defendants as reckless according to the Model Penal Code:

A person acts recklessly with respect to a material element of an offense when he consciously disregards a substantial and unjustified risk that the material element exists or will result from his conduct. The risk must be of such a nature and degree that, considering the nature and purpose of the actor's conduct and the circumstance known to him, its disregard involves a gross deviation from the standard of conduct that a law-abiding person would observe in the actor's situation.

(Proposed Official Draft, S 2.02(2)(c))

Curley argues that the defendants consciously disregarded a risk since they claimed they believed Mrs Morgan to be consenting, therefore we must 'assume that [they] considered the possibility that she was not consenting and rejected it' (1995: 569). In other words, since Mrs Morgan gave the defendants plenty of evidence to believe that she was not consenting, they had to consider it and then *consciously disregard the risk that she was not consenting*. The other part of the criteria for recklessness is 'substantial and unjustified risk.' A substantial risk is 'one where there is a significant probability of the outcome risked.' Determining significant probability requires justification, and Curley argues (p. 569) that 'If the harm to be anticipated in acting on a false belief is very great, and the good which may be lost in failing to act on a true belief are slight, then it will not take a very high probability to make the risk a substantial one.' The defendants acted recklessly because their belief in consent to sex, particularly in the context of the victim's protests, disregarded the substantial risk that she was not consenting. In this case, against her vehement protests, they continued their assault.

The problem with Curley's analysis is that he assumes that a jury would not find a defendant honestly believed that a woman was not consenting in a context like the Morgan case. And yet on the heels of this came the Cogan case described at the beginning of the chapter.

The fact that juries might find such a belief honestly held and hence, under the *Morgan* rule, be forced to acquit, makes for questioning the legitimacy of acquittal on an unreasonable belief. Unreasonable mistakes of consent to sex are, as Marcia Baron reminds us, possible 'if the defendant was indifferent as to whether his partner consented, or at best cared about it too little to attend to the matter and to stop if there was reason to think she wasn't consenting' (2001: 2). To engage in sex on the basis of an unreasonable belief is to omit to take reasonable care that we can demand of individuals when engaging in conduct that has substantial risks associated with it. Curley's and Baron's analysis is that 'an unreasonable mistake shows him to be culpable in roughly the same way that recklessness does' (Baron, ibid.). With some activities we do hold people responsible for their carelessness since that carelessness shows a total disregard for the welfare of others. We want the criminal law to protect against that kind of behavior. Consequently for rape, and possibly not for all crimes, for example bigamy, negligence is sufficient for culpability.

Is Glanville Williams correct in his assessment that to punish for unreasonable beliefs is to punish the stupid man? Baron raises an important issue in response, suggesting that if the man 'lacks the capacity to act reasonably,' for example because he is a low-functioning retarded person, then a different defense is justified, namely one of diminished capacity or even insanity (p. 14). But this is a different kind of case that does not impugn on the *mens rea* standard for rape involving individuals in society who cannot conform their behavior to the criminal standards, but not because they hold false beliefs. Outside of these cases of individuals with diminished mental capacities I do not think that there are genuine cases where the person cared enough to try to discover whether his partner was consenting and to desist if he thought there was some doubt about her consent. In the cases of Morgan and Cogan the defendants did not exhibit as evidence that they cared whether their victims were consenting; there was blatant evidence to the contrary and they failed to investigate whether it was genuine.

Unreasonable beliefs about sexual consent are those when the defendant shows no regard for the consent of his partner. Consequently there is nothing unjust about holding him criminally liable for rape. Further, to exculpate on the basis of unreasonable beliefs gives men *no reason* to be careful about whether the person they are having sex with is consenting. Incentives in the law will go in the other direction, encouraging men to be oblivious and encourage in themselves the most outrageous fantasies about women and sexual consent.

Is it Reasonable to Believe that 'No' Means Yes?

Moving beyond unreasonable mistakes, there is also controversy about when it is *reasonable* for men to believe women are consenting to sex. The *actus reus* of rape, even with our proposed revised statute of sex without consent, still requires the *mens rea* that the man be at fault about the woman's lack of consent, so that if the man *reasonably* believed the woman was consenting then he cannot be held liable for the rape. In order to show a reasonable belief in consent to successfully mount a mistaken belief defense the defendant must establish, first, that he was *in fact* mistaken about consent – that is, that he really held a false belief about the woman's consent – and, second, it must be true that his mistake was *reasonable*. Juries must decide on both aspects of this claim. The first is a question of fact that is often difficult to establish because, of course, defendants lie about what they believed or didn't believe. Moving to the second point, when is a belief in consent reasonable? In *People v. Rusk*, where the defendant ignored the victim's verbal refusals, disregarding her question that if she had sex with him would he then not kill her, illustrates what some feminists contend is a standard of 'reasonable belief' based on what men in a sexist society would believe reasonable in the circumstances, namely that, since he did not use 'excessive' force and she did not strenuously resist, it is reasonable to believe that she was consenting.

Turning to more mundane cases, consider the claim that men believe, reasonably according to many (including many juries), that 'no' can mean yes. The classic scene illustrating this view is from *Gone with the Wind* in which Rhett Butler sweeps Scarlet off her feet and carries her up stairs to her room while she was screaming for him to put her down and leave her alone. The next morning, presumably after sexual intercourse, she is happy and contented. A couple of decades later we get in a Mitch Miller song ('The Yellow Rose of the 1950s: 'Your lips tell me No! No! But there's Yes! Yes! In your eyes,' and in the late 1990s a country music song by Holly Dunn entitled 'When I Say No I Mean Maybe.' There are hundreds of other culture narratives that reinforce the stereotype that women say 'no,' resist, and yet mean 'yes.' Berkowitz in the Pennsylvania acquaintance rape case admitted that his victim repeatedly said 'no' but that he took it as amorous moaning rather than as rejection. That same story is told, retold, and unfortunately accepted by police, prosecutors, judges, and juries.

We should consider the implications of what has been called by some the 'gender gap' in sexual communication.

> Men and women frequently misinterpret the intent of various dating behaviors and erotic play ... a woman may believe she has communicated her unwillingness to have sex—and other women would agree, thus making it a 'reasonable' female expression. Her male partner might

> still believe she is willing—and other men would agree with
> his interpretation, thus making it a 'reasonable' male
> interpretation. The woman, who believes that she *has*
> conveyed her lack of consent, may interpret the man's
> persistence as an indication that he does not care if she
> objects and plans to have sex despite her lack of consent.
> She may then feel frightened by the man's persistence, and
> may submit against her will.
>
> (Robin Weiner, 1993: 147, 149)

Going along with these facts is a vast discrepancy
between the number of women who claim that they
were forced to have sexual intercourse by an acquaintance and the very small number of men who claim to
have forced a woman to have sex. Outside of imagining
that the women or men are deluding themselves about
what happened, there is obviously a significant number
of men who are not aware that their partner has not
consented to sex. Are those men consciously disregarding a risk that their partner might not be consenting?
Are they acting unreasonably?

Many rape reformers have argued that 'no' means no
and that the law should treat any disregard of a 'no' as
culpable. Susan Estrich, among others, argued that the
law ought to recognize that 'no' means no and
understand that it is not reasonable for men to believe
that when women say 'no' they mean yes. They cannot,
therefore, escape criminal liability by claiming that they
reasonably believed the victim was consenting, that is,
using the mistake defense (McGregor, 1996). On the
other hand even Stephen Schulhofer, who advocates
rape reforms to protect women's sexual autonomy,
argues against the reformist strategy that the law ought
to recognize that 'no' means no. Schulhofer rejects these
reforms, claiming that they are destined to fail because
of the 'widely held beliefs' about women's sexual
desires that will make it reasonable for men to believe
and jurors to believe that women are consenting to sex
when they say 'no.' He worries that, since the belief that

women sometimes mean yes when they say 'no' is so widely held, it will lead to acquittals on the ground that the defendant made a reasonable mistake about her consent. Schulhofer claims: 'In most states, verbal resistance—saying "no"—still isn't sufficient to bring criminal safeguards into play. [One reason for this] is the continued hold of the old idea that women who say "no" sometimes mean yes. A readiness to find consent still permeates our culture' (1998: 11). Discussing the negligence standard he continues:

> Unfortunately, the negligence standard does little to solve the enforcement problems that anti-rape reformers are concerned about. When a man claims 'mistake,' he may be insincere or sincere but exceptionally insensitive. More often the difficulty is that his beliefs about the woman's consent are perfectly consistent with widely held attitudes that ['no' sometimes means yes].
>
> (p. 259)

Schulhofer is arguing that we should not accept the reformist view that the law ought to hold men criminally liable for rape unless they reasonably believe that the woman is consenting, and that it is not reasonable to believe that when a woman says 'no' she means 'yes I consent.' However, unless he or others have evidence to support this argument then it would be absurd on the face of it to have the law understand that when people say 'no' they mean yes. Outside of an Orwellian world this would appear insane. How do individuals say or mean *no* in this world? With a 'yes?'

The evidence that Schulhofer and others such as Husak and Thomas advance for the reasonable inference on the part of a man that an explicit 'no' means yes are empirical studies that show that roughly 35–40 percent of women sometimes say 'no' when they desire sex (Muehlenhard and Hollabaugh, 1988). Other studies show that a fair number of women said 'no' initially or engaged in resistance behavior when they

intended to engage in sexual intercourse eventually.
Throughout there is a discussion of women's *real
preferences and desires* as support for the inference
about consent. What Schulhofer and others who argue
this way are doing is offering evidence about women's
possible *mental states as evidence for consent*. There are
two problems with this view. First, on a performative
theory of consent, mental states alone are not consent.
It is the *act*, performed with the mental state to consent,
that is consent. Second, as already discussed, showing
or establishing *desire* for sex is different from showing
that one *has consented* to sex, as one can desire
something and yet refuse to consent to it. There is
nothing inconsistent with saying that a woman desired
sex with a man but did not consent to the sex.
Consequently, the argument that we should not use
'no' to mean no, or reject consent, is without basis.
Schulhofer's argument is that saying 'no' sometimes
means that women desire sex. We can acknowledge that
but still maintain that women have not *consented to
sex*. Hence, the law should take 'no' to mean no. Does
that mean that a 'no' could never be overcome, in other
words that, once a woman says 'no,' any sex that
followed would be rape? No, it does not. The fact that a
person declines to consent at one point does not entail
that she would not consent in the future. A woman
saying 'no' should signal that the man discontinue his
sexual advances. The legal presumption, without
further evidence, should be that there is no consent. If
she then says that what she meant was 'no, not now, but
maybe later' then she is open to a proposal at a later
time. If she says nothing more at the time than 'no,' and
on a later date the man attempts to secure consent
again, then the earlier 'no' does not reign over this later
occurrence. Also she might say 'no' and then when he
stops, say 'what I meant was no, I don't want to do that
(for example, have intercourse) but I do want to do
something else (have oral sex).' Merely saying the word

'no' should have the effect of *no consent*. But that presumption could be overcome in the context of other things said. Nevertheless, the law should not understand that 'no' means yes. The law should take that 'no' means no.

Reasonable Beliefs and Social Conventions

Douglas Husak and George Thomas III take the argument further and advance that we base our determination of whether a man's belief is reasonable or not upon social conventions – in this case the relevant conventions surrounding consent to sex. Husak and Thomas argue that studies indicate that women often use nonverbal behaviors to consent to sex. Given this social convention about sexual consent, it is then reasonable for men in these circumstances where women say 'no' or engage in physical resistance to believe they are consenting. Furthermore, Husak and Thomas claim that 'it is not impossible for the social convention [women's consent to sex] to interpret 'no' as yes when it comes on the heels of an incomplete rejection strategy [physical behaviors such as resisting]' (1992: 122). It is reasonable for men to take silence and even a clear 'no' as consent, thereby establishing mistaken belief on their part and undermining their liability for rape. Husak and Thomas reject the strategy of many rape commentators of changing statutes, for example requiring affirmative consent, thereby foreclosing the defense of reasonable mistaken belief in these sorts of cases. They argue that this would fail to do justice in individual cases; men who rely upon these social conventions about sexual consent would not receive fair treatment from the criminal justice system.

Husak and Thomas rest their argument on empirical findings that show that individuals are more likely to express sexual consent nonverbally. Consent to sex is typically given by a set of conventions that do not depend on words. According to Husak and Thomas then it is reasonable for men to believe that women are consenting to sex without verbal assent. Men and women, they claim, were more likely to use 'indirect strategies to have sex' – nonverbal means such as body language and seduction (McCormick 204). Similarly, rejection is also frequently nonverbal. Here they cite a Canadian study in which 48 percent of the women ranked saying 'no' as the most important way to communicate nonconsent, and 34 percent thought that the most important ways to refuse consent was by indirection, that is, by being 'unresponsive or passive.' In another Canadian study 23 percent of the women who did not want to engage in the initiated sexual activity made no verbal refusal. What Husak and Thomas see as following from this is that a man might well mistake consent to sex when the woman did not intend to convey it. They believe that a man might perceive a woman's behavior as sexual when she does not intend it to be sexual, or he might perceive her sexual cue as promising more intimacy than she desires. If the women corrects these misperceptions by indicating that she does not desire the level of intimacy he seeks, Husak and Thomas believe that there are three avenues of mistake possible. First, the man might believe that some indications of resistance are not genuine, what some researchers call 'token resistance.' And, since they purportedly show that resistance is often expressed nonverbally or in 'incomplete rejection strategies,' this increases the likelihood that the man might doubt the sincerity of the rejection. Second, the man might realize that the woman does not want to have sex at that moment, but still believe that she can be persuaded to want sex at a later time or place. 'No,' as they put it, may not mean 'never.' Here Husak and Thomas use the survey which concluded that 36 percent of women refused in ways that implied that the advances might be accepted later. Finally, the man might believe that, even if the woman cannot be persuaded to want to have sex, she can be persuaded to have sex as a way of bestowing a favor on him – what one study called 'compliant' sex (Husak and Thomas III, 2001: 95ff.). With these findings, Husak and Thomas believe that there is a lot of room for men to reasonably believe that women are consenting to sex. In their view, even an explicit verbal rejection is grounds for reasonable belief in consent since women often reject an initiated sexual activity but permit a different type to continue. Men have been exposed to the cultural message that 'good girls' say 'no' whether they mean it or not, and 'even though most women only rarely engage in "token" resistance to sex, several studies have concluded that many women do so on some occasions' (1992: 96). Given these reasons a man could reasonably infer that the woman is consenting when she says nothing, says 'no,' or engages in rejection behavior.

What these data say to me is that there are such ambiguous 'conventions' about consenting to sex that mistakes are highly likely to occur in many circumstances. For example, one study showed that a large number of women who did not want sex made no verbal refusal, and another 23 percent who did not want to engage in the initiated sexual activity remained passive and unresponsive. What would it be reasonable for men to infer when a woman says nothing and/or remains passive and unresponsive? They should *not* reasonably infer that she is consenting because of her failure to give a verbal refusal. In their studies a full third of the women refused in some nonverbal fashion. And yet I think that is often assuming (that is, what Husak and Thomas are assuming) that if she didn't say 'no' or do anything to establish her refusal it is reasonable to believe she *is* consenting. Yet the studies they cite would contradict that conclusion in many instances.

Moving from saying nothing to cases where there is an explicit 'no,' Husak and Thomas still think that verbal refusal is not sufficient grounds for the man reasonably to believe that his female partner is not consenting. It is reasonable for men to think women are consenting because there is a possibility that they might agree to some other type of sexual activity and, as stated above, because men believe that women engage in 'token' resistance. Even if we grant that some women who say 'no' actually do want to engage in sexual activity (one study showed that 39 percent of women had done so at *some* time), why would that make it reasonable to believe on any given occasion? Why wouldn't that look more like what one wants to believe is the case, or merely that these men are engaging in wishful thinking? This approach to reasonable mistakes does not take seriously the worry about false positives; it does not guard against the statistically large number of times that women are genuinely not consenting to sex. Granted that sometimes the man who does not accept 'no' as meaning no – relying on the convention that the woman might move to another type of sexual activity if he persists and the cultural message that good girls can't say yes – might truly believe that the woman is consenting, is his reliance on those beliefs enough given that, when he is mistaken, someone has been raped?

More has to be said too about the nature of social conventions. Does the fact that 39 percent of women at some time have permitted some other sexual activity to continue after an initial refusal make a convention? I would understand social convention to mean something that happens all the time, like tipping waiters or shaking hands with acquaintances, and not something that happens even half of the time. Also what do the statistics really say? They report that women claim that they only rarely engaged in 'token' resistance to sex. Let us take 100 women and say that 50 percent of them said that they had at some time engaged in token resistance to sex and suppose they each have had 100 sexual encounters. Suppose that what they mean by 'rarely' is 15 percent of the time, then 750 out of 10 000 sexual encounters had involved token resistance.[2] The probability that a man would be wrong if he relied on this so-called convention would be astronomically high. He would be *right* only seven times out of 100. Imagine the same odds with a revolver with 10 chambers and nine bullets. How comfortable would you feel about someone preparing to shoot at you while assuring you that 10 percent of the time you would not be hurt? Husak and Thomas conclude that, since a 'substantial' portion of women engage in 'token resistance,' it is reasonable to believe that women consent to sex even in the face of resistance. They understand less than half and just a little more than a third to be substantial portions of the population, and even those women who admitted engaging in token resistance said they had only done it *rarely*. This is not my understanding. It is unimaginable in any other important area of our lives that we would allow a reliance on such a weak probability of success.

Since I do not think that Husak and Thomas have shown that there are clear conventions about consent to sex, and since their data can be interpreted in contradictory ways – is a woman's passive behavior part of the romantic ideal of conquest or is it a genuine refusal to consent; is her verbal refusal real or token resistance? – it is unwarranted to use these 'conventions' as a basis for reasonableness. Relying on token resistance, a man would only truly believe in consent in a small fraction of cases, which cannot possibly be reasonable.

One other variation thrown into this issue from Husak and Thomas that mistakes can occur because men and women sometimes engage in sex when they do not want to – 'unwanted sexual activity.' Earlier I said that consent does not entail that the activity is wanted, so I agree with them that we should not make that inference. But what, if anything, follows about reasonable mistake? The clear paradigm of so-called 'compliant sex' is individuals in a relationship. Not so clear are the cases that Husak and Thomas cite, namely, of men who have been rejected and who attempt to see if, with some force, he can get the woman to engage in compliant sex. They cite studies showing that men are at least twice as likely to see force as justified in overcoming a woman's refusal. But because men *believe* that they are justified does not make them justified. Interestingly, the fact that so many men report that they believe they are justified in using force to gain sexual satisfaction supports my earlier claim about the social construction of sex. Men's belief in their justification to use force to get compliant sex does not sound as if they think they need genuine consent. These are not social conventions unless we mean that men's beliefs are based on sexist conventions. What they may believe is justified and what the law should protect them against are two separate questions. Husak and Thomas cite a study in which one third of the men approved of force to achieve sex 'when a partner has a change of mind concerning intercourse.' That is not a belief in the women's consent, but rather a belief in what they think they are entitled to. This is what MacKinnon means about our social construction of sex as entitling men to sex. That entitlement includes the assumption that they can get it by force if necessary. Husak and Thomas say that 'it seems likely that many men who use minor force to overcome resistance at the initial stage believe that consent will be forthcoming (even if the consent is to unwanted sex)' (2001: 100). Why suppose that the man believes that and why suppose that it is reasonable for him to believe that?

In Husak and Thomas's view, reasonable belief would stretch to an absurd extent: repeated 'nos' would not be sufficient to undermine it; adding physical resistance might do it but presumably a man might still believe that this is what 'good girls' do and thereby hold onto his belief in consent. This view of reasonable but mistaken belief totally undermines the reason for having consent as the desideratum for permissible sex. All of these reasonable mistaken beliefs mean that someone is raped but the offender is not a rapist. If these so-called sexual conventions were really social conventions like tipping, with a consistency of use, then it might be reasonable to use them as a basis for belief in consent. But, when all we have are statistics telling us what 35 percent of women do and what men *believe* about sex, that does not make a convention and should not be used to justify mistakes. Particularly troubling is the fact these statistics are based upon a conquest picture of sexual relationships and not one in which the parties can acknowledge sexual interest or lack of it and express a choice about their desires.

Granted, it would be unfair to change the legal requirements of sexual offenses and keep them secret and then convict individuals on the basis of those laws. In general, however, there is nothing unfair about changing and promulgating the legal rules even if those changes go against social conventions. If a cogent argument is made that going against social conventions will prevent other injustices from occurring, then the weight of evidence may be on that side, and the law may reasonably change the legal requirements. Husak and Thomas cite empirical studies that show that, in the social conventions surrounding sexual consent, many women say nothing when they are consenting to sexual relations. Those studies also suggest that 39 percent of college women have said 'no' when they intended to have sex. Nevertheless, since these statistics suggest that a significant percentage of women said nothing or said 'no' and meant no, the suggested strategy of Husak and Thomas would leave those women unprotected. The law should protect the negative freedom of those women. Indeed, if is it reasonable to believe that 'no' means yes then when is it reasonable to believe that 'no' means no? What would that 'reasonable man' take *no* to look like? In saying that a belief is reasonable he would have to have a view about the other alternatives, for example, if she does this then she is consenting; if she does that she is not. Yet it would seem that a man who takes no to mean yes does not seem to have an adequate picture (a reasonable one?) of what would count as rejection. He might believe that women who do not want sex with him must resist to the utmost. But surely it is unreasonable (and unfair) for women to have to engage in violent behavior in order to avoid the advances of this man.

Husak and Thomas suggest that social conventions are always changing, citing the elimination of the resistance requirement and the restrictions on admission of the victim's sexual history as reflective of such change. They forget that those requirements changed as a result of feminist law reformers exposing the injustice of the law persisting with them. Admittedly, social conventions do change but the pace of change may be too slow for avoiding serious harms. The women who want sex can presumably learn to say so, but the women who do not want sex under the Husak and Thomas analysis are left without alternatives (they have already said 'no', or failed to say 'yes'). Why aren't Husak and Thomas worried about all the women who are sexually violated when they said 'no,' given their admission that many women say and mean 'no' and their wishes are not respected? Furthermore, they cite a study by Perper and Weis that suggests that 'not all men could distinguish seduction and incomplete rejection strategies' (1987: 471). The empirical studies seem to suggest that social conventions are not clear; men are inaccurately, at least in some circumstances, interpreting the signs of women. This fact provides even more support for the normative claims of rape law reformers who want to change social conventions by changing the law. Husak and Thomas admit that the risk of error on the part of men is great and since in the event of an error there is serious and irremediable harm to an individual's life, it seems reasonable for the law to intervene and force a change of social conventions. Nothing is lost by imposing an affirmative duty on men to ensure that the women with whom they are involved are truly consenting. The statutory change would make mistaken belief defenses much harder to mount.

Husak and Thomas have argued that mistakes about consent would be reasonable if based on social conventions about how people behave in sexual situations. If men rely upon social conventions as the basis of the reasonableness of their beliefs about consent then that should be sufficient to exculpate them. Social conventions are generalizations about peoples' behavior within particular contexts and in a particular society. There are different kinds that differ from society to society and across time. For example the convention for tipping in the United States is to leave between 15 and 20 percent of the bill for all meals in restaurants. Failure to do so is seen as an insult or social faux pas. The conventions about sexual consent that Husak and Thomas discuss are different in that they are not as ritualized or consistent, begging the question of whether they should be called 'social conventions' at all since they fail to be practiced consistently. What Husak and Thomas do is report statistical behavior of individuals in sexual situations, admitting that what is worth noting about the conventions is that a person can consent without conforming to them and that a person can conform to the conventions without consenting. To consent is not then merely to act according to these social conventions. Notice the difference, whereas, for example, if one fulfills all the felicity conditions for marriage and at the appropriate time says 'I do,' then engaging in those social conventions will make one married.

How then do we avoid these mistakes in consent? If the law wants to protect women's sexual autonomy then it should not only look for defeaters of consent, external and internal conditions that would undermine consent, but also it should require positive signs of consent. Consent to a sexual encounter should not be inferred from the failure to refuse as statistics show that women often refuse by nonverbal means. The law needs to specify that parties must give positive signs of assent to the interaction. Threatening actions or gestures on the part of the man should undermine the credibility of consent but, additionally, the fact finder should look for positive signs of consent from the woman, what she said and did. Antioch College's proposal that required students wanting to engage in sexual conduct to explicitly consent to sex was ridiculed in the media as taking the spontaneity out of sex, making it too analytical, too 'unsexy.' These criticisms are exaggerated (and maybe unwarranted) and rely upon an unflattering view of women – that they are not supposed to want sex and must be pressured into it – assuming something like the conquest model. Otherwise, why is it unsexy and unspontaneous to have parties to a sexual encounter positively agree to have sex with one another? It is these traditional stereotypes that encourage and foster in women conflicting attitudes about their sexual desires and stifle their developed sexual autonomy. Standards that require women to be honest and open about their sexual preferences and that require men to be clear about women's willingness to engage in sex are needed. Without them we will continue to run the risks of women being forced into sex and men possibly unwittingly engaging in non-consensual sex. If the cultural and legal norms permit women to enter into sexual relationships without positive expressions of consent then men continue to believe that it is permissible to proceed without those signs. Requiring women to acknowledge and express their desires about sex encourages autonomy by requiring individuals to be informed about their desires, express their desires, and be accountable for those desires.[3]

On this account, mistaken belief in consent is only justified in cases where the woman said 'yes' and did not mean it or when she gave positive signs in the absence of threats, threatening circumstances or intimidation; for example, she undressed herself or the man or was sexually caressing him. Positive signs in the absence of threatening circumstances would make it reasonable for the man to believe that the woman was consenting. Husak and Thomas are correct to say that affirmative assent to sex is not the current practice of consent to sex. The studies show that there are multiple practices at work which I am sure have changed dramatically since the 1950s. A society that values sexual autonomy will want to encourage fully voluntary participation in sex, which requires men and women to understand their sexual desires and to feel free to act upon them. If the sexual revolution does anything, it should make women more aware of their sexual feelings and permit them to explore them without outmoded stereotypes or pornographic models of their desires. To insure fairness to women and particularly men in the course of changing the legal standard for consent, the changes need to be promulgated and people educated about their details. Education about sexuality and standards of consent are long overdue. Other areas of the law have changed the standards of what counts as consent. In those areas too the change was to foster more autonomous choice.

Consent figures centrally in unaggravated rape, providing the key to understanding the moral wrongness and seriousness of this form of rape. How should we think about the moral status and force of consent? Autonomous persons can be analogized to sovereign nations who may rightfully control their borders. The law, in a manner of speaking, backs up agents' rights to control their own borders. Valuing autonomy is valuing the self-governing person. Autonomous agents are ones who are left to identify their own interests, make choices which fit into larger life plans, and make decisions about their own good. One way that we respect autonomous agents is to leave them room for choice and to respect the choices they make. From the moral point of view, concern about personal autonomy and self-determination is represented by guaranteeing agents control over their domain through their power of consent. Consent can play this role only if there are fairly rigid standards about what counts as consent. Indeed, if consent is inferred from the mere fact of silence or submission through intimidation or implicit threats, then consent does not provide agents with a significant instrument with which to police their boundaries.

Notes

1   Also note that for statutory rape the offender does not have to be aware of the victim's status as underage to be guilty of the offense.
2   The study cited by Husak and Thomas says that in a US sample 38 percent of women admitted engaging in token resistance; of those 44 percent said they only did it once and 41 percent reported doing so two or three times.
3   See Naomi Wolf's discussion in *Promiscuities* (New York: Random House, 1997, 136) about how society encourages girls to be unaware of their sexual choices and not acknowledge them.

Chapter 8

What is the Harm of Rape?

Rape, as I have maintained throughout, conjures in people's minds pictures of strangers wielding knifes or guns and threatening to use them if their victims do not submit to sex. I have reported that the statistics for rape belie that scenario since most commonly the attacker has no weapon. He forces himself on his victim with threats or superior strength, or in a slightly different scenario, which in fact turns out to be the most prevalent form of rape, the victim knows the attacker – he is a date, her boss or other acquaintance, and the victim is deceived or intimidated or too incapacitated to consent. In all of the above scenarios, I have argued, the events seriously wrong their victims. Rape has other victims as well, by striking terror and fear in *potential* victims. Many (perhaps most) women find themselves structuring their activities around the fear of rape. Whether it is not working late at the office for fear of dark and deserted parking areas or not studying late at the library for fear of walking across the campus at night, these are all curtailment of women's liberty based on the fear of rape. At the baseline, what differentiates rape from other crimes is *sexual intercourse or contact without consent* – nonconsensual sex is rape. The guns, knives, threats, beatings and intimidation create the fear and are the various ways of exerting power over the victim. They are additional wrongs to the victim and they help the attacker to perpetrate the wrong of rape. Many of the difficulties with rape involve cases where there are no 'weapons' such as knifes or guns or 'excessive' physical force, and the victims were not physically abused beyond the rape itself. These are the kinds of cases, as we have discussed, where it is extremely difficult to get police and prosecutors to press charges and, if those cases do get to trial, it is difficult for juries to 'see' them as genuine rapes. Yet, according to some surveys, most rapes involve no weapon or excessive physical force whatsoever (Warsaw, 1994).

In this book I have focused on nonaggravated rape, that is, rape involving no weapons or excessive physical force. I have argued that the law and society have taken too narrow a view about what constitutes rape. Part of the problem was statutory, that is, the statutes required a showing of force. But part of what motivates and maintains the narrow conception of rape has been myths about sexuality generally. These include views about women feigning disinterest in sex and, consequently, *needing* to be forced into it, and about men's inability to control their own sexuality and thereby being excused when they don't, so that police, prosecutors, and juries saw some force and overriding verbal protests as consistent with legitimate sex. All these factors lead away from a focus on nonconsenual sex alone and to the search for extreme physical force to find rape. But I have argued that this narrow approach, leaving out all nonconsenual sex that is not secured with a weapon or extreme violence, is unjustified. In this chapter I will consider what exactly is the harm of rape.

How is the Victim Wronged?

Without weapons or 'excessive' physical force what is the *wrong* of rape? The victim is not necessarily bruised or beaten, she is not bleeding. The wrong then must be in the fact that the sex is nonconsenual. According to Shafer and Frye, writing on rape in the 1970s: 'We would not want to say that there is anything morally wrong with sexual intercourse *per se*, we conclude that the wrongness of rape rests with the matter of the woman's *consent*.'[1] This is obviously the approach that I have been taking, focusing on the issue of consent, but I would like to introduce a caveat to that approach about the harm of rape. In some ways we have all been too captivated with a legalistic understanding of what makes rape wrong, so that a law professor's statement that 'consent turns an act of rape into an act of lovemaking' describes the legal perspective understanding (Hampton, 1999: 134). But this statement misrepresents the victim's experience, the problem being that it sees the experience of rape as merely sexual intercourse (making love) with the absence of consent. It does not see that the character of the act from the victim's perspective is entirely different from consensual sexual intercourse or lovemaking. So saying that 'consent turns an act of rape into an act of lovemaking' is to give the legal account of the wrong. In other words, what the law looks for, or should look for, is consent. But, from the victim's point of view, the nature of the act itself is entirely different from consensual lovemaking. This is what leads some commentators to undervalue the nature of the wrong of rape (for example, Jeffrie Murphy's sarcastic suggestion that nonconsensual sex could be compared with forcing someone to eat sushi). The fact that the victim's consent is overridden is central as an element of the offense of rape, yet we should not stop there when trying to understand the wrong or harm from the victim's perspective.

Notice, too, that consent may be overridden or circumvented in other kinds of cases and yet the injury will not be analogously serious. What explains the seriousness of the injury of rape is what the consent *ranges* over. Sex, sexuality, our bodies and control over them are central to who we are. One does not have to have an overly romantic view of sexual relationships to conceptualize a significant difference in the experience of consensual sexual interactions and nonconsenual ones. Rape is such a serious violation because it transgresses this central zone for our identity, it exposes us and makes us a tool or thing for someone else's sexual ends.

The scope of our power of consent ranges over our 'domain,' that is, our body and property. Being a *person* is conceptually linked to having a domain which we control through our power of consent. Persons have particular traits and capacities which define person-hood. Which exact traits and capacities an individual has to have to qualify as a person is controversial, yet it is generally accepted that people must be capable of identifying their own interests, making choices which fit into larger life plans based on their interests, and must have the ability to communicate those interests and choices to others. Persons have autonomy rights over most issues within their domain, just as sovereign nations have control over what happens within their borders. Personhood can, however, come in degrees; for example, children, incompetents, and the insane are not total persons in the sense described, that is, they do not have the power to consent over the range of issues which 'full persons' have. Others act on their behalf and in their best interests.

Rights carve out a person's domain. The physical body is the physical locus of the person. Competent adults have an interest in controlling what happens to their bodies through their power of consent. That any nonconsensual touching violates a person's domain is reflected in the criminal laws of murder and assault, including sexual assault. Modern liberal theory claims that we have an autonomous right over, among other things, what happens to our bodies. Following from that, even the most minor nonconsensual touching of another's body violates that right. But just violating one's right to not have one's body touched may not be enough, for example, we wouldn't prosecute for grabbing someone's shoulder (but notice that we might, however, for grabbing a woman's breast). Some border crossings may be too minor to warrant the coercive arm of the law, but why one touch is minor and another is not often turns on whether it is construed as sexual or not. Being sexual makes the touching more serious than it would otherwise be.

Let us consider what makes some unconsented-to border crossings more serious than others. One way of thinking about the gravity or seriousness of an injury is to ask how 'close' (metaphorically) a particular offense is to the personal and intimate aspects of ourselves and how close to the person does it come. Imagine one's domain in terms of concentric circles with the inner ones more central to personal integrity, identity, and dignity, to whom one *really* is. Offenses to the inner circles then constitute more serious crimes because they 'touch' the person in a more profound way (Feinberg, 1984: 37). Those more serious wrongs have to do with loss of control, pain, humiliation, loss of personal integrity, loss of sense of security, and loss of self-esteem. We have been assuming, which we must for establishing the severity of crimes, that people are roughly the same in what they care about and thus in how they assign levels of seriousness. These assignments depend on what people in fact care about and how they define their personhood. This, I think, may differ culturally, although I believe that most cultures attach a similarly high value to the sexual lives and the sexual parts of their bodies. Nevertheless, the fact that the ordering of seriousness and even of the offenses themselves may differ culturally is not an objection to this analysis since what we are proposing is a criminal code for US culture.

In the outer circles on this model we will have the level of offense associated with stealing someone's newspaper, or some other trivial theft, when the sense of personal space, dignity, and identity have not been affected at all. Car theft however is a more serious offense since then the thief has violated something within one's power of consent. But most of us do not have an extreme personal attachment to our cars, and, even if we do, we do not feel violated in some private and personal way, for example, humiliated, degraded, physically hurt. If the car is insured then the injury will be very minor indeed, as the insurance company will simply replace the car. Other crimes move closer into our personal, private, and intimate self; for example, breaking into someone's house is a greater violation than car theft regardless of the value of the stolen possessions. Burglaries involve the violation of personal space, privacy, and sense of security in one's home; the stealing of property is a distinct and separable injury. The uninvited or unconsented-to invasion of one's house is serious because it intrudes on our private space, literally and figuratively on the things which we choose to share only with people close to us, with whom we would normally let down our guard.

Although there are some bodily invasions that are trivial, for example, patting someone on the back when he dislikes it, generally, the more 'serious' offenses are ones where consent ranges over that part of our domain that concerns our bodies and, particularly, our sexual lives. Much of our personal identity is tied to our gender and sexual expression and hence to our sexual self-determination. In society, sexual interactions are regarded as personal, private, and intimate relationships. Sexual relationships are not generally performed in public and are usually assumed to be performed by partners who have a close and caring relationship. Moreover, it is commonly believed that sexual relationships are imbued with significance and meaning beyond the physical act. Another reason for the seriousness of sexual offenses is that they force the victim to relinquish control over this aspect of her life and that most individuals believe they are most vulnerable and exposed. In sexual interactions, unlike in other interactions, it is even more important that we are able to control whom we are intimate with, since sexual relationships expose us more than other relationships and thereby make us more vulnerable. This is a reason why sexual touching, even as a 'joke,' is offensive. It makes the recipient merely a sexual being, vulnerable and exposed. It is a way of exerting power over another, particularly women, by reducing them to their sexual selves alone. This provides the justification for many sexual harassment offenses. 'Hostile environment' sexual harassment occurs when there is, in the workplace, sexual touching or sexual references, even when those occur in the form of jokes. Taking away the power to consent to sexual relationships, to control this most personal part of our domain, is an extremely grave injury. All unconsented-to border crossings show disrespect for the victim, but some more than others.

Rape not only denies the ability to control a central part of one's domain, but in doing so, it makes the victim a mere object, an instrument of her attacker's sexual gratification. Rape makes the victim feel dehumanized, denigrated, and humiliated. The attacker takes something that should be a wonderful and pleasurable experience and so distorts it as to fundamentally change the character of the act. Rape victims often recount that they feel 'dirty' and defiled by the experience. The victim is made to feel that she has an inferior status, sexually and morally. Furthermore, the terror of the experience of being violated in this way contributes to the gravity of the offense, as does the psychological trauma that lingers as a result. There is a surprising amount of consensus about how 'serious' individuals take the crime of rape to be. In a notable study by Thorsten Sellin and Marvin Wolfgang (1964) respondents rated 'forcible rape' as second to murder, well ahead of armed robbery and 'aggravated assault.'

The moral wrongness of rape consists in violating the autonomous right to control one's own body and one's sexual self-determination, and the seriousness of rape derives from the special importance we attach to sexual autonomy. The importance we attach to controlling our sexual lives should have a significant impact on the role of consent in sexual interactions and on whether consent should be implied from the circumstances. The wrongness and seriousness of rape are understood in terms of nonconsensual sexual relations, and not necessarily in terms of the 'incidental' assaults that may accompany it. Whereas the law often focuses on the *forceful* nature of the attack, this account of wrongfulness maintains that the focus should be on the nonconsenual aspect of sexual violation.[2] Nonconsenual sex constitutes a serious wrong to a person. The harm of rape may be secured with a weapon or with threats, but those are not required for nonconsenual sex to be wrong.

Moral Injury to Personal Status

So far we have been discussing the harm of rape in terms of undermining the victim's consent which violates her sexual autonomy. Here I would like to consider a different wrong, one with which Jean Hampton (1999) argued that a particular kind of *moral injury* occurs. That moral injury is the expression of disrespect for the value of the victim, in other words, a diminishment of that person's worth. Hampton's argument that this moral injury occurs with all wrong-doing may be difficult to support, whereas the argument that moral injury occurs with *many* types of offenses, particularly sexual offenses, is persuasive. I will support the narrower claim that some offenses involve moral injury. In all cases of nonconsenual sex, besides the physical wounds and psychological harm, the claim is that there is an injury to the person's status as an equal. A moral injury is not the same, Hampton cautions as the 'material or psychological damage to that over which a person has a right [for example, her possessions, her body, her psychological well-being] and comes about because of a wrongful action' (p. 123). It is an *expression* of inferior status, of diminishment; the act of rape *expresses* that degradation or inferior worth of the victim. Failure to secure consent for sexual activity is an injury to the acknowledgment of the victim's value as a fully fledged person worthy of respect.

The idea of moral injury assumes, Hampton argues, a certain conception of value, like the Kantian conception of value that all persons have equal, intrinsic value. That value is not dependent upon characteristics such as race, gender, or intelligence, or even upon the good deeds one has done, but rather on our capacity for rational autonomy. Each of us is, as Kant said, an end-in-herself, each equally deserving of respect. We are not objects or things but subjects and ends. What moral obligations we owe each other are not dependent on factors about individual characteristics or attributes, but rather we owe each other equal moral consideration because people have intrinsic value. This conception of persons' worth informs liberalism and modern democracy. Each person deserves 'equal concern and respect' as Ronald Dworkin has said.

The concept of moral injury also assumes a certain theory of how human behavior expresses meaning. Some wrongful actions *express* the inferiority of the female victim; they 'say' that the victim is worth less than the offender. The treatment, either intentionally or unintentionally 'means' or provides evidence of the offender's belief in his superiority. Not all wrongful behavior is done intentionally for that purpose, but the fact that the offender treats his victim as inconsequential *expresses* his belief in his superiority and the inferiority of the recipient of the action. Human behavior is meaningful like language and gets its meaning from conventions in society (not unlike the way words' meanings are conventional). Whether bowing, burping, or shaking hands, actions have a meaning in a social context and are understood by members of society. We understand the meaning of behavior by knowing or learning the conventions of that society. Etiquette or manners of a society are conventional – they are not matters of 'common sense,' as Judith Martin has said. Their primary use is to convey respect for others. Failure to behave according to the customary standards expresses disrespect for others.

Many of our actions – from sarcastically saying to the restaurant owner as you storm 'That was the best meal I have ever had,' to walking out in the middle of a presentation, to refusing to shake someone's hand – express particular meanings that are conventional. Flaunting conventional behavior can send messages about the value of a person. By loudly walking out on someone's presentation of a paper expresses disrespect and contempt for the speaker. Sometimes one doesn't intend to express a particular meaning and later can be embarrassed to find out what was 'heard.' For instance, imagine that the reason former US president Jimmy Carter didn't shake the black-activist politician Jesse Jackson's hand was that Carter had a cold and didn't want to spread his germs. Nevertheless, what Jackson 'heard' was disrespect as the failure of white men to shake hands with black men in the racist south meant that whites thought themselves as superior. Shaking hands expresses greetings to someone considered an equal (this may explain the fact that until recently it was not the practice for men to shake women's hands) and failure to do so expresses belief in the inferior status of the recipients.

An extremely explicit example of some behaviors conveying meaning about the value of others would be cross burning on a black person's lawn. That action *expresses the meaning* in American society that the actor believes that the occupant *qua* black person is inferior to white people and it carries a threat of violence to come. Other behaviors are less explicit yet their meaning is understood. Since we suppose that persons, as equal agents, are deserving or entitled to certain kinds of treatment that respect their equal worth, human behavior that fails to accord that treatment is a harm to their status as an equal. In not treating persons in the way they are entitled, they are insulted (and when we see disrespectful treatment of others we become indignant). The treatment expresses the message of their inferiority, but they are also harmed by not receiving the kind of treatment they deserve.

This is the kind of harm that Hampton labeled 'moral injury,' which is an expressive harm (see p. 123). Some wrongful actions have, over and above their direct physical or psychological damage, this expression of diminution or degradation of the victim's value. The act does not *actually* degrade or make the person less valuable because, according to the Kantian analysis, that cannot be done. Nothing can literally make a human being less valuable, but people can treat others as if they were less valuable, as if they were inferior. Consider the case in Texas a few years ago in which three white men tied a black man to the back of a pickup truck and dragged him along a dirt road until he was literally pulled apart. The method of killing that man was to intentionally reduce him to a thing or object – treating him like a sack of potatoes. The killing expressed the message 'loud and clear' that the killers thought that their victim, as a black man, was inferior to them and, conversely, that they were superior. The moral injury, the expressive meaning of the murder was clear and certainly was understood by the African-American community as well as by others.

All murder is wrongful and all murder sends a message of disrespect or devaluation of the victim, but racially motivated murders, murders that are expressing a message of inferiority to all members of a targeted group, inflict a moral injury on all members of that race. The victim is a token for the group; obviously she is harmed in other ways as well, but the moral injury – the expression that her racial group is inferior to the perpetrator's – is an injury to her *qua* member of that group and to its other members. Some of the indignation and anger expressed over racially motivated crimes comes from hearing the message of the inferiority of that racial group. We are angered by the treatment of members of groups that is meant to indicate their inferiority and the superiority of the members of the group from whom the perpetrators come. Racially motivated crimes against African-Americans harm them by expressing the message of inferiority in society that once condoned the unequal status of black people and that, to some extent, still countenances the position of their inferiority.

Rapes express very clearly the message of the inferiority of women. The rapist, whether the violent rapist or the subtler 'date rapist,' sends the message that this woman is for his enjoyment, an object to be used for his pleasure. His actions express her inferiority to him since he does not feel the need to bother to investigate whether she is really consenting, even in the face of evidence that she was not or may not be. Her physical and verbal rejections are not worth investigating as to whether they were 'real' since her interests do not really matter. For him, her wishes and desires are irrelevant. He is superior to her, his desires matter and hers do not, making her an object rather than an equal person. Sending this message is the expressive moral injury of rape. The message of inferiority, of what women are for, is received by all women, not merely by the woman who experiences the rape. Not wanting to diminish the real physical and psychological harms to rape victims, I am not claiming that all women experience those harms, which are very real and serious. But there is something peculiar about rape and the response that women have to other women being raped. They are indignant to the harms of another and have a deep response that goes beyond the worry that they might too be a victim. Women are *resentful* of the treatment. What accounts for that response might just be that women understand or hear the message that is being expressed by the rapist. Being a woman in western (American) society, where sexual violence is high, means being vulnerable to rape and thereby 'hearing' the message about devaluing women. The indignation and resentment, combined with the fear that women have about rape, are based on this moral injury. The prevalence of rape makes the message pervasive. The impotence of the legal response to the epidemic of rape reinforces societal acceptance of the message. The rapist aims, whether consciously or not, to establish his mastery of men over women and the law unwittingly may be supporting him. The message of inferiority is extremely insulting. The harm is intensified due to the pervasiveness of rape, and the legal reinforcement of the message of women's inferiority further denigrates women as a group. Rape is therefore a moral injury to women as a group.[3]

Moral injury is objective in that it is not dependent on the victim feeling a particular way or believing she has received dishonoring treatment; although most victims of rape certainly do psychologically experience the message of inferiority, of their diminishment. Being used for someone else's sexual purposes is deeply insulting and humiliating, along with the other harms. Indeed that fact that some victims so internalize the message of devaluation may account for the shame that many feel about *being* a victim of rape. They feel shame because they *feel* less valuable as a person, and the societal response to rape of blaming the victim exacerbates that feeling of inferiority. Society often says to victims of rape 'If you only had not done x, this wouldn't have happened,' where x is 'looking sexy,' or 'dressing a particular way,' or 'drinking alcohol,' or 'went to a man's apartment,' and so on. Saying that moral injury does not require the agent to believe she has been treated as inferior is important since some people so lack self-respect or self-worth that they do not recognize when they have been treated as a thing, and thereby wronged. These individuals, sadly, would not notice when some treatment was sending them a message of inferiority because they see themselves as deserving poor treatment (they may in fact see themselves as inferior). Women with what is called 'battered woman syndrome' often see themselves as not having value and thereby deserving the abusive treatment by their husbands. Nevertheless, the rest of us can recognize when another person is treated as inferior in status to the wrongdoer.

Asking for consent is a requirement for treating another person as an equal, so the failure to get consent before proceeding with a sexual relationship expresses deep disrespect for the victim. What Hampton has proposed is that we see rape as expressing a particular kind of moral injury to the victim – the expression of degradation or diminishment of her status. The meaning of the rape involves the victim's worth and the wrongdoer's worth and we can 'read off' the expression of the offender's superiority. In the case of rape, the diminishment in the victim's worth is tied to group membership. Women are the target of rape in society and women get the message that the rapist sends. In this sense, the moral injury of rape is shared by women as a group.

Is Consent All That Matters?

Most liberal theorists, as we have discussed, suppose that consent makes *legally* permissible any sexual activity, arguing that consent is necessary and sufficient for permissible sexuality. But should consent legitimize all sexual behavior? Earlier I said that to answer this question requires first that we elaborate on the standards of consent as absurdly weak standards tell us little about whether consent constitutes necessary and sufficient conditions for permissible sexuality. The other important question is whether we are talking about what is *legally* permissible or *morally* permissible. In general, these are not the same since many things are legally acceptable but not morally acceptable.

Considering legal permissibility we might suppose that, with a more robust theory of consent for sexual relationships, many worries about 'immoral sex' would dissipate. But is that because we assume that individuals would never consent to 'immoral sex?' Obviously if one assumes that consent makes all sexual interactions morally permissible this issue is a nonstarter. But what I am supposing is that there are certain relationships that involve, for example, the kind of moral injury discussed in the previous section. That moral injury arises because of the degrading or exploitative treatment of one person by another. The relationship is therefore immoral. But isn't it possible that someone might still consent to that relationship? What I am imagining is that it is immoral for one person to treat another person in a fashion that is humiliating and/or makes them an object of ridicule and/or is dangerous for them even if the person consents. This will have to be examined further but, for the time being, let us imagine that there are instances such as this and they are immoral because they are exploitative and involve moral injury. The cases are rare, I would argue, and more often than not nonconsenual, but the person who has been abused by her experiences in life (analogously the 'battered woman') might well consent to an exploitative relationship. The contemporary rhetoric about sex has extended the idea that consent legitimates any sexual behavior – even from a moral point of view. What I am suggesting is that consent does not make all sexual relationships morally acceptable.

Returning to the earlier observations of Catherine MacKinnon and Andrea Dworkin regarding western society's views about sexuality, they argue that sexuality is socially constructed on the basis of views of male domination and female submission. We have been socialized to erotically respond to men's domination of women. Men see women as objects, tools for their use, specifically, for their sexual gratification – the objectification of women by men for men's sexual pleasure. The irony of this social construction of sexuality is that women too are socialized, at least to some extent, to respond to the subjugation. They will sometimes volunteer or 'consent' to the use or even abuse of themselves for the sexual gratification of men. MacKinnon and Dworkin would say therefore that this social construction of human sexuality that entails the instrumental use of individuals is immoral.[4]

What is interesting about the MacKinnon/Dworkin view of sexuality is that Immanuel Kant had similar views and argued that it was immoral because sexual desire leads to the use of persons as mere things for the satisfaction of one's own desires (Herman, 1993: 49–67). According to Kant, the instrumentalization of another person denies their autonomy by dictating how they will behave in order to secure one's own satisfaction. The instrumentalization is also a denial of that person's subjectivity as one does not ask about their wants or desires and only focuses upon one's own desires. Kant's reason for thinking that sexual desire involves this immoral instrumental treatment of one's partner seems to be that he thought that the sensations in a person's own body were so intense that they drove out, for that period of time at least, all other thoughts, including thoughts of respect for the humanity of the other person that are characteristic of the moral attitude. For Kant, however, since both parties have the same sexual satisfaction interests they will permit themselves to be used in this object-like manner, to dehumanize and to be dehumanized. Kant thinks that this is an essential feature of sexuality generally, not just of male sexuality. He also seemed to think that it drove out every end-like consideration of the pleasure or experience of the sexual partner. One becomes completely absorbed in their own bodily pleasures, while the other becomes merely an instrument to the first's pleasurable sensations.

Unlike MacKinnon and Dworkin, Kant does not see this view of sexuality as asymmetrical or as part of a system of social hierarchy. Like Kant, the former believe that human beings are owed respect and that this respect is incompatible with treating a person as an instrument of sexual gratification, which includes the rejection of the person's autonomy and subjectivity. They again part company with Kant in denying that this lack of respect for the humanity of the other person is essential to sexual desire, arguing that it is western culture's construction of the erotic, particularly for men, to see its paradigm as domination and instrumentation. Pornography reinforces and extends this image.[5] Women too can internalize these images of what is sexy and desirable and eroticize being dominated and used as objects for another's enjoyment. The objectification that Dworkin and MacKinnon discuss is asymmetrical in that women are objects for men's pleasure. Hierarchy for them is the cause of the problem exemplified by the asymmetrical structures of power. If we disagree with Kant that all sexual desire entails this wrongful utilization (that there can be sexual desire that is a mutually satisfying mingled experience of pleasure) then, in other words, we don't believe that it is the nature of sexual desire to be wrongfully utilized. And yet if we acknowledge with MacKinnon and Dworkin that, at least to some extent, western society does eroticize domination and subjugation, we can then criticize as immoral the construction of sexuality as the asymmetrical instrumental use of women by men.

In the noninstrumental use model, both parties may temporarily give up their autonomy in a good way that enhances receptivity and sensitivity to the other (to fully enjoy sex one must 'let down one's guard') and without instrumentalizing or becoming oblivious to the other's desires. Because of space limitations, I cannot expand on this view of sexuality but a fully developed view would include, I believe, the encouragement of women's erotic potential not as nonhuman objects of men's desires but as fully fledged sexual beings with significant sexual desires and power. A society committed to equality and one that acknowledges the importance of sexuality in the full development of lives will want to encourage that development.

Turning to the immorality of sexuality, in Kantian terms sexual activity that involves solely the instrumental use of another for one's own sexual gratification and/or that denies the person's status as a full participant, their autonomy, their wishes or wants and subjectivity is morally wrongful. It involves the expression of moral injury. Sexual practices or acts where the perpetrator gets pleasure from treating the other as an object only of his sexual enjoyment do not comport with the dignity of humans, because they demean and degrade that person, treating them as subhuman. Arguably, sexual desire based on this instrumentalization effects all women since it conceptualizes that it is what women are for. Who they are, what their wishes and desires are, do not matter. The victim is a token of a type, namely the group of women who do not need to be respected since they are for sex. This is where the feminist argument against pornography jumps off, claiming that the basis of much pornography is to represent women solely as objects for men's sexual gratification. The argument is that pornography legitimizes immoral sexuality. Sexual conduct that involves the *mere* utilization of another person for one's own sexual gratification without regard for her autonomy and subjectivity is immoral. The gang rape cases at St. John's and Florida State University are apt examples of immoral sexuality. Even outside the question of consent, these would represent immoral types of sexuality since each victim is being used solely as an instrument for others' sexual gratification.[6]

What should the law's response be to immoral sexuality? Lois Pineau argued that immoral sexuality should be evidence of rape. She proposed the model of 'communicative sexuality,' arguing that in intimate situations we have an obligation to take the ends of others as our own:

> Assuming that each person enters the [sexual] encounter in order to seek sexual satisfaction, each person engaging in the encounter has an obligation to help the other seek his or her ends ... But the obligation to promote the sexual ends of one's partner implies the obligation to know what those ends are, and also the obligation to know how those ends are attained ... [I]n the practice of a communicative sexuality, one which combines the appropriate knowledge of the other with respect for the dialectics of desire.
>
> (Pineau, 1989: 234–35).

She further argues that communicative sexuality should be viewed as the norm for sexual encounters with which reasonable women would agree and, following from this view, 'the guilt of date rapists [is located] in the failure to approach sexual relations on a communicative basis' (Ibid., 240).

Pineau goes too far. The law is not interested, nor should it be, in the mere fact that sexuality is immoral.

The crime of rape cannot be analyzed as not approaching a sexual encounter on a communicative basis. 'Communicative sexuality' may be an *ideal* for sexuality but we would want to say that failing to engage in it is rape. An ideal is one that the law can support by rejecting norms that are so far along the continuum from communicative relationship that they differ in kind. But we would not want the outcome that, for example, I could be convicted of rape for not performing some sex act that I know my partner wants me to perform. What this returns us to is the importance of the consent of the parties involved. If communicative sexuality has a role, it is an evidentiary one in helping to establish that the victim did not consent. Furthermore, one might communicate that one desires a kind of sex that is not in line with what Pineau envisions as the ideal, for example sadomasochistic sex. If the partner went along with this, even though not liking it, would that be a case of rape? It is not true that every time someone has sex it is for personal enjoyment or sexual satisfaction. There may be other reasons that make individuals willing to consent to sexual encounters. The communicative sexuality model goes too far in indicating one acceptable form of sexuality. Sexual freedom should mean opportunities for women and men to experiment sexually – the only constraint being that the actions are truly consensual. If sexual expression is one of the important ways of expressing oneself then individuals should be free to explore those parameters. Pineau is correct, nevertheless, to point out that when consent is in doubt it is reasonable to look for communicative characteristics. If they are missing and the sexual relationship is exploitative, one-sided, for example, we should use communicative norms to judge how likely it would be that anyone would consent to it. Unless we have some compelling reason to believe that the woman consented when there is an absence of the communicative characteristic, then that is strong evidence of rape.

There can be immoral sex even when there is consent, but the fact that sex is immoral should not make it criminal. This is consistent with the liberal principles that the law should not punish immorality per se, even when it involves another person. So in those rare cases where women do consent to immoral sex that is degrading and exploitative, then the law should not interfere. On the other hand, since there is a strong presumption that women do not consent to sex that is immoral – that is harmful to them, that does not involve their own pleasure, that makes them an object of ridicule – those characteristics should lead the law to presume that they have not consented. Standards of consent are based upon what the choice of a reasonable person would be and, since we are trying to determine whether the reasonable or average woman would consent, the relevant question should be what is reasonable from a woman's point of view.

In matters of sexual self-determination, one always has the option of withholding consent. The choice to engage in sexual activity is based upon the pleasure or other goods secured through the activity. In general, a person can consent, without wanting to, to something that one has reservations about; but it does not follow, as we have argued, that consenting is just a matter of choosing between disagreeable alternatives and picking the most 'reasonable' choice. The latter view is consistent with coercion. Particularly in sexual matters, the reasons for consenting should be based on positive goods to be received from the encounter and not on avoiding evils. When trying to determine if a woman consented to a sexual relationship the question of whether the reasonable woman would find the circumstances and/or the kind of sex attractive and enjoyable should be asked. This question is neglected in most jurisdictions and women are held to have consented in

circumstances and to acts which most women would be
revolted by.

In the St. John's case, if it had been asked whether the
reasonable or average woman would have consented
freely and knowingly to oral and anal sex with a group
of men in the described circumstances then the answer
would clearly have been no. Most women would not
find the circumstances of this case pleasurable; in fact,
most would find them revolting. What reason could the
victim have had to consent to this form of sexual
contact? If she had received money for the sex then, at
least, there would be *a* reason for her granting consent.
Given the actual circumstances, however, there is no
reason to suppose that the victim consented, so we
should presume as a matter of evidence that she did not.
The burden then, under this account, would shift to the
defendant to show that the victim did in fact consent or
that it was reasonable for him to believe that she did.
The law often utilizes presumptions to guide the fact-
finding process. When the facts given are best explained
by a presumed fact, then the jury may presume that fact
unless given some reason to the contrary. It operates
thus: 'If B is presumed from A, then on a showing of A,
B must [may] be assumed by the trier in the absence of
evidence of non-B' (Kaplan and Waltz, 1984: 752).
Once the prosecution has established some facts
essential to the crime – for example, that the defendant
had sex with the victim and that he did so under
circumstances where the reasonable or average woman
would not consent – then the jury may presume
nonconsent and that the defendant knew that the victim
was not consenting, or knew it was possible that she
was not consenting (that is, he was reckless about her
consent). This approach, using a presumption of
evidence, retains the standard procedural guarantees
for the defendant, most important that he is innocent
until proven guilty. On the other hand, if the defendant
claims that a woman did in fact freely consent in

circumstances in which the reasonable woman or the average woman would not, he will be required to provide evidence to support his account. When logic tells us that the reasonable woman would not consent, we need a positive argument to rebut that presumption. Instead of requiring the *victim* to prove that she did not in fact consent in circumstances in which the reasonable woman would not, we shift the burden of that argument to the defendant.

Agents have a duty, before crossing the borders of others, not only to determine whether the other person is consenting but also they are accountable for having an awareness of the sorts of circumstances and actions which might prevent that other person from voluntarily consenting.[7] Clear instances where red flags should be raised are, for example, cases like *State v. Alston*, where the perpetrator had on previous occasions beaten his victim and had only minutes earlier threatened to 'Fix her face' if she refused his sexual advances. No defendant should be surprised that submission under those circumstances was less than fully voluntary. Because a person 'went along' with the aggressor or acted cooperatively, if the circumstances were such that it was reasonable for a woman to be fearful for her safety or otherwise threatened, or to find the circumstances undesirable for other reasons (having sex with a number of men), then the presumption in such contexts should be that there was no consent. This view is in line with other areas of the criminal law. If we find an event to which reasonable persons would not normally consent, whether it involves one's death, transfer of one's money, or, for example, a beating, we presume that it done without one's consent. It is not that a person could not consent to another's doing these things, but rather that it is unlikely. Similar understanding is called for here, keeping in mind what average women are like and what they might find desirable to consent to. If the circumstances are not ones that the reasonable woman would consent to then we should presume that the victim did not.

What about Sadomasochists?

Are sadomasochistic relationships immoral even if they are consensual? Do they, for example, involve the kind of moral injury that Hampton introduced us to? This is a complicated question that I think is beyond the scope of this project to analyze. Instead I am interested in questioning whether sadomasochism can be used as a defense in a rape case. Consider the case of *People v. Jovanovich* (2000), in which New York's highest court let stand a lower appellate court decision which held that *consent* can be a defense to violent assault and battery occurring within the context of a sadomaso-chistic encounter. The case involves a male graduate student at Columbia who was sentenced to 15 years in prison for kidnaping, assaulting, and sexually abusing a female Barnard College student. The two New York students met online and frequently discussed in emails their mutual interest in sadomasochism. The victim admitted in an email to being in a sadomasochistic relationship with another man, and described in intimate detail her fantasies, which included being tortured (Hanna, 2001). At trial, the victim testified that when the two met in person for the first time, she voluntarily went to Jovanovich's apartment and agreed to be tied to a futon as part of a sexual encounter. But she also testified that she never consented to being tortured for twenty hours. Jovanovich poured candle wax on her, bit her, shoved an object in her rectum, and refused to release her even after she invoked a 'safe word' which meant 'stop.' Neighbors testified that they heard screams coming from the apartment and friends corroborated her injuries. The defendant did not take the stand, but his attorney Jack Litman, who also defended the 'Preppie murderer' Robert Chambers (see below), claimed that this was all part of a consensual sadomasochism encounter.

Using New York's Rape Shield Law, the trial judge refused to permit the introduction of portions of the email correspondence relating to the victim's experience with sadomasochism. The Supreme Court of New York, Appellate Division, reversed the conviction and ordered a new trial. The Supreme Court held that, although the defendant had no constitutional right to engage in sadomasochism, the email statements would have underscored his own state of mind regarding the reasonableness of consent. Thus, the court said that in the 'interests of justice,' the emails should have been admitted. The court will accept then consent to private sexually motivated violence. This case raises many more questions than it answers. For example, is there any limit on the violence that one person can perpetrate on another as long as it is sexually motived? Can it lead to death as in the 1986 Robert Chambers case where the victim died, allegedly as a result of the sex act that involved choking her at the point of climax? (See *Los Angeles Times*, 17 March 1988.) Once a person consents to a sadomasochistic relationship are there no limits to the relationship, no ways out of it? The victim in the Jovanovich case stated that she said the 'safe' words and yet he continued disregarding her verbal signs to stop. Also we should remember that the criminal law does not permit consent to any other assault, so this decision was far outside the norm for criminal jurisprudence. Even the court's statements make the decision all the more puzzling:

> There is no available defense of consent on the charge of assault. ... Indeed, while a meaningful distinction can be made between an ordinary violent beating and violence in which both parties voluntarily participate for their own sexual gratification, nevertheless, ... a person cannot

avoid criminal liability for an assault that causes injury or
carries with it a risk of serious harm, even if the victim
asked for or consented to the act. ... And, although it may
be possible to engage in criminal assaultive behavior that
does not result in physical injury, we need not address
whether consent to such conduct may constitute a defense,
since the jury clearly found here that the complainant was
physically injured.

(*People v. Jovanovich*, at 168 n. 5)

Sadomasochistic relationships cause problems for liberals who want to maintain that, if individuals
genuinely consent to some activity, then it is not the
government's business to interfere with that activity.
Particularly with sexual choices, liberals have been
eager to keep the government out of individuals' sexual
practices. But these cases present themselves as especially challenging for me as a person reconsidering rape
laws in the light of the abuses of the law and society
against women. For my current vantage, it would seem
that allowing defendants to claim that the victim of
sexual brutality consented opens the door that I have
been trying to close, namely, taking out of consideration as consensual sexual relationship those that, in the
face of it, seem unreasonable from the women's point of
view. So, if a man is permitted to claim that the brutal
treatment was part of a sexual ritual that they shared
and consequently that he believed, and had reason to
believe, that his partner was consenting, then we open
the door to a vast array of cases that seem unreasonable.
I recognize that the woman who wants to engage in an
sadomasochism relationship will see the relationship as
reasonable, and I imagine she will see it as pleasurable
as well. But the practitioner of sadomasochism must
acknowledge that if the law does not protect her from
genuine abuses that arise within the context of a
sadomasochistic encounter, then she could be seriously
harmed by such a system. Since the abuses from
allowing the defense of belief in consent for sexual

violence are great (consider, for instance, *Regina v. Morgan*), and the use of that defense is extremely prevalent, and the loss by not permitting it is not that great, consequently, the law should not permit the defense of belief in consent to sexual violence.

Saying that does not mean that sadomasochistic practices themselves should be prohibited. For example, in a case dubbed 'Paddleboro,' police in Attleboro, Massachusetts raided a private BDSM (bondage, discipline, and sadomasochism) party and arrested the host and a guest who had paddled another woman with a large wooden spoon, allegedly causing bruising and bleeding.[8] The victim had not complained and was presumably a consensual attendee of this party. Targeting individuals who engage in consensual sadomasochism limits sexual autonomy and does not protect individuals from harm. Nevertheless, even without targeting sadomasochism there has to be limits on the amount of violence that is acceptable. Where these lines are drawn, I am not sure, although I am inclined to only permit the injuries to be slight. But my argument is that a defendant could not use consent as a defense to sexual violence, consequently individuals engaging in this kind of activity run a risk.

Where Do We Go From Here?

My argument throughout this book is that we must empower women by taking their words and actions seriously. Once society and the law stop treating women as if they do not know what they want and are afraid to say it when they do, we may find that women are empowered to express their own sexual desires. We may find that there are a lot more women who do feel free to consent to sex when they want to and refuse it when they don't. Having grown up in the 1960s and 1970s in the San Francisco Bay Area, my own experiences may not be representative of women of my age, but I think that they are of following generations. That is, many women like sex, feel comfortable with their sexuality, do not necessarily see that sex is exclusively associated with love, and feel comfortable consenting to sex. All those silly 1950s notions of sex that I thought were over in the 1960s have persisted and, in many ways, have been turned against women. Some women do retain more stereotypical views about sexuality, but certainly that is not the norm. And even if women do hold more traditional views about sex (whatever that means), that fact does not justify men making assumptions about their sexual consent. Certainly the law should not be in the business of legitimizing a system that does not require individuals to take responsibility for their sexual choices and the choices of others. Whatever one's view are about sex and sexual relationships, anyone wanting a sexual relationship should be very clear about consent. It should not be enough to assume that 'She cannot say she wants it because that would mean in her mind that she was a slut' and, consequently, think that it is acceptable to force sex upon her, thinking that 'she really wants it.' And particularly the law should never accept outmoded stereotypes about women and consent as a justification for belief in consent. The law should take people at their word and back up their words with the force of the law. That is to take people seriously. That is also to make men and women take responsibility for their words and actions. If a woman is unable to say she wants sex, then she is going to go without sex. In a world in which men and women understand and enjoy their sexuality and are not ashamed about it, they will feel permitted to be sexual with people they want. Sexuality is an intrinsically good thing, contrary to the aberrant messages of western society. We have not taught young people about sex, its pleasures and powers, and consequently we leave many young adults with these outmoded notions about male and female sexuality.

Equal sexual autonomy would mean that we teach males and females about sexuality in ways that are to be celebrated. On page 171 of her book *Harmful to Minors* (2002), Judith Levin discusses what we ought to be teaching adolescents about sex. She says:

> The achievement of equality does not require that we desexualize boys as we have girls. The masculine self-recognition of sexuality is something to be celebrated. Rather, the message to boys about their own as well as girls' sexuality should be that it is as variable as the people in whom it resides, and that any individual girl can be expected sometimes to want sex with a particular person, and sometimes not to. Placing girls on a pedestal of purity is not the same as respect. It only perpetuates the division of the female population into virgins and whores, a division upheld with dreary diligence by our nation's schoolchildren. The task for boys is to listen and discern a partner's clues. ... Boys can also expect girls to listen to them. In this way neither gender is cast as the permanent aggressor or resister, expert or innocent. ... We have evidence that this is already happening and that practice in listening bears fruit over time. A heartening study of sexual consent conducted by Charlene Muehlenhard and Susan Hickman at the University of Kansas ... showed that while college women and men often make their willingness to have sex known in different ways, they almost universally understand the cues from a partner of the other sex. And—good riddance to bad myths—'a direct refusal (saying 'no') was not perceived as representative of sexual consent by either women or men,' Muehlenhard wrote me. 'They seemed to agree that 'no' meant 'no.'

Notes

1 Carol M. Shafer and Marylin Frye, 'Rape and Respect,' in Mary Vetterling-Braggin, Frederick Elliston, and Jane English (eds), *Feminism and Philosophy* (Totowa NJ: Rowman and Littlefield, 1977, 334). Though much has been made of a very limited number of feminists who argued that all heterosexual relationships are coercive, most feminists have not maintained that view. Most

feminists have worried about the unequal power relationships and the role of consent in heterosexual relationships.

2 Any nonconsenual sex will involve some force – forced penetration – but this has not been recognized as force.

3 Rape as an instrument of war is a variation of this expressive harm. Rapes in war or other conflicts are using women to symbolize the inferiority of her group – whether ethnic, racial, national, religious, or whatever. Taking 'their' women and raping them is meant as an insult to that group – the woman is the vehicle for sending the message of her group's inferiority and the attacker's superiority. The 'meaning' of the act is very clear.

4 MacKinnon and Dworkin do not talk about 'immorality' at all, but I am assuming that that is what they would say about these relationships.

5 For examples of other cultures' construction of sexuality, particularly women's sexuality as not entailing being an object, see Naomi Wolf's discussion of India and China's view in *Promiscuities* (1997).

6 Prostitution may be distinguished from these other instrumental use cases since, on the assumption that the woman is voluntarily a prostitute and is engaging in the activity in exchange for money, that means she is getting something out of the interaction. I am not sure that everything that occurs within the prostitute's relationships can be handled this way.

7 This raises the issue of whether criminal liability should be based upon 'objective' or 'subjective' standards. This dispute often surfaces in determinations of whether a defendant intended to bring about a given result. According to 'objectivists,' a person intends the natural and probable consequences of his acts, and his intention for purposes of imposing criminal liability is established by reference to the 'reasonable person.' If the reasonable person would have foreseen that a given consequence would follow from his conduct, then the defendant is held to have intended that result. 'Subjectivists' contend that what a defendant intends depends only on what he in fact foresees. This debate is crucial in cases in which a reasonable person would have foreseen a given consequence, though the particular defendant did not.

8 Paddleboro Information website at http://www.paddleboro.com (visited 2 November 2000); Cindy Rodriquez, 'Group Creates Defense Fund to Support S&M Accused,' The Boston Globe, 27 July 2000, at B6.

Bibliography

Cases and Primary Printed Sources

American Law Institute, *Model Penal Code and Commentaries*, Part II. Section 213 (Philadelphia, 1980).

Berkowitz v. Pennsylvania, 537 Pa. 143; 641 A.2d 1161; 1994 Pa. LEXIS 179.

Boro v. Superior Court, 163 Cat. App. 3d 1224, 210 Cal Rptr. 122 1985.

Bowers v. Hardwick, 478 U.S. 186; 106 S. Ct. 2841; 92 L. Ed. 2d 140; 1986 U.S. LEXIS 123; 54 U.S.L.W. 4919.

Brown v. State, 127 Wisconsin 193, 199–200 (1906).

California Penal Code, Sec. 261.5 West Supplement (1981).

Coley v. State, 616 So.2d 1017, 1023 Florida Court of Appeal (1994).

Commonwealth v. Berkowitz, 641 A.2d 1161 Pennsylvania (1994, 1995).

Commonwealth v. Biggs, 467 A.2d 31 Pennsylvania Superior (1983).

Commonwealth v. Goldenberg, 338 Massachusetts 377; 155 N.E.2d 187; 1959 Massachusetts LEXIS 651; 70 A.L.R. 2d 814.

Commonwealth v. Helfant, 398 Massachusetts 214, 217, 496 N.E.2d 433, 437 (1986).

Commonwealth v. Mlinarich, 345 Pennsylvania Superior 269, 498 A.2d 395 Pennsylvania Superior (1985).

Commonwealth v. Richter, 551 Pennsylvania 507; 711 A.2d 464; 1998 Pennsylvania LEXIS 844.

Davis v. State of Florida, 538 So. 2d 515 (Florida App. 2 Dist. 1989).

Don Maran v. People, 1872.

Goldberg v. State, 41 Maryland App. 48, 395 A 2d 1213 (1979).

Gonzales v. State, 516 P.2d 592 Wyoming (1973).

Hart v. Commonwealth, 131 Virginia 726, 729 (1921).

In re. B.G., 589 A.2d 637, 638–42 New Jersey Superior Court Appeals Division (1991).

Jackson v. State, 890 P.2d. 587, 593 Court of Appeal (3 March 1995).

Louisiana v. Powell, 438 So. 2d 1306 Court of Appeal (1983).

McNair v. State, 108 Nevada 53; 825 P.2d 571; 1992 Nevada LEXIS 21.

Michael M. v. Superior Court of Sonoma County, 450 U.S. 464 (1981).

Model Penal Code, see American Law Institute.

Natanson v. Kline, 186, 187 Kansas; 354 P.2d 670; 1960 Kansas LEXIS 398 (1960).

People v. Barnes, 42 California 3d 284, 289, 721 P2d 110, 119, 228 California Rper 228, 299 (1986).

People v. Burnham, 76 California App. 3d 1134, 222; California Rptr 630 (1985); 222 California Rper. 630; California App. (1986).

People v. Dohring, 59 New York 374, 394 (1874).

People v. Evans, 85 Misc. 2d 1088, 379 New York State 2d 912 (1975).

People v. Hale, 142 Michigan App. 451, 453, 370 NW 2nd 382 383 (6 May 1985).

People v. Hough, 159 Misc. 2d 997; 607 New York State 2d 884; 1994 New York Misc. LEXIS 10.

People v. Jovanovich, 95 New York 2d 846, 2000 (leave to appeal granted, decision without published opinion); 700 New York State 2d 156 Appeals Division (1999).

People v. Rusk, 289 Maryland 230, 424, A.2d 720 (1981).

Perez v. State, 94 S.W. 1036, 1038, Texas Criminal Appeal (1906).

Regina v. Cogan, 2 All ER, (1975).

Regina v. Malone, 2 Criminal Appeal Rep. 447 (1998).

Regina v. Morgan, A.C. 182, House of Lords (1976).

Schloendorff v. Society of New York Hospital (1914).

State v. Alston, 61 North Carolina App. 454, 300 S.E. 2d 470 (1984).

State v. Davis, 497 S.W. 2d 204 (Mo. App. 1973).

State v. Draghi, 23/25 90 New York Superior Court (1991).

State v. Dutton, 450 N.W. 2d 189 Minnesota Court of Appeal (1990).

State v. Mitchell, No. 01C01-9612-CR-00502 Tenn. Criminal Appeal (1999).

State v. Thomas, No. B9198729, Palo Alto Municipal Court, Preliminary Examination (13 November 1991).

State v. Thomson, 792 P.2d. 1103 Montana (1990).

Whittaker v. State, 50 Wisconsin 519, 520, 522 (1880).

Other Printed Sources

Anderson, Elizabeth, 'What is the Point of Equality?' *Ethics*, January 1999.

Archard, David, *Sexual Consent* (Boulder CO: Westview Press, 1998).

Archard, David, 'The *Mens Rea* of Rape,' in *A Most Detestable Crime*, ed. Keith Burgess-Jackson (New York: Oxford University Press, 1999).

Aristotle, *Nicomachean Ethics*.

Arizona Republic, '3 Strike Deals in Gang-Rape Case Pleas Likely: Youth Held 2 Years,' 6 March 1999.

Austin, John, *How to Do Things with Words* (New York: Oxford University Press, 1962).

Baker, Brenda, 'Consent, Assault and Sexual Assault,' in *Legal Theory Meets Legal Practice*, ed. Anne Bayefsky (Edmonton: Academic, 1988)

Baron, Marcia, 'I thought she consented,' *Philosophical Issues*, 11 (2001).

Bechhofer, Laurie and Andrea Parrot, *Aquaintance Rape: The Hidden Crime* (New York: Wiley, 1991).

Beneke, Timothy, *Men on Rape* (New York: Harper & Row, 1988).

Bentham, Jeremy, *An Introduction to the Principles of Morals and Legislation* (Oxford: Clarendon Press, 1907).

Berger, Vivian, 'Not So Simple Rape,' *Criminal Justice Ethics*, 7, 1 (1988).

Bienen, Leigh, 'Rape III – National Developments in Rape Reform Legislation,' *Women's Rights Law Reporter*, 6 (1980).

Blackstone, William. *Commentaries on the Law of England* (London: Dawsons of Pall Mall, 1966)

Brett, Nathan, 'Sexual Offenses and Consent,' *Canadian Journal of Law and Jurisprudence*, 11, 69, 1998.

Brownmiller, Susan, *Against Our Will: Men, Women and Rape* (Penguin: Harmondsworth, 1976).

Chamallas, Martha, 'Consent, Equality, and the Legal Control of Sexual Conduct,' *South California Review*, 777, 836 (1988).

'Rape and Rape Law: Sexism in Society and the Law,' *California Law Review*, 61 (1973).

Curley, E.M., 'Excusing Rape,' in Joel Feinberg, *Philosophy of Law* (Belmont CA: Wadsworth Publishing Company, 1995).

Dahl, Robert A., 'Equality Versus Inequality,' *Political Science and Politics*, 29, 639 (1996).

Davis, Michael, 'Setting Penalties: What Does Rape Deserve?,' *Law and Philosophy*, 3 (1984).

Denno, Deborah, 'Sexuality, Rape, and Mental Retardation,' *University of Illinois Law Review* (1997).

Dressler, Joshua, *Understanding Criminal Law* (New York: Matthew Bender, 1987).

Dripps, Donald, 'Beyond Rape: An Essay on the Difference Between the Presence of Force and the Absence of Consent,' *Columbia Law Review*, **92**, 7 (1992).

Dworkin, Andrea, *Intercourse* (New York: Free Press, 1987).

Dworkin, Roger, 'The Resistance Standard in Rape Legislation,' *Stanford Law Review*, **18**, 680 (1966).

Dworkin, Ronald, *Taking Rights Seriously* (Cambridge: Harvard University Press, 1977).

Estrich, Susan, *Real Rape* (Cambridge MA: Harvard University Press, 1987).

Fairstein, Linda, 'Men, Women and Rape,' *Fordham Law Review*, **63**, 1 (1994).

Fairstein, Linda, *Sexual Violence: Our War Against Rape* (New York: William Morrow, 1993).

Feinberg, Joel, *Harm to Others* (New York: Oxford University Press, 1984).

Feinberg, Joel, *Harm to Self* (New York: Oxford University Press, 1986).

Feinberg, Joel, *Philosophy of Law* (Belmont CA: Wadsworth Publishing Company, 1995).

Fox-Genovese, Elizabeth, *Feminism Is Not the Story of My Life* (New York: Doubleday, 1995).

Frankfurt, Harry, 'Freedom of the Will and the Concept of Person,' in *The Importance of What We Care About: Philosophy Essays* (Cambridge: Cambridge University Press, 1988).

Fried, Joseph, 'St John's Juror Tells of Doubts in Assault Case: He says he went along to acquit,' *New York Times*, 14 September 1991.

George, William H. and Jeanette Norris, 'Alcohol, Disinhibition, Sexual Arousal, and Deviant Sexual Behavior, *Alcohol Health and Research World*, **15** (1991).

Gilbert, Neil, *Public Interest*, Spring 1991.

Goodman, Ellen, 'Date – or Rape?,' *Boston Globe*, 2 May 1991.

Griffin, Susan, 'Rape: The All-American Crime,' *Ramparts* (1971).

Hampton, Jean, 'Defining the Wrong and Defining Rape,' in *A Most Detestable Crime* (New York: Oxford University Press, 1999).

Hanna, Cheryl, 'Sex Is Not a Sport: Consent and Violence in Criminal Law,' *British Columbia Law Review*, 239 (2001).

Hart, H.L.A., *Punishment and Responsibility* (Oxford University Press, 1968).

Hart, H.L.A., *Law, Liberty and Morality* (New York: Vintage Books, 1996).

Hazelton, Peter, 'Rape Shield Laws: Limits on Zealous Advocacy,' *American Journal of Criminal Law*, **19** (1991).

Henderson, Lynne, 'Getting to Know: Honoring Women in Law and Fact,' *Texas Journal of Women & Law*, **2**, 41, 56 (1993).

Henderson, Lynne, 'Rape and Responsibility,' *Law and Philosophy*, **11**, 1 and 2 (1992).

Herman, Barbara, 'Could it be Worth Thinking about Kant on Sex and Marriage?,' in *A Mind of One's Own: Feminist Essays on Reason and Objectivity*, ed. Louise M. Antony and Charlotte Witt (Boulder, CO: Westview Press, 1993).

Hirshman, Linda and Larson, Jane, *Hard Bargains* (New York: Oxford University Press, 1998).

Houston Chronicle, 'Acquittal of Husband Spurs Anger: Wife Accused of Raping Him,' 18 April 1992.

Hume, David, 'Of the Original Contract,' in *Hume's Ethical Writing*, ed. A. MacIntyre (Notre Dame: University of Notre Dame Press, 1965).

Hurd, Heidi, 'The Moral Magic of Consent,' *Legal Theory*, **2** (1996).

Husak, Douglas and George Thomas III, 'Date Rape, Social Conventions, and Reasonable Mistakes,' *Law and Philosophy*, **11**, 1 and 2 (1992).

Husak, Douglas and George Thomas III, 'Rapes Without Rapists: Consent and Reasonable Mistake,' *Philosophical Issues*, **11** (2001).

Kaplan, John and Jon Waltz, *Evidence* (Mineola NY: The Foundation Press, 1984).

Koss, Mary P., Thomas E. Dinero, Cynthia Seibel, and Susan Cox, 'Stranger and Acquaintance Rape: Are There Differences in the Victim's Experience?,' *Psychology of Women Quarterly*, **12** (1988).

Kramer, Karen, 'Rule by Myth: The Social and Legal Dynamics Governing Alcohol-Related Acquaintance Rapes,' *Stanford Law Review*, **47** (1994).

LaFree, Gary, 'Official Reactions to Social Problems: Police Decisions in Sexual Assault Cases,' *Social Problems*, **28** (1981).

Landers, Ann, *Chicago Tribune*, 27 June 1991.

Langton, Rae, 'Free Speech and Illocution,' *Legal Theory*, **4** (1998).

Larson, Jane E., 'Woman Understand So Little, They Call My Good Nature "Deceit": A Feminist Rethinking of Seduction,' *Columbia Law Review*, **93** (1993).

Legrand, Camille, 'Comment: Rape and Rape Laws: Sexism, Society and Law,' *California Law Review*, **61** (1973).

Levin, Judith, *Harmful to Minors* (Minneapolis: University of Minnesota, 2002).

Locke, John, *Second Treatises of Government*, ed. C.B. MacPherson (Indianapolis: Hackett, 1980), Book II, C.P. viii, Sect. 120.

Los Angles Times, 'The Nation,' 17 March 1988.

MacKinnon, Catherine, *Towards a Feminist Theory of the State* (Cambridge MA: Harvard University Press, 1989).

Malm, Heidi, 'The Ontology of Consent,' *Legal Theory*, **2** (1996).

Martin, Judith, *Miss Manners' Guide for the Turn-of-the-Millennium* (New York: Pharos Books, 1989).

McCormick, 'Come-ons and Put-offs: Unmarried Students' Strategies for Having and Avoiding Sex,' *Psychology of Women Quarterly*, 4 (1974).

McGregor, Joan, 'Rape, Consent, and the Reasonable Woman,' in *In Harm's Way: Essays in Honor of Joel Feinberg*, eds Jules Coleman and Allen Buchanan (Cambridge: Cambridge University Press, 1994).

McGregor, Joan, 'Why When She Says No She Doesn't Mean Maybe and Doesn't Mean Yes: A Critical Reconstruction of Consent, Sex and the Law,' in *Legal Theory*, 2 (1996).

McGregor, Joan, 'Law's Failure to Protect Women's Sexual Autonomy as Injustice,' in 'Proceedings of the Twentieth World Congress of the International Association for Philosophy of Law and Social Philosophy,' 2003.

Mill, John Stuart, *On Liberty*, ed. Alburey Castell (Arlington Heights IL: AHM Publishers, 1947).

Milloy, Ross E. 'Furor Over a Decision Not to Indict in a Rape Case,' *New York Times*, 25 October 1992, § 1 at 30.

Mosher, Donald and Anderson, Ronald D., 'Macho Personality, Sexual Aggression, and Reactions to Guided Imagery of Realistic Rape,' *J. Res. Personality*, 20 (1986).

Muehlenhard, Charlene and Hollabaugh, Lisa, 'Do Women Sometimes Say No When They Mean Yes?,' *Journal of Personality and Social Psychology*, 54, 872 (1988).

Murphy, Jeffrie, 'Some Ruminations on Women, Violence, and the Criminal Law,' in *In Harm's Way*, eds Jules Coleman and Allen Buchanan (Cambridge University Press, 1994).

New York Times, 'Woman in Florida Rape Inquiry Fought Adversity and Sought Acceptance: For

Woman in Florida Rape Inquiry, a Fast Jump Up the Economic Ladder,' 17 April 1991, A17.

New York Times, 'Rapist Who Agreed to Use Condom Gets 40 Years,' 15 May 1993, § 1 at 6.

Olsen, Frances, 'Statutory Rape: A Feminist Critique of Rights Analysis,' in *Feminist Legal Theory*, eds Katharine Bartlett and Rosanne Kennedy (Boulder CO: Westview Press, 1991).

Paglia, Camille, *Sex, Art and American Culture* (New York: Vintage, 1992).

Paglia, Camille, *Vamps and Tramps* (New York: Random House, 1994).

Panichas, George, 'Rape, Autonomy, and Consent,' *Law and Society Review* 35, 231 (2001).

Pateman, Carol, *The Sexual Contract* (Stanford: Stanford University Press, 1988).

Perce, Gregory, 'The Tuskegee Study,' in *Contemporary Issues in Bioethics*, eds Tom Beauchamp and LeRoy Waters, 6th edn (Belmont: Wadsworth, 2003).

Perper, Timothy and David Weis, 'Proceptive and Rejective Strategies of U.S. and Canadian College Women,' *Journal of Sex Research*, 23 (1987).

Pineau, Lois, 'Date Rape: A Feminist Analysis,' *Law and Philosophy*, 8 (1989).

Pollack, Daniel, Naphtali Harcsztark, Erin A. McGrath and Karen R. Cavanaugh, 'The Capacity of a Mentally Retarded Person to Consent: An American and Jewish Legal Prespective,' *New York Law School Journal of International and Comparative Law*, 20, pp. 197–247, (2000).

Rhode, Debra, *Justice and Gender* (Cambridge MA: Harvard University Press, 1989).

Richardson, Deborah and Jennifer L. Campbell, 'Alcohol and Rape: The Effect of Alcohol on Attribution of Blame for Rape,' *Personality & Social Pyschology Bulletin*, 8 (1982).

Roiphe, Katie, *The Morning After: Sex, Fear, and Feminism on Campus* (Boston: Little, Brown, 1993).

Russell, Diana, *Sexual Exploitation: Rape, Child Sexual Abuse, and Workplace Harassment* (Newberry Park CA: Sage, 1984).

Sanday, Peggy Reeves, *A Woman Scorned* (New York: Doubleday, 1996).

Shafer and Frye, 'Rape and Respect,' in *Feminism and Philosophy*, eds Mary Vetterling-Braggin, Frederick Elliston, and Jane English (Totowa NJ: Rowman and Littlefield, 1977).

Schulhofer, Stephen J., 'The Gender Question in Criminal Law,' *Social Philosophy & Policy*, 7, 2 (Spring 1990).

Schulhofer, Stephen J., 'Taking Sexual Autonomy Seriously: Rape Law and Beyond,' *Law and Philosophy*, 11, 1 and 2 (1992).

Schulhofer, Stephen J., *Unwanted Sex: The Culture of Intimidation and the Failure of the Law* (Cambridge MA: Harvard University Press, 1998).

Sellin, Thorsten and Marvin Wolfgang, *The Measurement of Delinquency* (New York: John Wiley & Sons, 1964).

Simmons, A. John, *Moral Principles and Political Obligations* (Princeton: Princeton University Press, 1979).

Smith, Patricia, 'Social Revolution and the Persistence of Rape,' in *A Most Detestable Crime*, ed. Keith Burgess-Jackson (New York: Oxford University Press, 1999).

Sommers, Christine Hoff, 'Do These Feminists Like Women?,' *Journal of Social Philosophy*, 21 (Fall/Winter 1990).

Sommers, Christine Hoff, *Who Stole Feminism? How Women Have Betrayed Women* (New York: Simon and Schuster, 1994).

Tong, Rosemary, *Women, Sex, and the Law* (Totowa: Rowman and Littlefield, 1984).

'Victims of Rape: Hearing Before the House Select Committee on Children, Youth, and Families,' 101st Congress, 2d. Session 5 (1990).

Warshaw, Robin, *I Never Called it Rape* (New York: Harper Perennial, 1994).

Washington Post, 'Man cleared of Marital Rape,' 18 April 1992, A2.

Weihe, Vernon and Ann Richards, *Intimate Betrayal: Understanding and Responding to the Trauma of Acquaintance Rape* (Thousand Oaks, CA: Sage Publications, 1995).

Weiner, Robin, 'Shifting the Communication Burden: A Meaningful Consent Standard in Rape,' *Harvard Women's Law Journal*, **6** (1993).

Wertheimer, Alan, *Consent to Sexual Relations* (Cambridge University Press, 2003).

West, Robin, 'Legitimating the Illegitimate: A Comment on *Beyond Rape*,' *Columbia Law Review*, **93** (1993).

West, Robin, 'The Difference in Women's Hedonic Lives: A Phenomenological Critique of Feminist Legal Theory,' in *At the Boundaries of Law*, eds Martha A. Fineman and Nancy S. Thomadsen (New York: Routledge, 1991).

Westen, Peter, *The Logic of Consent*, unpublished manuscript.

Wigmore, John Henry, *Evidence in Trials at Common Law*, rev. ed. James Chadbourn (Boston: Little, Brown, 1970), Vol. 3A, sec. 924a.

Yale Law Journal, 'Forcible and Statutory Rape: An Exploration of the Operation and Objectives of the "Consent Standard",' **62**, 233 (1952).

Williams, Glanville, *The Proof of Guilt* (London: Stevens and Sons, 1963).

Williams, Glanville, 'Lords' Decision of the Law of Rape,' *The Times*, 8 May 1975, p. 15.

Wolf, Naomi, *Beauty Myth* (London: Chatto & Windus, 1990).

Wolf, Naomi, *Fire with Fire* (New York: Fawcett Columbine, 1994).

Wolf, Naomi, *Promiscuities* (New York: Random House, 1997).

Index